S0-BIF-673

MEDICINE IN A CHANGING SOCIETY

Lawrence Corey, M.D.

Senior Fellow in Medicine, Department of Internal Medicine,
Division of Infectious Disease, University of Washington,
Seattle, Washington

Michael F. Epstein, M.D.

Chief Resident, Children's Hospital,
Massachusetts General Hospital,
Boston, Massachusetts

Steven E. Saltman, M.D.

Endocrinologist,
Fullerton Internal Medicine Clinic,
Fullerton, California

SECOND EDITION

ILLUSTRATED

The C. V. Mosby Company

Saint Louis 1977

SECOND EDITION

Printed in the United States of America

Distributed in Great Britain by Henry Kimpton, London

The C. V. Mosby Company
11830 Westline Industrial Drive, St. Louis, Missouri 63141

Library of Congress Cataloging in Publication Data

Corey, Lawrence, comp.
Medicine in a changing society.

Bibliography: p.
Includes index.
1. Medical care—United States. 2. Social medicine—United States. I. Epstein, Michael F., joint comp. II. Saltman, Steven E., joint comp. III. Title.
[DNLM: 1. Physician-Patient relations. 2. Social medicine. WA30 M488]
RA395.A3C74 1977 362.1′0973 76-46313
ISBN 0-8016-1044-3

GW/VH/VH 9 8 7 6 5 4 3 2 1

CONTRIBUTORS

AGNES W. BREWSTER

Formerly Director, Health Economics Branch,
Public Health Service,
U.S. Department of Health, Education, and Welfare,
and Senate Special Committee on Aging

BERTRAM S. BROWN, M.D.

Director, National Institute of Mental Health,
U.S. Department of Health, Education, and Welfare,
Rockville, Maryland

WILBUR J. COHEN, Ph.D., LL.D.

Professor of Public Welfare Administration,
Dean, School of Education,
The University of Michigan,
Ann Arbor, Michigan

BARBARA COOPER

U.S. Department of Health, Education, and Welfare,
Office of the Commissioner,
Social Security Administration

LAWRENCE COREY, M.D.

Senior Fellow in Medicine,
Department of Internal Medicine,
Division of Infectious Disease,
University of Washington,
Seattle, Washington

AVEDIS DONABEDIAN, M.D., M.P.H.

Professor of Medical Care Organization,
Department of Medical Care Organization,
School of Public Health,
The University of Michigan,
Ann Arbor, Michigan

MICHAEL F. EPSTEIN, M.D.

Chief Resident, Children's Hospital,
Massachusetts General Hospital,
Boston, Massachusetts

I. S. FALK, Ph.D.

Professor Emeritus of Public Health (Medical Care),
Yale University School of Medicine;
Chairman, Technical Subcommittee,
Committee for National Health Insurance;
Executive Director,
Community Health Center Plan, a federally qualified Health Maintenance Organization (HMO),
New Haven, Connecticut

EDWARD M. KENNEDY

U.S. Senator from Massachusetts,
Member, Committee on Labor and Public Health,
Chairman, Subcommittee on National Science Foundation,
Chairman, Subcommittee on Health,
Member, Select Committee on Nutrition and Human Needs,
Member, Special Committee on Aging

LORRIN M. KORAN, M.D.

Associate Professor of Psychiatry,
Department of Psychiatry and Behavioral Science,
Health Sciences Center,
S.U.N.Y. at Stony Brook

MARC LaLONDE, P.C., M.P.

Minister of National Health and Welfare,
Ottawa, Canada

VICENTE NAVARRO, M.D., D.M.S.A., Dr. P.H.

Editor-in-Chief International Journal of Health Services,
Department of Health Care Organization, School of Hygiene and Public Health,
Johns Hopkins University,
Baltimore, Maryland

FRANK M. OCHBERG, M.D.

Director, Division of Mental Health Service Programs,
National Institute of Mental Health
Washington, D.C.

ALBERTA PARKER, M.D., M.P.H.

Clinical Professor of Community Health,
School of Public Health,
University of California,
Berkeley, California

STEVEN E. SALTMAN, M.D.

Endocrinologist,
Fullerton Internal Medicine Clinic,
Fullerton, California

ROBERT E. SCHLENKER, Ph.D.

Vice President,
Organized Health Delivery Systems,
InterStudy,
Minneapolis, Minnesota

JOHN D. THOMPSON

Professor of Public Health,
Chief, Division of Health Services Administration,
Yale University School of Medicine;
Professor of Nursing Administration,
Yale University School of Nursing;
Professor, Yale University Institution for Social Policy Studies,
New Haven, Connecticut

H. ASHLEY WEEKS, M.A., Ph.D.

Former Research Scientist Department of Medical Care Organization
School of Public Health
University of Michigan
Ann Arbor, Michigan

LEONARD WOODCOCK

President, International Union, United Auto Workers;
Chairman, Committee for National Health Insurance

To Tom,
whose model we followed.

To our families,
whose support we received.

PREFACE
TO THE SECOND EDITION

In the five years since the first edition of *Medicine in a Changing Society,* much has changed in the process and content of traditional medical education. Many of the reforms that were innovative at the time of our original edition, such as student participation in course-planning and education and courses on alternatives in health care delivery schemes, are now commonplace. What has not changed, however, is the basic purpose of our original and continuing endeavor to illustrate the importance of social change in the clinical practice of medicine.

By describing the extent of the health delivery gap, providing background concerning the historical origins of these problems, and introducing many of the current proposals for solving these issues, we hope to provide some perspective and orientation to the importance of the patients' social milieus in the proper management of health and illness.

As in the original edition, our intent in this book is not directed toward comprehensively covering all the areas or defining all the problems of medical care organization. Rather, our goal is to acquaint students of medicine and other health professions with current viewpoints and developments concerning the major controversies in the United States about the social institution of health care.

Since the rhetoric surrounding health care delivery has changed substantially during the last 5 years, we have extensively revised and updated this edition. New chapters covering concepts of primary care, health maintenance organizations, progressive patient care, and alternatives for financing health care have been added. In addition, revisions have been made in the sections on organizing services and measuring the quality of health care in order to include a reevaluation of the impact of many of the new programs of the late 1960s, such as community mental health centers, Medicare, and Medicaid. Comprehensive chapters describing consumer expectations of health professionals and health services, as well as a description of the currently proposed national health insurance proposals, have been included. Finally, a provocative article illustrating the goals of the Canadian national health plan and the impact it has had on the health of a nation has also been included.

As editors, we have now switched roles—from students to teachers. Our desire for partnership in learning, as expressed in the preface to our first edition, has, however, not changed. For it is still the student who has supplied us with the impetus and desire to continue our endeavors in this area of health maintenance and care.

In addition, we would like to extend our appreciation to the contributors for their adherence to our format and time constraints. We would also like to thank Melvin A. Glasser, whose constructive comments, encouragement, and remarkable insight into the controversies regarding health care delivery were instrumental in the original conception and continued development of this book. In addition, we would like to thank Ms. Carol Adams, Ms. Andrea Valesko, and Ms. Hetty Jackman, whose tolerance and assistance in the preparation of the manuscript were indeed remarkable.

Lawrence Corey

Michael F. Epstein

Steven E. Saltman

PREFACE
TO THE FIRST EDITION

This book represents the result of a process that began many months ago and involved many medical students, physicians, and other health professionals. The book's importance as a pertinent commentary on the problems—and their potential solutions—facing America's health system will depend on its reception and use by both health professional and student. In another sense, however, its value is already assured, for the events that led to the publication of this volume and their implications for medical education are important in themselves.

Formerly, all facets of a student's 4-year sojourn at a medical school were determined by committees wholly composed of faculty members and deans. The influence of medical students on their own education was limited to the indirect method of data collection by questionnaires. These surveys sought student opinion on general educational techniques and goals as well as on specific lecturers, lectures, and topics. Once gathered, however, the information was frequently not used. There were few or no formal channels of communication between students and faculty—no students were members of curriculum-planning committees and no students were members of faculty appointment or promotion committees. When students were able to distribute questionnaire results to the faculty through school newspapers, bulletin boards, or letters, the faculty was frequently more concerned with sampling errors and "representativeness" of the survey than in its underlying significance.

At The University of Michigan this trend changed between 1968 and 1969. The sophomore class, having experienced the frustrations previously described in their freshman year surveys, began to press for real changes in teaching techniques, schedules, and even in some cases, subject matter. They sought the opportunity to become active participants in policy-making in the school. No overwhelming desire was present to completely change structure or function; the students wished only to significantly influence the educational process from which they hoped to benefit.

Students successfully sought appointments to the committee planning the clinical medicine curriculum; evening meetings were held to promote exchange among students, faculty, and administration; and finally the class organized a "discuss-in." This event represented a turning point for student involvement in medical education at The University of Michigan.

Frustration with a public health course led students to boycott scheduled discussion group meetings one afternoon in the fall term. For the first time there was an open confrontation between the School of Public Health's view that the students were receiving what they needed in order to become good physicians and the student's view that in today's society it is not possible to be an effective physician without understanding the social issues and moral, ethical, and organizational problems that derive from the setting in which medicine is practiced. The students called an ad hoc class meeting in a large lecture hall. The dean of the School of Public Health, the professors who planned the curriculum, and the associate deans of the Medical School were invited and, although given only minutes notice, attended the meeting. No longer could they ask of the student leaders, "Who do you represent?" The entire class of 205 students sat in front of them asking questions, answering queries, and expressing opinions and views. The passive approach was finished. The initiative had successfully passed from a few students to the entire class.

The administrations of the Medical School and the School of Public Health (they are separate entities) agreed to open discussions between faculty and students. During the discussions, the students recognized that the curriculum at The University of Michigan Medical School had provided for intermittent and uncoordinated sessions, from time to time, on the social aspects of medicine. They expressed the belief that these efforts, lacking focus and organization and given inadequate time, were not meeting the needs of medical students who would be required to practice in a society undergoing rapid change. They further insisted that formal curriculum recognition be given for a course on medicine in a changing society.

As a result of joint student-faculty discussion (in which the editors of this volume represented the students), the Medical School faculty accepted the constructive nature of the curriculum criticism and went even beyond the expectations of the students in agreeing to the inclusion of a new course in the formal curriculum for second-year students, further stipulating that its organization and development would be placed wholly in the hands of the student committee.

On the basis of extensive analysis and discussion of student interests and needs, the Student Curriculum Committee instituted the proposal, Medicine in a Changing Society. The program began in the fall of 1969.

This book is based on the presentations made in the new course now under way at The University of Michigan Medical School. Its contents have the following basic aims: (1) to provide more knowledge about how health services are and are not being provided in the society, (2) to make possible an in-depth understanding of the problems inherent in the present method of delivery of health care, (3) to develop insights into how current developments in society are affecting the delivery of health services, (4) to stimulate thinking about selected proposals that hold the promise of more effectively relating the medical profession to a changing society.

In addition, other direct and indirect results of that fall 1968 meeting continue to develop today. Some specific reforms at The University of Michigan Medical School are as follows: (1) students are voting members of all medical school standing committees; (2) students are voting members of each department's curriculum committee; (3) students now take part in the faculty retreats that formulate long-range medical center plans; (4) students are represented on several medical center-community committees dealing with community health problems; (5) students are members of search committees for new departmental chairmen; (6) students have been given the opportunity to plan and present their own courses during official university time.

These developments, which directly affect medical education, represent important changes in actual teaching and policy-making at The University of Michigan Medical School; however, we believe that their main importance is in their reflection of a change in attitude. The medical student is no longer viewed as a hollow container to be filled with facts and concepts during the 4-year undergraduate training period but is increasingly being seen as a partner in the process of medical education and in the dynamic changes affecting the profession as a whole.

The partnership of student and faculty in medical education is long overdue and is eminently rational. The ideal partnership is not one that joins two groups with identical resources, but rather one that joins groups that offer different but complementary views and talents. No two groups are better suited for a successful partnership than student and teacher. Sharing the general goals of the profession, they bring different backgrounds, experience, and immediate interests. The combination of the two views has the potential for greater improvement in traditional methods and for increased impetus to implement newer approaches and methods.

The changing role of medical students, as described, is reflected to an even greater extent in the problems and issues with which this book deals. In no field has student participation and contribution been greater than in the area of defining and meeting our profession's responsibility to society. Student groups at many medical schools have been active leaders in the organization and staffing of programs designed to deliver care to the community and in the presentation of symposiums and the establishment of groups organized to study the problems inherent in this delivery. Student participation has not only made many of these community service programs possible but also has further strengthened the position of the student as an active participant and partner in medical education.

In any publication, especially one by students, numerous people are instrumental in its creation. As editors, we would like especially to acknowledge Drs. John Weller, George DeMuth, and Robert A. Green of The University of Michigan Medical School for the encouragement and opportunity given to us in organizing our program, and Mrs. Emily Reece, whose assistance in the preparation of the manuscript was invaluable.

Lawrence Corey

Steven E. Saltman

Michael F. Epstein

CONTENTS

Part one

INEQUITIES IN HEALTH CARE—THE NEED FOR CHANGE

1 Society and health: the dilemma, 3
LAWRENCE COREY, MICHAEL F. EPSTEIN, and STEVEN E. SALTMAN

2 The society—its influence on health care and delivery, 9
VICENTE NAVARRO

3 Health care goals for Americans—1975, 36
LEONARD WOODCOCK

4 Income and disease—the pathology of poverty, 53
H. ASHLEY WEEKS

5 The elderly and disease—Medicare and Medicaid—help and hindrance, 66
AGNES W. BREWSTER

Part two

ISSUES AND PROPOSED SOLUTIONS—ORGANIZATION OF HEALTH SERVICES

6 Primary care—definition and purpose, 83
ALBERTA PARKER

7 The hospital—its role and limitation in the health care system, 107
JOHN D. THOMPSON

8 Health maintenance organizations, 131
ROBERT E. SCHLENKER

9 Community mental health centers—impact and analyses, 141
BERTRAM S. BROWN, LORRIN M. KORAN, and FRANK M. OCHBERG

10 Measuring the quality of medical care, 151
AVEDIS DONABEDIAN

11 Policy issues in national health insurance, 175
WILBUR J. COHEN

12 Financing and cost controls in medical care, 188
I. S. FALK

13 Legislative realities of national health insurance, 206
EDWARD M. KENNEDY

14 The Canadian health care system—its impact on the health of the society, 215
MARC LaLONDE

Part one

INEQUITIES IN HEALTH CARE—THE NEED FOR CHANGE

1

Society and health: the dilemma

LAWRENCE COREY
MICHAEL F. EPSTEIN
STEVEN E. SALTMAN

In traditional terms, the maintenance and restoration of physical well-being, health, have always been the sole domain of the physician. Modern society, however, in its increasingly sophisticated awareness has extended this concept of health to include not only physical comfort but also the mental and social well-being of the individual. Consequently, it has come to expect the physician to recognize and attend to psychosocial as well as physical ailments. Today physicians are expected to be diagnosticians, counselors, psychologists, social workers, laboratory technicians, businessmen, and committed community workers; yet as health professionals, they are untrained in all except the scientific requirements of their occupation. In fact, their professional education is largely a process that increases their isolation from the community.

The boom in biological sciences within the last 25 years has brought with it an emphasis on producing the scientific physician—highly trained, specialized in analyzing data, and skilled in the diagnosis and treatment of organic disease. Taught by scientists with Ph.D. degrees for the first 2 years and by medical specialists in the last 2 years, medical students are well inculcated with the importance of laboratory and clinical investigation. In the quest to master the technical tools necessary to the scientific physician, students are educated in an atmosphere in which the "good patient" is the sick patient, the individual with multiple physical, radiological, and laboratory abnormalities. Students are forced to focus on the patient and the disease as objects; thus, their subjective feelings and understandings of their own and their patient's worlds are left unattended.

In contrast to these realities, most medical school catalogs list two primary goals: (1) to provide the opportunity to learn the technical and scientific skills required to treat disease and (2) to learn the necessary techniques to understand the social and cultural milieu of the physician-patient relationship. During the physician's formal training, however, appropriate emphasis on the second goal has been lost. By graduation, physicians have been prepared to take immediate, scientifically based action in treating ill individuals, but they are often unable to visualize and understand the social context in which both they and their patients function.

The theory that if one is to foster sensitivity and creativity one must educate people in an environment that rewards these principles has been lost in the technological advances in the study of cellular substructure. This is not to say that health professionals and educators must trade technical competence for tenderness. Instead, the concept that health is more than the absence of disease must permeate medical school curricula.

Medicine plays multiple roles in society. It goes beyond its licensed role of curing and preventing disease by functioning at a personal level in reassuring and allaying the anxiety of the individual who turns to a physician. At a sociological level it provides the organization and development of health services. Quite clearly, social and cultural attitudes and values play a major role in the utilization of health services by the public as well as in the implementation of the programs by members of the health professions. Although all medical educators agree that in order to adequately assess the extent of a patient's illness the physician requires knowledge of the person's family, home, and community relationships, the harried house officer's or student's assessment is largely mechanized through a rote series of questions, such as "How much alcohol do you drink?" "How many packs of cigarettes do you smoke per day?" "What do you do for a living?" "How many people live with you?" "Do you have Blue Cross?"

Excluded from the curriculum and hence from the student-physician's developing process of understanding each patient is the sociological context in which medicine is practiced. Questions regarding consumer expectations of health professionals' roles, the health needs of the community, the influence of social and economic class on the receipt and utilization of services, and the evaluation of types of organizations designed to deliver health services are of central importance in practicing health care. Yet most medical school curricula devote little or no time to these questions, and many students are not fully aware of these problems, much less of the possible solutions.

For years exhortation about the "massive crisis" in health care has come from medical, political, sociological, and economic platforms. Yet the impetus to discuss these aspects of health within the formal training years of the medical profession has not come until recently. Probably the prime moving force in promoting this increased concern in the behavioral and social issues facing medicine has been the students themselves. Surveys at many medical schools indicate that changes in student attitudes toward medical practice have occurred. The role models of the fee-for-service, solo practitioner and the academic physician, although still present in large numbers, are increasingly being replaced by physicians having community medicine orientations. Concerned with the social problems in which health is involved—poverty, malnutrition, population control, pollution—students desire to develop better ways of delivering health care to communities.

Professions exist because the people believe they will be better served by licensing specially trained experts to minister to their needs. Society, through its privilege of professional monopoly and its financial subsidization of medical education, places an obligation on the physician, an obligation that many believe is not being adequately fulfilled.

It is indeed difficult for the individual physician, who assumes the daily responsibility and often staggering work hours of a waiting room full of patients, to believe he is not meeting his community or societal responsibility. However, health workers must concern themselves with the overall health of the society, and thus they must also be concerned with those who do not have access to their offices. It must be recognized that providers of care are not performing their role on an organizational level if everyone in their community is not receiving health care. For society, through its financial subsidization of both medical education and health services, is now demanding that the health care needs of all segments of the community be met by medical care providers.

To accomplish universal accessibility to health care will require, however, a change in the medical environment of the teachers, students, and recipients of care. This change in framework must present new models of medical care—models on both individual and societal levels. On an individual level the role model of the primary care physician must be strengthened. The prolonged adolescence of medical education is accompanied by an increasing emphasis on compartmentalization and specialization of teacher, student, and recipient of care. Inpatient care is stressed, complex medical problems are "exciting," and preventative care is quietly glossed over. There are few role models of primary care physicians on medical school faculties, although recognition of this problem on a faculty level is now occurring. However, if society is to ensure that primary care physicians for medically indigent areas are going to be trained, certain incentives to ensure these goals will be necessary. Whether these incentives take the form of financial inducements to practice in medically indigent areas or admission preference to persons who are likely to return to primary care is still controversial. What is not controversial, however, is that the recipients of medical care are asking for a change in their medical environment, a change that allows greater accessibility, less fragmentation, and better quality and cost control.

This book is an attempt to illustrate to students in the health professions the realities of social change and the proposed and necessary adaptations in the delivery system required to successfully accommodate this change.

The initial articles in the book are directed at delineating current problems.

Dr. Navarro in the initial chapter presents us with the historical background for our present system of medical care—how the economic and social class structure of the United States determines the nature and function of the U.S. health sector and how the debated questions of what services to provide and for whom are determined largely by whoever is dominant in the process of defining and directing these questions.

Mr. Woodcock, head of the Committee for National Health Insurance, then stresses the fact that health care is not a problem of only the poor but rather one that extends across all social strata. The average American worker spends one twelfth of his earnings on health care; 8.4% of our total gross national product is spent on health, yet gaps in coverage exist for most Americans—gaps that they wish to close.

In the next chapter Dr. Weeks then emphasizes the direct relationship that income has to health. Increased maternal mortality, increased prenatal mortality, decreased life span, and percentage of bedridden disability days are all related to poor education and low income. Documented evidence shows that hypertension and hypertensive heart disease occur significantly more often in the poor, whether they are black, white, or oriental or live in urban or rural locales. Within the United States, there is a pathology of poverty.

Nowhere, however, has there been a greater gap between promise and performance than in health care to the elderly. Even with Medicare the elderly are paying for health services at a record rate. Dr. Agnes Brewster reviews the inequities in our present Medicare program, analyzes their effects on the health economy over the last 10 years, and makes recommendations for including these programs in a larger health insurance scheme.

With these issues delineated in the initial chapters of this book, the problem of developing practical programs for improved health care is then explored. The issues are varied, and many innovative proposals for solving selected areas of concern have been launched. These programs are approached from an organizational, financial, and evaluative viewpoint.

Since primary care is the area of major deficiency in our present health system, knowledge of what constitutes primary care, how it is presently being delivered, and what should be included in a comprehensive primary care system are all important concerns. Dr. Alberta Parker reviews these concepts and then delineates the framework and goals of a well-integrated primary health care system.

As noted by John D. Thompson, the hospital is only one cog in a health care system. As such, the concerns of hospital administrators, directors, and staff must extend beyond the walls of their institution if they are to provide the personalized yet efficient and economical medical care that patients, third party payers, and regulatory agencies are now requiring.

The concept of integrated medical services, pioneered after World War II by the prepaid group practice plans and extended during the 1960s by the neighborhood health centers has now been officially institutionalized in the health maintenance organization (HMO). Dr. Shenker reviews the structure, function, and organization of presently existing HMOs and discusses the difficulties that these organizations encounter in delivering comprehensive health care.

The impact that a comprehensive health care service can have on the health of a community is then discussed by Drs. Bertram Brown, Lorrin M. Koran, and Frank Ochberg. Drs. Brown, Koran, and Ochberg retrace the experience of community mental health centers and indicate that even though inroads toward health can be made through a reorganization of service, these comprehensive health centers cannot operate in a vacuum. The shift of mental health patients out of inpatient facilities into inadequately financed and understaffed outpatient facilities cannot, however, upgrade the overall mental health problems of a community.

Other issues within the health care field include quality and cost control of health services. Dr. Avedis Donabedian reviews the problems encountered in measuring the quality of medical care and discusses the goals, proposed methodology, and current realities of the proposed PSRO guidelines.

The last section of the book examines the issue of national health insurance. Wilbur Cohen, former Secretary of Health, Education, and Welfare, discusses the currently proposed programs for national health insurance. Dr. I. S. Falk then discusses the area of major controversy within various national health insurance schemes, alternatives toward the financing of health care delivery systems. Dr. Falk discusses the advantages and disadvantages of some of the proposals that Dr. Cohen describes.

Senator Edward Kennedy, the principal advocate of national health insurance legislation within the U.S. Senate, then discusses the legislative realities of a national health insurance scheme. His viewpoints and perspective provide insight into the formulation, process, and type of health care scheme the United States may eventually enjoy.

The final chapter by the Honorable Marc LaLonde, Minister of Health of Canada, is a review of the impact that the Canadian Health Care scheme has had on the health of a nation. This article provides perspective on the role that the organization of medical services can have as an instrument of social, economic, and medical change.

The reader will recognize the following recurring ideas in this presentation:

1. Obtaining high quality medical care is a problem affecting all socioeconomic strata in America; this problem is, however, accentuated among the people who most frequently need medical care—the elderly and the poor.
2. Financial barriers to health exist, are associated with increased morbidity and mortality among the poor, and must be removed if we are ever going to have "public health within the United States."
3. Maldistributed and fractionated health services need correction.
4. Medical care services must be organized into a system that emphasizes health maintenance and prevention.
5. Health knowledge and technology require the expertise of many—health professionals, administrators, and consumers.
6. Many methods of instituting change within our present delivery system exist; however, these methods require a new vitality and vigor.
7. Social, economic, and medical change can be effected by an innovative and comprehensive health care delivery mechanism.

To illustrate how the people who are involved in health care delivery must adapt to the present social climate is our aim; to challenge both our colleagues' and our teachers' established convictions toward the practice of medicine is our hope. If either of these aims is successful, we will consider our endeavor to have been worthwhile.

2

The society—its influence on health care and delivery

VICENTE NAVARRO

■ Sociological, economic, and medical literature frequently attributes the present status of the American health sector to the value system of middle class American society. In this chapter, Dr. Navarro postulates that the present economic structure of the United States determines and maintains a social class structure, both outside and within the health sector; furthermore, it is the different degrees of ownership, control, and influence that these classes have on the means of production, reproduction, and legitimization in the United States that determine the current status of the health sector. It is further postulated that the value system is not the cause but a symptom of these class controls and influences.

In trying to understand the present composition, nature, and functions of the health sector in the United States, one is hampered by a great scarcity of literature, both in the sociological and in the medical care fields, that would explain how the shape and form of the health sector—the tree—is determined by the same economic and political forces shaping the political and economic system of the United States—the forest. In fact, health services literature reveals what C. W. Mills[1] and N. Birnbaum[2] have found in other areas of social research: a predominance of empiricism, leading to dominance of experts on trees who neither analyze nor question the forest but accept it as given.

Health services research, like most social research, has become more and more compartmentalized, with its practitioners turning into narrower and narrower specialists, superbly trained in their own fields, but with less and less comprehension of the total. And yet, the hegelian dictum that "the truth is the whole" continues with its undiminished

I want to express my great appreciation to Christopher George for editing this paper, to Janet Archer for preparing the figures and tables, and to Loetta Wallace for assisting me and typing the manuscript.

validity. There is a need for explanation of how the parts are related to each other, and it is in meeting this need that our empiricists have fallen short and, for the most part, have remained silent. It is to break this deafening silence that this chapter has been written. Although admittedly full of assumptions, perceptions, and values, it will try to show that the composition and distribution of health resources are determined by the same forces that determine the distribution of economic and political power in our society. Indeed, I would postulate that the former cannot be understood without an understanding of the latter.

The article is divided into three sections. The first is an analysis of the current social class and economic structures of the United States, both outside and within the health sector. The second analyzes the different degrees by which social class influences and controls the financing and delivery of care in health institutions, and the third analyzes the effects of class on the organs of the state. It is theorized that these social class influences on the institutions of production, reproduction, and legitimization determine the composition, nature, and functions of the health sector.

THE CLASS STRUCTURE OF THE UNITED STATES, OUTSIDE AND WITHIN THE HEALTH SECTOR

In attempting to explain and understand the composition, functions, and nature of the health sector, one must first look outside the health sector and address a key question in any society—who owns and who controls the income and wealth of that society? Thus, I have to revive a forgotten paradigm in social analysis in the United States: that of social class structure. In so doing, I am going against the mainstream of our sociological research, which assumes that this category has been transcended by the present reality of the United States, where it is considered that most of our population is middle class. Actually, it is assumed in most of the press and in most of academia that the contemporary United States is being recast in a mold of middle class conditions and styles of life. Moreover, this situation is considered to be the result of social fluidity and mobility that is believed to falsify past characterizations of the United States as a class society. This conclusion, however, seems to confuse class consciousness with class interests. Indeed, the social reality that establishes the level of social aspiration of the American population as the consumption pattern of the middle class and the assumed concomitant absence of class consciousness do not deny the existence of social classes. In fact, as C. W. Mills pointed out,

> . . . the fact that men are not 'class conscious', at all times and in all places does not mean that there are no classes or that 'in America everybody is middle

class'. The economic and social facts are one thing. Psychological feelings may or may not be associated with them in rationally expected ways. Both are important, and if psychological feelings and political outlooks do not correspond to economic or occupational class, we must try to find out why, rather than throw out the economic baby with the psychological bath, and so fail to understand how either fits into the national tub.[3]

Actually, there is not even convincing evidence that class consciousness or awareness does not exist. According to a study conducted in 1964, 56% of Americans said that they thought of themselves as "working class," about 39% considered themselves "middle class," and 1% said they were "upper class." Only 2% rejected the whole idea of class.[4]

An analysis of the social structure of the United States shows that there are indeed social classes in this country. There are a relatively small number of people on the top, who own a markedly disproportionate share of personal wealth and whose income is largely derived from ownership. Many of these owners also control the uses of their assets. But, increasingly, this control is vested in people who, although wealthy themselves, do not personally own more than a small part of the assets they control—the managers of that wealth. Both the owners and the controllers of wealth constitute what can be defined as the upper class, or for reasons to be defined later, the corporate class, and they command, by virtue of ownership or control or both, the most important sectors of economic life.

At the other end of the social scale is the working class, composed primarily of industrial or blue collar workers, the workers of the services sector, and also the agricultural wage earners, although the last form a steadily decreasing part of the labor force. In 1970 these groups represented 35%, 12%, and 1.8% of the labor force, respectively.[5] This working class remains a distinct and specific social formation "by virtue of a combination of characteristics which affect its members in comparison with the members of other classes."[6] It is also primarily from their ranks that the unemployed, the poor, and the subproletariat come.

Between the "polar" classes is the middle class, consisting of (1) the professionals, including doctors, lawyers, middle rank executives, academicians, and others, whose main denominator is that their work is intellectual as opposed to manual and whose work usually requires professional training; (2) the business middle class, associated with small and medium-sized enterprises, ranging from businessmen employing a few workers to owners of fairly sizable enterprises of every kind, who are the owners and controllers of O'Connor's competitive sector or of Galbraith's market sector of our economy; (3) the self-

Table 1. Occupational and social class distribution in the United States*

Distribution of labor force		Social class	Estimated annual median income (1970)
Percentage (1970)	Occupational group		
1.3%	Corporate owners and managers	Corporate class	$80-100,000
14%	Professionals and technicals	Upper middle class	18,000
6%	Business middle class executives	Upper middle class	16,000
7%	Self-employed, Shopkeepers, craftsmen, and artisans	Lower middle class	8,500
23%	Clerical and sales workers	Lower middle class	6,500
35%	Manual workers	Working class	6,000
12%	Service workers	Working class	4,000
1.8%	Farm workers	Working class	2,600

*Adapted from Bownell, V., and Reich, M.: Workers and the American economy: data on the labor force, Boston, 1973, New England Free Press; Consumer income: income growth rates in 1939 to 1968 for persons by occupation and industry groups, for the United States, Current population reports, Series P60, no. 69, Boston, 1970; Giddens, A.: The class structure of the advanced societies, London, 1973, Hutchinson University Press.

employed shopkeepers, craftsmen, and artisans, a declining sector of the labor force, representing less than 8% of that force; and (4) the office and sales workers (the majority of the white collar workers), the group that has increased most rapidly within the labor force in the last two decades and that today represents almost a quarter of the labor force of the United States and of most Western European countries. This last group differs in its career prospects, conditions of work, status, and style of life from the industrial working class, and its own view of itself is definitely not working class. In terms of median income, however, it was closer at $6,000 per worker (in 1968) to the blue collar worker's median income of $5,800 and to the service worker's $4,000 than to the median income of any of the other three middle class groups, for example, the median income of the professionals, which was $14,000.[7]

For reasons of brevity, and recognizing the simplifications that this categorization implies, I will continue in this paper to refer to groups 1 and 2 as the upper middle class and groups 3 and 4 as the lower middle class. Table 1 shows, in summary form, the percentage of the popula-

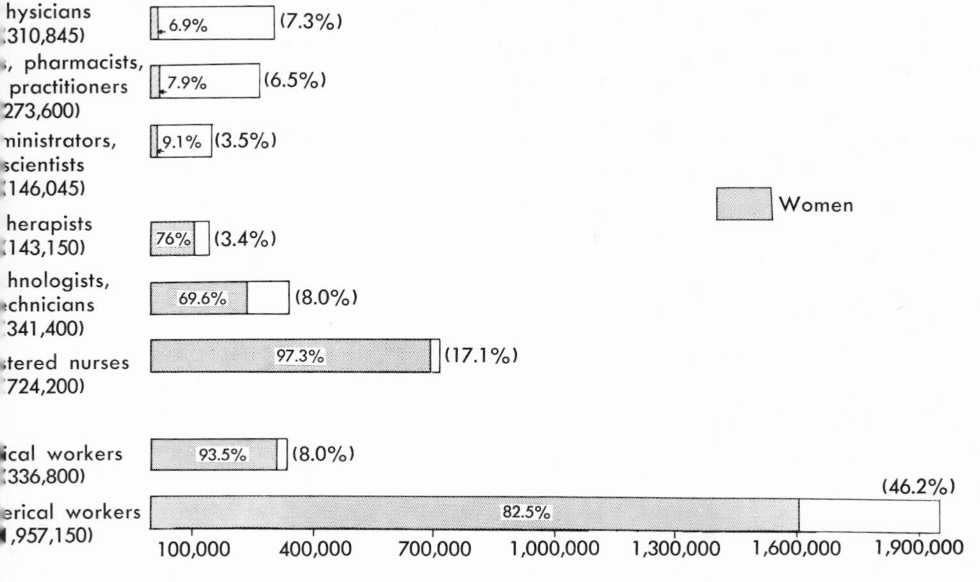

Fig. 1. Persons employed in the delivery of health services in the United States, by sex, in 1970. (Numbers in parentheses indicate percentage of total health labor force represented by that occupational category.)

tion and of the labor force in each occupational category and social class and gives the annual median income for each category.

The distributions of wealth and income follow these class lines, with the highest possession of both at the top and the lowest possession at the bottom. Moreover, these distribution patterns of wealth and income have remained remarkably constant over time. In the last retrospective study of the distribution of income, published in the 1974 annual *Economic Report of the President* and widely reported in the press, it was found "that the bottom 20 per cent of all families had 5.1 per cent of the nation's income in 1947 and had almost the same amount, 5.4 per cent, in 1972. At the top, there was a similar absence of significant change. The richest 20 per cent had 43.3 per cent of the income in 1947 and 41.4 per cent in 1972."

This class structure in our society is also reflected in the composition of the different elements that participate in the health sector, either as owners, controllers, or producers of services. Indeed, considering just the health sector and analyzing the owners, controllers, and producers of services in health institutions, we find that members of the upper class and, to a lesser degree, the upper middle class (groups 1 and 2 of the middle class in the previous categorization) predominate in the decision-making bodies of our health institutions, for example, the boards of trustees of foundations, teaching hospital institutions, medical schools, and hospitals. For the producers and the members of the labor force in the health sector we can see the distribution shown in Fig. 1. At the top we find the physicians, who are mainly of upper middle backgrounds and who had in 1970 a median annual net income of $40,000, which places them in the top 5% of our society. I should add that the majority of persons in this group are white and male, besides being upper middle class. They represent 7.3% of the whole labor force in the health sector.

Below, very much below, the upper class of the health sector, we find the level called paraprofessional. This could be defined as equivalent to the lower middle class, office worker category of the previous categorization (category 4), for example, nurses, physical therapists, occupational therapists, and others, whose annual median income was approximately $6,000 in 1970. They represent 28.5% of the labor force in the health sector. This group is primarily female and is part of the lower income group; 9% of it is black.

Below this group we find the working class per se of the health sector, the auxiliary, ancillary, and service personnel, representing 54.2% of the health services labor force, who are predominantly women (84.1%) and who include an overrepresentation of blacks (30%). This group's median income was $4,000 in 1970.

If we look at income distribution in the health sector, as we did for society in general, we find a similar structure, although here again we find a great scarcity of information and empirical data. Fig. 2, however, shows the trend in the differentials of median income among the different groups of producers in the health sector. Here we can see that there has been a very dramatic increase in the income differentials between the top and bottom income groups of the health industry.

Much has been written about the reasons for these income differentials. According to the orthodox economic paradigm, "every agent of production receives the amount of wealth that agent creates" and "every man receives all that he creates." Thus, workers' incomes depend on their productivity, "on the amount of capital available, on the one hand, and on workers' skills and education, on the other."[8] According to this interpretation, the conditions for social mobility are (1) increased education, to improve the workers' positions in the market for their skills and (2) equal opportunity for each worker in the competitive labor market. The strategy, then, is to increase educational opportunities and to break the race and sex discrimination, which prevents the market forces from functioning properly. This paradigm is shared, incidentally, by the majority of people in the black and women's liberation

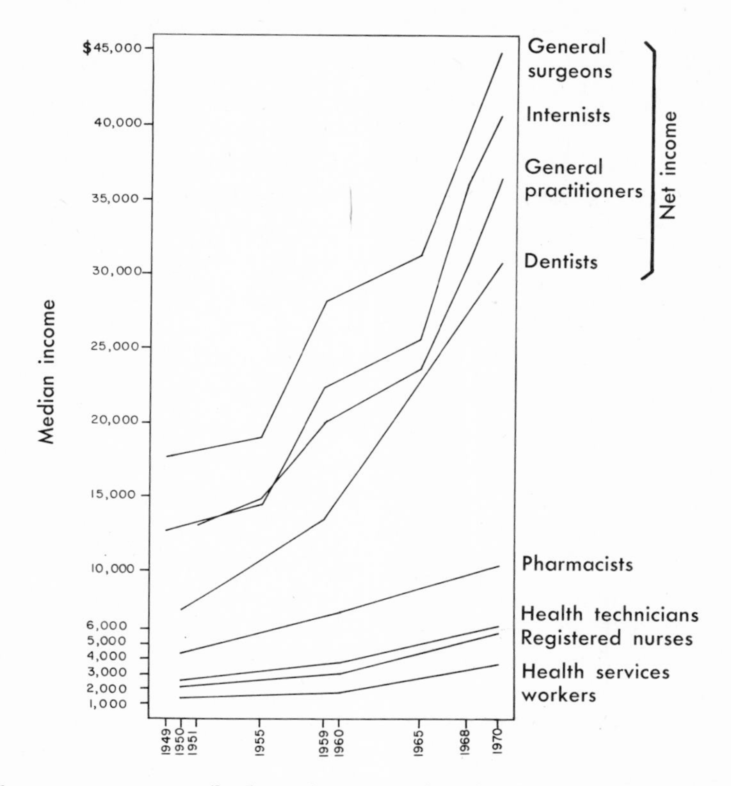

Fig. 2. The rise in income of selected personnel in the delivery of health services in the United States, 1949-1970.

movements within and outside the health sector. However, absent in this analysis is the concept of property and class.

Empirical evidence, however, seems to question the main assumptions of the liberal paradigm. Regarding the social mobility that is supposed to be the result of the widening of opportunities and of the free flow of labor market forces and that is supposed to have caused the withering away of the social classes, Westergaard[9] and others have recently shown that, although there has been some mobility among the different social groups or strata within each social class, there has been practically no mobility among social classes. In addition, the primary result of education, rather than being the transmission of skills to aid upward mobility, seems to have been the perpetuation of social roles within the predefined social classes. Indeed, Bowles and Gintis,[10] among others, have indicated how education, labor markets, and industrial structures interact to produce distinctive social strata *within* each class. A similar situation prevails in the health sector, where Simpson[11] and Robson[12] in England and Kleinbach[13] in the United States have shown

(1) how the social class backgrounds of the main groups within the health labor force have not changed during the last 25 years and (2) how education fixes and perpetuates those social backgrounds and replicates social roles.

In the United States in 1968, only 17% of the physicians were the children of craftsmen or skilled and unskilled laborers, who represented 57% of the whole labor force, while over 31% of the physicians were children of professionals, who represented 4.9% of the labor force.[11] Actually, it is quite interesting and, I would add, not surprising to note that while the underrepresentation of women and blacks among new entrants to the medical schools slowly, but steadily, diminished over the last decade, the underrepresentation of entrants with working class and lower middle class backgrounds remained remarkably constant during the same period. Indeed, women, who represent 51% of the U.S. population, made up 6% of all medical students in 1961 and 16% in 1973, while blacks, representing 12% of the overall U.S. population, went from 2% to 6% of all medical students during the same time period. During these years the percentage of medical students who came from families earning the median family income or below, representing approximately one half of the population, remained at 12%. This percentage has remained the same since 1920.[14]

This evidence would seem to indicate that there is not an automatic trend toward diminishing class differences or bringing about social class mobility within and outside the health sector of the United States at present. As in the past, experience seems to show that, as Harold Laski used to say, "the careful selection of one's own parents" remains among the most important variables explaining one's own power, wealth, income, and opportunities.[6] The importance of this selection, moreover, seems to be particularly vital at the top.

It would seem, then, that the liberal paradigm does not sufficiently explain the current composition of the labor force and its class and income structure. Indeed, I would postulate that a better explanation of that structure would be that the inequalities of income, wealth, and economic and political power are functionally related to the way in which the means of production and reproduction of goods, commodities, and services and the organs of legitimization in the United States are owned, controlled, influenced, and directed.

According to this interpretation, property and control of and/or influence on those means of production, reproduction, and legitimization are not just marginal factors in explaining class structure and income differentials, as the liberal paradigm would suggest, but key explanatory ones. Thus, in this alternative explanation, the overall distribution of wealth and income depends on who owns, controls, influences, and directs the means of production, reproduction, and legitimization in the different sectors of the U.S. economy. Overall income differentials among social classes, then, do not have as much to do with the free operation of the labor market forces as with the patterns of ownership and control of the main means of income-producing wealth and of the organs of legitimization—communication, education, and the agencies of the state. Education and other means of socialization are not the means of creating upward mobility among social classes but actually are the means of perpetuating patterns of control and ownership.

In summary, social classes and income differentials are the result of the different degrees of ownership, control, and influence that different social classes have over the means of production and consumption and over the organs of legitimization, including the media, communications, education, and even the organs of state. Moreover, these class influences determine not only the nature of the economic sectors in the United States today but also the nature of the social sectors, including that of the health services.

THE CONTROL OF THE FINANCIAL AND HEALTH DELIVERY INSTITUTIONS

Before discussing the controlling influences in health services, it is important to examine the different sectors of the American economy and the position of health services within them.

O'Connor[15] and Galbraith,[16] among others, have recently defined three different sectors in the United States economy: the planned or monopolistic sector, the market or competitive sector, and the state sector.

The *planned* or *monopolistic sector,* which employs about a third of the labor force, is characterized by being capital intensive as opposed to labor intensive, national in contrast to regional or local, and highly monopolistic both in economic concentration and in economic behavior (such as in the use of price fixing). Important characteristics of this sector are its requirements for economic stability and planning and a tendency toward vertical integration (for example, the control of raw materials from the point of extraction to the process of production and distribution) as well as horizontal integration (as in the control of different vertical sectors of the industry and the establishment of conglomerates). If we look at the social makeup of this sector, we find (1) the corporation owners (the stockholders) and the controllers (or managers), who Galbraith[16] says together make up the "corporate community" and whom Miliband[6] labels the "large business community," and whom, according to my own definition outlined before, we would call the corporate class; (2) the technocracy or professionals, group 1 of my categorization of the middle class; (3) the blue collar workers, highly unionized in this sector, who correspond to the industrial working class of my previous categorization; and (4) the white collar workers, the technical and administrative workers, or lower middle class.

The second sector, the *market* or *competitive sector,* used to be the largest of the three sectors but today is the smallest and continues to decline. It employs less than one third of our labor force, with the largest proportion of workers being in services and distribution.[15] It is characterized by being labor intensive, local or regional in scope, with a relatively weak labor force and low unionization. Examples of workers in this sector are people working in restaurants, drug stores, and commercial display. The social makeup of this sector consists of (1) the owners and controllers (executives) of small scale, localized industries and services, group 2 of my own categorization of the upper middle class, (2) small percentages of blue collar workers, (3) small percentages of white collar workers, and (4) a large sector of service workers, who are primarily auxiliary and ancillary personnel.

The third major sector is the *state sector,* which is made up of two subsectors. The first subsector produces goods and services under the

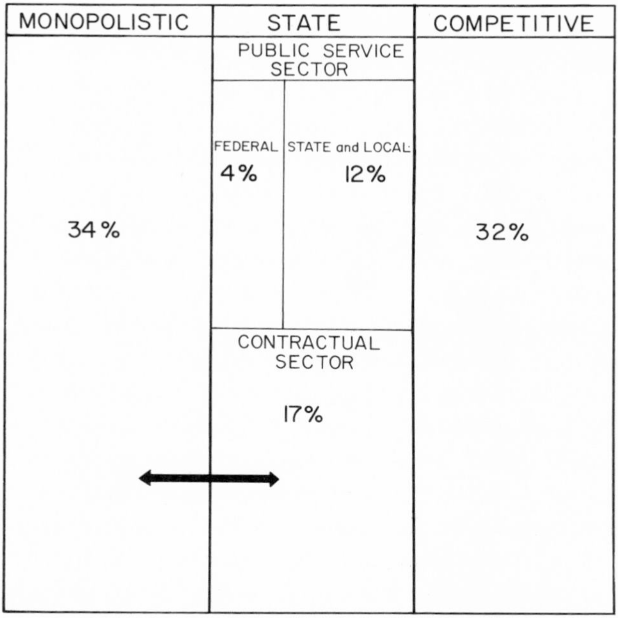

Fig. 3. Approximate percentage of labor force in each sector of the U.S. economy.

direction of the state itself, for example, the public health services, and the second involves production organized by industries under contract from the state. The contracts, such as for military equipment and supplies, are mainly with corporations belonging to the monopolistic sector. In terms of social makeup, the first subsector, employing close to 17% of the labor force, has characteristics similar to that of the market system, while the other—the contractual one—also employs 17% of the labor force and is part of the monopolistic sector. Fig. 3 summarizes the percentage of the labor force in each sector and Table 2 the main characteristics of the production and labor force in each sector.

Of these three sectors, the most important one for an explanation of the present economic system of the United States and also, according to my postulate, for a partial explanation of the situation in the health field is the monopolistic sector. Actually, the owners and controllers of that sector, the American corporate class, have a pervasive and dominant influence over the patterns of production and consumption of the United States. Their influence affects the most important means of production and distribution in the United States as well as the means of value generation, including the media, the educational institutions, and the organs of the state. I believe that in the health sector that same class, augmented in this case by the upper middle classes (the professionals and the business middle class of my categorization), maintains a dominant influence on (1) the financial and health delivery institutions, (2) the health teaching institutions, and (3) the organs of the state in the health sector.

A main characteristic of the United States and most Western economies is the high concentration of economic wealth in the monopolistic sector. At the top in 1967, a few giant corporations (958 or just 0.06%) held a majority of all assets ($1,070 billion or 53.2%), while at the bottom, a large number of small corporations (906,458 or 59% of the total) held a very small, almost minuscule portion of corporate assets ($31 billion or 1.5%)[17] (Table 3).

This concentration of corporate economic power replicates itself in the several sectors that constitute the economy of the United States. For example, in the key area of manufacturing, in 1962 a mere 100 firms (out of a total of 180,000 corporations and 240,000 unincorporated businesses) owned 58% of the net capital assets of all the hundreds of thousands of manufacturing corporations. Another way of expressing this extraordinary degree of concentration is, as Hunt and Sherman point out, that "the largest 20 manufacturing firms owned a larger share of the assets than the smallest 419,000 firms combined."[17]

Another sector within the corporate side of the economy is the financial capital sector, which includes the banks, trusts, and insurance

Table 2. Production and labor force characteristics of each sector of the U.S. economy

Monopolistic	State		Competitive
	Contractual	**Service**	
Characteristics of production	Primarily manufacturing Economic concentration Highly monopolistic Vertical and horizontal integration (conglomerates) National and international	Primarily service Economic deconcentration Monopolistic Vertical and sectorial Federal, state, local	Primarily trade and service Economic deconcentration Competitive Vertical and sectorial Regional and local
Characteristics of labor force	Predominantly male Nonwhites underrepresented Unionized Salaries relatively high	Predominantly female Nonwhites proportionally represented Nonunionized Salaries medium	Predominantly female Nonwhites overrepresented Nonunionized Salaries low

Table 3. Distribution of corporate assets (all U.S. corporations, 1967)*

Size (lower limit in dollars)	Corporations (percent)	Assets owned (percent)
0	59.00	1
100,000	29.00	5
500,000	10.00	10
5,000,000	1.94	31
250,000,000	0.06	53
TOTAL	100.00	100

*Adapted from Hunt, E. K., and Sherman, H. J.: Economics: an introduction to traditional and radical views, New York, 1972, Harper & Row, Publishers.

companies. Highly concentrated itself, this group exerts a dominant influence in the corporate sector, primarily through lending to the corporations. Actually, as a congressional committee report indicated recently, accumulated evidence shows that corporations are not self-sufficient in terms of financial capital but are increasingly dependent on the financial institutions for their capital needs. This dependency leads to influence on corporate policies by the financial capital institutions, through ownership of corporate stocks and the interlocking of directorships on their boards.

Not surprisingly, the top financial institutions are also important in the health industry, the second largest industry in the country. According to the *National Journal,*[18] the flow of health insurance money through private insurance companies in 1973 was $29 billion, slightly less than half of the total insurance, health and other, sold in this country in that year. About $15 billion, or over half of this money, flowed through the commercial insurance companies. Among these companies we find, again, a high concentration of financial capital, with the ten largest commercial health insurers (Aetna, Travellers, Metropolitan Life, Prudential, CNA, Equitable, Mutual of Omaha, Connecticut General, John Hancock, and Provident) controlling close to 60% of the entire commercial health insurance industry. Most of these top health insurance companies are also the biggest life insurance companies, which along with the banks are the most important controllers of financial capital in this country. Metropolitan Life and Prudential, for instance, each control $30 billion in assets, making them far larger than General Motors, Standard Oil of New Jersey, and ITT.[19] These financial entities have close links with banking, and through the banks they exercise a powerful influence over the top corporations.

The importance of this influence, defined by the Subcommittee on Government Operations of the U.S. Senate and others as dominance over the overall economy, is reflected in the present debate on the different proposals for national health insurance, on whether to "open the doors" to the commercials or keep them out of the coming national health insurance scene. It actually speaks highly of the great political influence and power of these financial capital institutions that all the proposals except one (the Kennedy-Griffith proposal, whose main constituency was the trade unions of the monopolistic sector, the AFL-CIO and UAW) have left room for and even encouraged the involvement of the commercials in the health sector. The Nixon and the Ford administration's proposal, for example, would increase the flow of money through the private insurance industry (including commercial health insurance) from $29 billion to $42 billion, with another $14 billion handled by the private carriers in their role as intermediaries in the publicly financed segment of the proposal.[18] Actually, it was the power of the commercial insurance companies that determined a change in the Kennedy-Griffith proposal—to acceptance of the role of these companies in the new Kennedy-Mills proposal. In fact, the decision of the Kennedy-Mills proposal to retain the insurance companies' role was based on recognition of that industry's power to kill any legislation it considers unacceptable. The bill's sponsors thus had to choose between appeasing the insurance industry and obtaining no national health insurance at all.

Thus, the same financial and corporate forces that are dominant in shaping the American economy also increasingly shape the health services sector. Although the largest financial powers in the premium market in the health sector, the commercial insurance companies are not the only ones. They compete with the power of the providers, expressed in the insurance sector primarily through the Blues—Blue Cross and Blue Shield. The controllers of both the commercials and the Blues, although sharing class interests, have opposite and conflicting corporate interests. Actually, it is likely that the predominance of financial capital in the health sector, and specifically of commercial insurance, could mean the weakening of the providers' control of the health sector, analogous to the way in which the predominance of the monopolistic sector—financial and corporate—has meant the weakening of the market or competitive sector. If this should come about, we would probably see the proletarianization of the providers, with providers being mere employees of the finance corporations, the commercial insurance companies. In this respect, unionization of the medical profession would be a symptom of its proletarianization, so the incipient but steady trend toward unionization of the medical profession may be an indication of things to come in the health sector.

THE CONTROL OF THE HEALTH REPRODUCTORY INSTITUTIONS

In order to understand the patterns of control and/or influence in the health sector, we have to look not only at the patterns of control in the financing of health services, but also at the patterns of control and influence in the health delivery institutions. Indeed, financial capital, the money or energy that moves the system, goes through prefixed institutional channels that are owned, controlled, and/or influenced by classes and groups that are similar to, although not identical with, those who have dominant influence through financing. We can group the institutions into (1) those that have to do with the reproduction and legitimization of the patterns of control and influence, such as the teaching institutions, and (2) those that deliver the services themselves. Following this categorization, we could speak of reproductive versus distributive institutions.

The former, in which I would include the foundations (for example, the Johnson, Rockefeller, and Carnegie Foundations) as well as the teaching medical institutions, are controlled by the financial and corporate communities and by the professionals, the corporate class and the upper middle class (1) of my initial categorization. As Professor MacIver writes,[20] "in the non-governmental [teaching] institutions, the typical board member is associated with large-scale business, a banker, manufacturer, business executive, or prominent lawyer," to which, in the health sector, we could add a prominent physician. For instance, one study showed that of the 734 trustees of thirty leading universities half were recognized members of the professions and half were proprietors, managers, or bankers.[21] Incidentally, it is quite misleading to assume that the class and corporate role of such board members is a passive one or that their function is one of rubber stamping what the administrators and medical faculty decide. In fact, their assumed passivity is really delegated control. Concerning the highest decisions, theirs is the first and final voice, and their primary role, as Galbraith has indicated, is to ensure that "the aims of higher education, of course, are to be attuned to the needs of the industrial [corporate] system," which is usually also referred to as the "private enterprise system."[22] In 1961, Dr. Pusey, then the President of Harvard, made this quite explicit when he said in a remarkable speech that "the end of all academic departments . . . is completely directed towards making the *private enterprise system* continue to work effectively and beneficially in a very difficult world."[23] This clearly ideological statement, from a supposedly unideological academic leader of a presumably unideological establishment, is meritorious for its clarity, conciseness, and straightforwardness. In fact, this commitment, which is far more typical than atypical of our academic institutions and foundations, cannot be dissociated from the predominant membership of corporate and business leaders on the boards of trustees of academia and foundations. The function and purpose of this dominant influence on the boards of trustees are to perpetuate the sets of values that will optimize their collective benefits as class and as corporate interests.

Allow me to clarify here that I do not believe that there is monopoly control of the value-generating system. However, I do think that the influence and control of that system are highly skewed in favor of the corporate and financial value system. And this dominant influence is felt not only in universities, foundations, and institutions of higher learning but also in most of the value-generating systems, from the media to all other instruments of communication. As Miliband says, all these value-generating systems do contribute to the

> . . . fostering of a climate of conformity, not by the total suppression of dissent, but by the presentation of views which fall outside the consensus as curious heresies, or, even more effectively, by treating them as irrelevant eccentricities, which serious and reasonable people may dismiss as of no consequence. This is very functional (for the system).[6]

Actually, another indication of this dominance of corporate values can be seen in the present debate in academia on national health insurance. In spite of the "hot" debate as to what type and nature of national health insurance "Americans may choose" and in spite of the critical nature of comments about our health sector made by many parts of academia and even the mass media, not one of the proposals and not one report in the media questions the sanctity of the private sector or its pattern of control of our health institutions. And a whole series of alternatives that would question the present pattern, such as different types of national health services as opposed to just national health insurance, are not even thought of or are quickly dismissed as being "un-American." The sanctity of "private enterprise values," however, has more to do with the pattern of control of the value-generating system by the financial and corporate interests than with the genetic-biological structure of the American population. As Marcuse has indicated, the success of the system is to make unthinkable the possibility of its alternatives.[23]

THE CONTROL OF THE HEALTH DISTRIBUTION INSTITUTIONS

The voluntary community hospitals are the largest component of the health distribution institutions. Analyzing the boards of trustees of

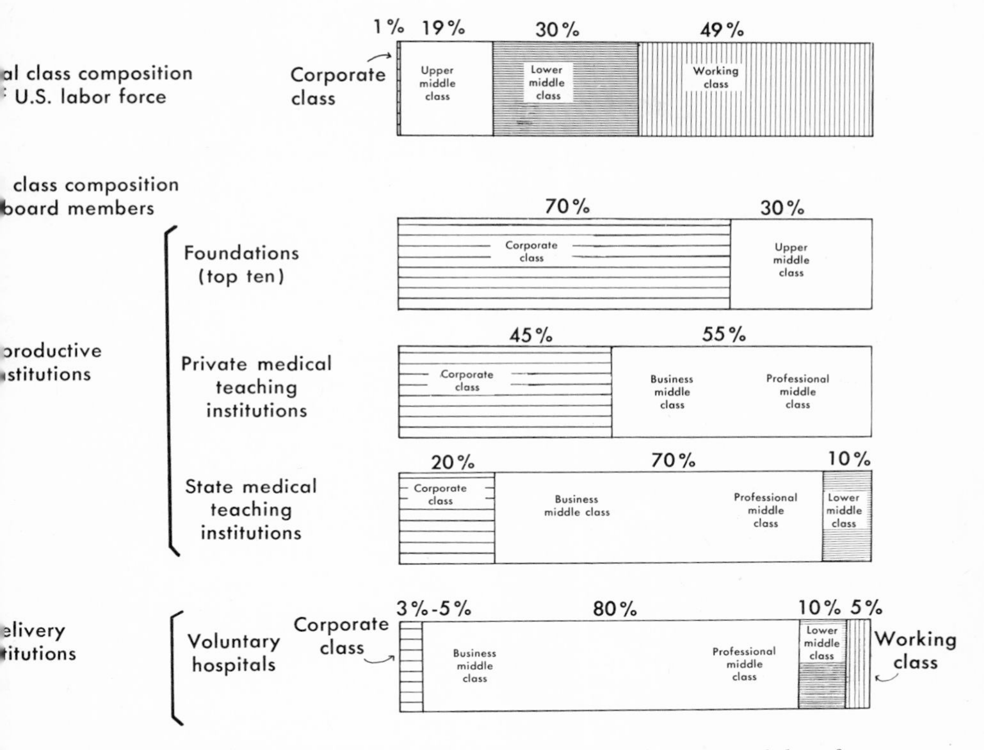

Fig. 4. Summary of the percentage class distribution of the U.S. labor force.

these hospitals, one sees less predominance of the representatives of financial and corporate capital and more of the upper middle class, primarily of sections 1 and 2 defined before—the professionals, especially physicians, and representatives of the business middle class. Even here, the other strata and classes—the working class and lower middle classes, which constitute the majority of the U.S. population—are not represented. Fig. 4 presents a summary of the percentage of class distribution of the U.S. labor force and how the classes are represented on the boards of the reproductive and distributive health institutions.

From the previous analysis it should be clear that I disagree with most of my colleagues, who perceive the present, basic dialectical conflict in the health sector of the United States—both in financing and in delivering health services—as being between the consumers and the providers. To me this is a simplification that obfuscates the nature of the distribution of economic and political power in the United States today both inside and outside the health sector. Although I would agree that the present delivery system seems to be controlled primarily by the providers and their different components—either the "patricians" or academia-based medical personnel, the practitioners or the AMA, and the hospital organizations or AHA—I would disagree with the proposition that there is an inherent control given to them by their "unique" knowledge or that the situation cannot be changed. Actually, the power of the medical profession is delegated power. As Freidson has indicated, "a profession attains and maintains its position by virtue of the protection and patronage of some elite segment of society which has been persuaded that there is some special value in its work."[24] But this section or segment of the population is not so much an economic elite as a class, the corporate class described before.

The great influence of the providers over the health institutions, which amounts to control of the health sector, is based on power delegated from other groups and classes, primarily the corporate class and the upper middle class, to which the providers belong. Their specific interests may actually be in conflict with the power of other groups or strata within the upper middle class and with the greater power of the corporate class. Indeed, as I have indicated elsewhere, the corporate powers of England and Sweden not only tolerated but even supported the nationalization of the health sector when the corporate interests required it, formalizing a dependency of the medical profession on those corporate and state interests.[25]

To define the main dialectical conflict in the health sector as one of providers versus consumers assumes that (1) providers have the final and most powerful control of decision making in the health sector and (2) consumers have a uniformity of interests, transcending class and other interests. Control of the health institutions, however, is primarily class control by the classes and groups described before and only secondarily control by the professions. The dialectical conflicts that exist are not, then, between the providers and the consumers, but instead there is conflict (1) between the corporate class and the providers over the financing of the health sector and (2) between the majority of the U.S. population, who belong to the working and lower middle classes and the controllers of the health delivery system, the corporate class, the upper middle class, and the professionals.

THE CORPORATE SYSTEM AND THE STATE

The final aspect of my analysis is the question of who has dominant influence over the state.

Before attempting to answer this question, let me describe what I consider to be erroneous answers. One of these is that government is run by business. As one of the proponents of this theory says, "Government is run by big business."[26] This idea is similar to Marx and Engel's statement in the *Communist Manifesto* that the "state is the executive committee of the bourgeoisie." I find such statements too much of a simplification. I find equally simplistic the idea, quite prevalent among our scholars, that the state organs are "above" business or that business is even actually antigovernment. I believe this explanation to be unhistorical and unempirical. Actually, in the executive branch of government,

> businessmen were in fact the largest single occupational group in cabinets from 1889 to 1949; of the total number of cabinet members between these dates, more than 60 per cent were businessmen of one sort or another. Nor certainly was the business membership of American cabinets less marked in the Eisenhower years from 1953 to 1961. As for members of British cabinets between 1886 and 1950, close to one-third were businessmen, including three prime ministers—Bonar Law, Baldwin and Chamberlain. Nor again have businessmen been at all badly represented in the Conservative cabinets which held office between 1951 and 1964.[6]

In respect to the legislative branch in 1970, as Hunt and Sherman point out:

> A total of 102 congressmen held stock or well-paying executive positions in banks or other financial institutions; 81 received regular income from law firms that generally represented big businesses. Sixty-three got their income from stock in the top defense contractors; 45, in the giant (federally regulated) oil and gas industries; 22, in radio and television companies; 11, in commerical airlines; and 9, in railroads. Ninety-eight congressmen were involved in numerous capital-gains transactions; each of them netted a profit of over $5,000 (and some as high as $35,000).[17]

It is, therefore, difficult to conclude from these figures that businessmen are antigovernment. Let me add that while these businessmen in the corridors of power may not necessarily think of themselves as business representatives holding state power, it is highly unlikely that their vision of national interest runs against the interests of the business community. Indeed, values and beliefs do not change when the call of government takes place. The appointment of businessmen to positions of power has also been the practice in the federal health establishment. In the dichotomy between business and labor, labor leaders have been a very small minority indeed in the key positions of either the executive or legislative branches.

This heavy involvement of businessmen in government, then, makes one begin to question the widely held belief that businessmen are against government. But, on the other hand, this involvement in and influence on the state should not lead to the opposite conclusion that businessmen are the government—at least not in the way that the land-owning aristocracy was the government in the eighteenth century.

Indeed, sharing the power of government with big business are other groups who represent different interests. In the executive branch of the federal health establishment, for example, powerful groups with whom the businessmen share power are the professionals of academic medicine—the patricians—and to a lesser degree, the practitioners. These two groups, while they are not the top decision makers (these are usually businessmen), do contol the next highest echelons of policy in the executive branch of the federal health establishment; for example, they are the Assistant Secretaries (and below) of health. The medical practitioners, who control the AMA, tend to exert more influence on the legislative branch of the federal government than on the executive.

There is indeed a diversity of interests in the health sector. Yet within this diversity that causes the plurality of sources of power in the federal establishment, there is a uniformity that unites these groups and sets them apart from other groups who do not share their basic characteristics of social origin, education, and class situation. As Professor Matthews notes:

> Those American political decision-makers for whom this information is available are, with very few exceptions, sons of professional men, proprietors and officials, and farmers. A very small minority were sons of wage-earners, low salaried workers, farm labourers or tenants . . . the narrow base from which political decision-makers appear to be recruited is clear.[6]

In fact, the majority of the governing classes belong, by social origin and by previous occupation, to our corporate and upper middle classes, as defined before.

Let me reiterate that I am not implying that the corporate class and the upper middle class, which predominate in and dominate the corridors of power, act and behave uniformly on the political scene. Indeed, they represent a plurality of interests that determines what is usually referred to as the "political pluralism" of our society. This plurality is reflected in the different programs put forward by the main political parties. In that respect, it is far from my intention to imply that all proposals for national health insurance, for example, are the same or that they represent the same groups. Differences *do* exist, but the nature of this political pluralism means that the benefits of the system are consistently skewed in favor of those classes mentioned before. As one observer of America has indicated, "The flaw in the pluralistic heaven is that the heavenly chorus sings with a very special accent . . . the system is askew, loaded, and unbalanced in favor of a fraction of a minority."[26] Moreover, the political debate that reflects that pluralism takes place within a common understanding and acceptance of certain basic premises and assumptions, which consistently benefit some classes more than others.

This is the situation not so much because of personalities but because of the inner logic of the system; it is a syndrome of the distribution of economic and political power within our system. It is because of this inner logic that, when there is government intervention, the distribution of possible benefits of that intervention is not random but rather is very predictable. And the answer to the question *cui bono?* (to whom the goods?) is predictably easy. Let me give as an example fiscal policies in general and taxation in particular. Titmuss[27] in Britain and Kolko[28] in the United States have shown that the two countries' systems of taxation have not weakened the income inequalities in either country but have actually accentuated them. A similar example in the health sector is the system of funding of most of the national health insurance proposals, which for the most part share the common denominator of being regressive.

With this introduction, let me describe, as I perceive them, the roles of state intervention as they relate to the health sector. I postulate that these roles are (1) the legitimization and defense of the private enterprise system and (2) the strengthening of that system. These categories are somewhat artificial, and thus their separation is one of convenience more than of necessity.

THE LEGITIMIZATION AND DEFENSE OF THE SYSTEM

According to Weber, the first role of any state is to assure the survival of the economic system. Thus the main role of the state is the legitimization of the economic and political relationship via the different mechanisms at the state's disposal. These mechanisms range from the exclusive use of force, through the armed forces and police, to the creation of social services, including the development of health services, with many mechanisms of intervention between these alternatives. Actually, it was none other than Bismarck, the midwife of the welfare state, who first used the social insurance mechanism as a way of coopting the forces threatening the capitalist system of that time. Social security legislation was passed in England and other countries for similar reasons.

Nor are we strangers to this mechanism in the United States. Piven and Cloward[29] have shown, for example, how welfare rolls are—and always have been—raised to reduce unrest among the poor. It was the function of welfare programs to integrate those sectors of the population who have felt increasingly alienated from the political system and to give them the feeling of being a part of the system in which those programs were introduced. As Moynihan has indicated about the antipoverty programs of the 1960s, "they were intended to do no more than ensure that persons excluded from the political process in the South and elsewhere could nevertheless *participate* in the benefits of the community action programs . . ."[29]

In that respect, the lateness of the United States to come to the welfare state stage may be caused by the lack of pressure, primarily on the corporate class, from any force that could obtain a concession from that class and achieve what the European Left has achieved for its constituents. The potential for threat does exist, however, and the perception of that potential is explicitly manifested in a continuous call for "law and order" and in expressed concern for the disintegration of the system. Indeed, the percentage of the American population who have expressed alienation from and disillusionment with their present system of government has achieved a record high in the history of the United States. A possible response by government to that popular alienation could be the establishment of measures such as income maintenance or national health insurance, aimed at integrating that alienated population into the political system.

THE STRENGTHENING OF THE PRIVATE ENTERPRISE SYSTEM

In creating a welfare state, however, the inner logic of the system, which is a product of the pattern of economic and political power as explained before, determines that the distribution of benefits brought about through state intervention is likely to benefit some groups more than others. Actually, it is because I believe the system functions this way that I am skeptical—as are others—about whether national health insurance will solve what is usually referred to as the "health crisis" in the United States. As Bodenheimer rightly points out, it is far from clear whose crisis national health insurance is supposed to solve—that of the financial interests of the insurance industry and of the providers themselves or that of the availability and accessibility needs of the majority of the population.[19] Not surprisingly, after making a comprehensive analysis of the flow of funds in the health sector, Bodenheimer postulates that "just as federal defense appropriations subsidize the military-industrial complex, national health insurance will subsidize the medical-industrial complex."

Again, state intervention is not uniform, since it depends on the interests of the dominant group in the area in dispute. This is shown by the fact that each of the different power groups in the health sector has put forward its own proposal aimed at optimizing its own interests. Thus each proposal has a rationale and ideology behind it that respond to the specific economic interests of its proponents. And, again, reflecting the power of the insurance industry, all proposals, except one, have allowed and even encouraged the involvement of insurance in the health sector, with state subsidization of the private insurance industry. For example, R. Fein indicated, in commenting on the Nixon proposal, that it is part and parcel of that proposal's strategy to strengthen the private market in health sector economic affairs.[30] The passing of this proposal, as well as the majority of the others, would strengthen the contractual segment of the state sector that I discussed in a previous section. As you may recall, following the categories outlined by O'Connor and Galbraith, I divided the state sector into two subsectors: (1) the contractual part, in which the state contracts and subsidizes the private sector, primarily the monopolistic or planned sector (such as in the case of the defense industry), and (2) the part that is owned and operated by the public sector per se, with services that are owned and run by the state (such as the public health services).

The first subsector, or contractual one, will be strengthened with the passing of the suggested national health insurance and would further expand what O'Connor calls the social-industrial complex. The rationale for that involvement, as *Fortune* magazine says, is that

> . . . implicit in the governmental appeals for help at all levels is an acknowledgement that large corporations are the major repository of some rather special capabilities that are now required. Business executives are increasingly identified as the most likely organizers of community-action programs, like the Urban Coalition and its local counterparts. Corporate managers often have the special close-quarters knowledge that enables them to visualize opportunities for getting at particular urban problems—e.g., the insurance companies' plans for investments in the slums. Finally, the new "systems engineering" capabilities of many corporations [have] opened up some large possibilities for dealing with just about any complex social problem.[15]

Medicare and Medicaid have already begun the expansion of the contractual subsector, and the rate of this expansion has established a record for the rate of growth of financial capital in United States. Indeed, from 1970 to 1973 the profits of the private health insurance industry increased by 120%, establishing an all-time record.[31]

Another objective of all the national health insurance proposals is to socialize the increasing costs of health insurance and to stop the increased drain of funds that health costs represent for both capital and labor. In 1966, for example, contributions to health insurance plans exceeded $8 billion, which was about 40% of total fringe benefits.[15]

The other subsector of the state sector, the public sector (city hospitals, public health service hospitals, and others), will have the responsibility of taking care of the load that is considered unprofitable or less profitable by the private sector. It is the perceived function of the state to strengthen the private sector through contracts and subsidies and by taking care of the unwanted responsibilities of the private sector.

In summary, then, the defined patterns of dominance within the state explain and ensure that state intervention is aimed at (1) legitimating those patterns of dominance and (2) strengthening the private sector and, of course, the groups that have dominance within it. And it is within this context of the functions and goals of state intervention that the debate regarding the different health insurance proposals must be understood. Thus the arguments of the proponents of the various alternatives are designed to convince the average citizens that the proposed insurance will improve their lives and, at the same time, to prove that the system is basically responsive to their needs. Yet, by the very nature of class dominance within the state, this intervention will predictably benefit some social classes, some economic groups, and some interest groups more than others.

That the proposals are more likely to benefit certain social classes more than others can be seen in the proposed systems of funding of the majority of national health insurance proposals, which are based for the most part on payroll taxes, social security taxes, premiums, or a combination of these—all of which are highly regressive systems of funding. Also, the likely benefit from these proposals to primarily the dominant economic groups in our society is clear in that the majority of the proposals rely on the insurance industry to administer the national insurance schemes, thereby guaranteeing not only the continuation of but also a dramatic increase in the flow of money through that industry. The awareness of this possibility by the insurance industry undoubtedly explains that $10 million campaign that the health and life insurance industry budgeted for 1974 and 1975 to "educate" our citizenry, through television and other media, on the "merits" of having the insurance industry "involved and responsible" for the administration of the proposed national health insurance schemes.[32]

Also, the provider interest groups will likely benefit to a large extent from whatever form of proposal may pass, sometimes sharing the benefits with the insurance industry and sometimes competing with it for those benefits.

Thus it is basically the patterns of dominance that condition the possibilities for change and the definitions of what is possible. Within these definitions and within these possibilities for change, it is unlikely, for example, that the funding for whatever insurance proposal may pass will be designed progressively to ensure that the largest burden of the funding will fall on the strongest rather than the weakest shoulders. Also, within the defined boundaries of what is possible and what is not, it is highly improbable that whatever system of control and regulation may evolve will profoundly change the patterns of governing our health institutions to become more responsive and accountable to the majority of those who either work in or are being served by those institutions. And, meanwhile, all the "political drama and political heat" goes on; the life of the average citizen is likely to remain the same. He is likely to repeat the old adage that "the more things change, the more they remain the same."

In summary, then, I have tried to show how the same economic and political forces that determine the class structure of the United States also determine the nature and functions of the U.S. health sector. Indeed, the composition, nature, and functions of the latter are the result of the degree of ownership, control, and influence that primarily the corporate and the upper middle classes have on the means of production, reproduction, and legitimization of American society. This interpretation runs contrary to the most prevalent interpretation, which assumes that the "shape and form" of the health sector is a result of American values that prevail in all areas and spheres of American life. But this explanation assumes that values are the cause and not, as I postulate, a symptom of the distribution of economic and political power in the United States. In fact, that explanation avoids the question of which groups and classes have a dominant influence on the value generating system and maintain, perpetuate, and legitimize it. According to my interpretation, they are the very same groups and classes that have a dominant influence over the systems of production, reproduction, and legitimization in other areas of the economy, including the organs of the state.

Let me emphasize, once again, that I do not believe these groups to be uniform or their dominant influence to be equivalent to control. Actually, I find this distinction between dominant influence and control a key one that has a number of implications, primarily in the area of strategies for stimulating change. Indeed, there is a plurality of interests among groups and among classes that explains and determines the political pluralism apparent today in the United States. Competition does exist. And a strategist for change has to be aware of and sensitive to the diversity of interests reflected in political debates. However, the competition that supports this pluralism is consistently and unavoidably unequal, skewed, and biased in favor of the dominant groups and classes.

The degree of skewedness in the distribution of economic and political power, both outside and within the health sector, is, as I have tried to show, very dramatic indeed. And at a time when much time and energy is spent in academia in debating what might be the perfect model for the health sector, it might have a salutary effect to emphasize that more important than the shape of the final product is the issue of who dominates the process. Thus, a primary intent of this chapter has been to show that the presently debated questions of what services to provide and for whom will actually be determined by whoever is dominant in the process of defining those questions and of formulating those answers.

REFERENCES

1. Mills, C. W.: The sociological imagination, New York, 1959, Grove Press, Inc.
2. Birnbaum, N.: Toward a critical sociology, New York, 1971, Oxford University Press.
3. Horowitz, I. L., editor: Power, politics and people: the collected essays of C. Wright Mills, New York, 1962, Oxford University Press.
4. Irish, M., and Prothro, J.: The politics of American democracy, Englewood Cliffs, N.J., 1965, Prentice-Hall, Inc.
5. Statistical abstract of the United States: 1970, Washington, D.C., 1970, U.S. Bureau of the Census.
6. Miliband, R.: The state in capitalist society: an analysis of the western system of power, London, 1969, Weidenfeld and Nicolson.
7. Bownell, V., and Reich, M.: Workers and the American economy: data on the labor force, Boston, 1973, New England Free Press.
8. Silverman, B., and Yanowitch, M.: Radical and liberal perspectives on the working class, Social policy **4**(4):40-50, 1974.
9. Westergaard, T. H.: Sociology: the myth of classlessness. In Blackburn, R., editor: Ideology in social science, New York, 1972, Fontana, pp. 119-163.
10. Bowles, S., and Gintis, H.: IQ in the U.S. class structure, Social Policy **3, 4, 5:**55-96, 1973.
11. Simpson, M. A.: Medical education: a critical approach, London, 1972, Butterworths.
12. Robson, J.: The NHS Company, Inc? The social consequence of the professional dominance in the National Health Service, International Journal of Health Services **3**(3):413-426, 1974.
13. Kleinbach, G.: Social structure and the education of personnel, International Journal of Health Services, **4**(2):297-317, 1974.
14. Kleinbach, G.: Social class and medical education, Cambridge, Mass., 1974, Department of Education, Harvard University, in press.
15. O'Connor, J.: The fiscal crisis of the state, New York, 1973, St. Martin's Press, Inc.
16. Galbraith, J. K.: Economics and the public purpose, Boston, 1973, Houghton Mifflin Co.
17. Hunt, E. K., and Sherman, H.: Economics: an introduction to traditional and radical views, New York, 1972, Harper & Row, Publishers.
18. Iglehart, J. K.: National insurance plan tops Ways and Means agenda, National Journal, **6**(11):387, 1974.
19. Bodenheimer, T., Cummings, S., and Harding, E.: Capitalizing on illness: the health insurance industry, International Journal of Health Services, **4**(4):569-584, 1974.
20. MacIver, R. M.: Academic freedom in our time, Staten Island, N.Y., 1967, Gordian Press, Inc.
21. Beck, H. P.: Men who control our universities, London, 1947, Kings Crown Press.
22. Galbraith, J. K.: The new industrial state, Boston, 1973, Houghton Mifflin Co.
23. Marcuse, H.: Repressive tolerance, Boston, 1972, Beacon Press.

24. Freidson, E.: Profession of medicine: a study of the sociology of applied knowledge, New York, 1970, Dodd, Mead, & Co.
25. Navarro, V.: A Critique of the present and proposed strategies for redistributing resources in the health sector and a discussion of alternatives, Medical Care, **12**(9):721-742, 1974.
26. Green, M. J., Fallow, J. M., and Zwick, D. R. ("Nader's Raiders"): Who runs Congress? New York, 1972, Bantam Books, Inc.
27. Titmuss, R.: Income distribution and social change, London, 1965, George Allen and Unwin Ltd.
28. Kolko, G.: Wealth and power in America, New York, 1968, Praeger Publishers, Inc.
29. Piven, F. F., and Cloward, R. A.: Regulating the poor: the functions of public welfare, New York, 1971, Vintage Books.
30. Fein, R.: The new national health spending policy, New England Journal of Medicine **290**(3):137-140, 1974.
31. Glasser, M.: The pros and cons of the private insurance involvement in the health sector, Policy and planning seminars, The Johns Hopkins University, April 18, 1974.
32. Washington Report on Medicine and Health, New York, 1974, McGraw-Hill Book Company.

3

Health care goals for Americans—1975

LEONARD WOODCOCK

■ As a nation, 8% of our gross national product is spent on health care. In 1975, the average automobile worker paid 1 month's wages to provide for less than adequate health care coverage. Mr. Woodcock outlines the financial and social reasons why consumers desire more participation in the health care process. He describes a system of health care delivery that he believes will overcome the lack of consumer participation, ineffective regulation, fragmentation of services, lack of access, and lack of cost control that are apparent in our present health care delivery system.

Safeguarding health is of the greatest importance to the worker and the worker's family. So is the amount of wages diverted to pay for necessary health benefits. The reasons in part explain why, for many years now, health benefits have been given high priority in UAW collective bargaining, as they have in most other unions. We have also bargained for life and related insurance, supplementary unemployment benefits, survivors' insurance, disability benefits, and substantial early retirement and pension programs. In 1973, as in a number of earlier years, the costs of these programs constituted a major portion of the entire collective bargaining settlements negotiated by the UAW with the major employers of the workers represented by the union.

The principal reason why labor unions in the United States and Canada have had to demand such substantial expenditures from collectively bargained benefit programs is that most of the social protection services provided through governmental programs in many other industrialized nations are lacking. Sixty-one other countries, now including Canada, have national health insurance programs, while the United States boasts only a limited Medicare program for our aged. Cash social security benefits are substantially higher in other countries than in the United States. In West Germany the average pension is 60% of final wage; in the United States, the average Social Security benefit is only about 30% of final wage.

UAW-negotiated health insurance benefits have been expanded gradually over time; from employer check-off of workers' health insurance premiums, through company partial payment to full payment of benefits; from company payments of the workers' premiums through employer-financed family and retiree coverage; from basic coverage through the addition of such innovative health insurance benefits as outpatient mental health care, nursing home care, prescription drug coverage, and, in the 1970s, a family dental care program. Today most UAW workers enjoy substantial though still not fully comprehensive health insurance protection, and, where geographically available, many may choose to join totally comprehensive prepaid group practice plans, most recently known as health maintenance organizations (HMOs).

CURRENT HEALTH CARE PROBLEMS

The United States has the highest level of medical competence of any nation in the world. Moreover, most American physicians, nurses, and other health providers are highly motivated to provide excellent care to their patients. However, this does not result in excellent care for all patients nor in care provided at reasonable cost to all patients. The crisis in health care continues to worsen not because there is a lack of medical know-how or a lack of dedication and commitment on the part of the American medical care providers, but because health care is the product of an obsolete, outmoded, Model T system—incapable of a rational and effective organization of health care manpower and facilities.

Some of our major health care problems include: (1) rapidly increasing and high costs, (2) a lack of comparable improvement in the health status of the American people, (3) a fragmented medical care delivery system with uneven quality in the provision of care, (4) individual hardship for millions of Americans because of inadequate insurance coverage, (5) lack of consumer participation in changing the delivery system, and (6) an ineffective, piecemeal, duplicative system of governmental regulation of health care.

Cost

As a nation, in 1974 we spent over $100 billion on health care, representing about 8% of our gross national product (GNP). This compares with about $26 billion and 5.2% of the GNP in 1960. On a more personal level the average married Chrysler auto worker in Michigan in 1975 spent approximately 1 month's wages to provide for considerably less than fully comprehensive coverage. Unless there is major intervention

Table 4. Estimated waste in the health care system*

Type of waste	Magnitude of waste	Cost per year
Unnecessary hospitalizations	10 million/year[1] at $1,000	$10 billion
Unnecessary hospital beds	60,000[2]	
	Construction costs, $50,000[3]	$3 billion
	Operating costs, $18,250/year/bed[2]	$1.1 billion
Unnecessary surgery	2 million operations/year[4] at $1,000	$2 billion
Drug promotion	Including advertising[5] and detailing	$1 billion
Unnecessary drugs	Overprescribed antibiotics,[6] tranquilizers, noneffective prescription drugs, worthless over-the-counter drugs	$2 billion
Unnecessary x-rays	$4.8 billion/year spent for diagnostic health and dental x-rays[7] (30% for "defensive" purposes)	$1.4 billion
	Total malpractice payments less than $100 million—1/14 of defensive x-ray costs/year	
Profiteering of private insurance industry[9]		$3 billion
	TOTAL waste per year	$23.5 billion

*Footnotes from Dr. Sidney Wolfe's testimony before the HEW Conference on Inflation, September 9, 1974.

[1]Although many experts have said that 30% of hospitalizations are unnecessary, comparison between prepaid health plans with incentives against unnecessary hospitalization and, for example, Blue Cross show the rate of hospitalization to be *twice as high* with Blue Cross (Inquiry **9:**70-76, 1972 and Federal Employees Benefit Programs 1961-1968, HSMWA, May, 1971)—429 days of hospitalization with prepaid plans and 934 days with indemnity insurers.

[2]1974 Study by Interstudy, Minneapolis, Minn.

[3]New Eng. J. Med. **291:**361, 1974.

[4]New Eng. J. Med. **282:**135, 1970. Dr. Bunker's study shows surgical rates in this country to be twice as high as in England. Rather than assuming that 8 million of the 16 million operations per year in this country are necessary (a conclusion which could also be derived from the two times higher rate of surgery with Blue Cross as opposed to prepaid plans—see ref. 1) a conservative estimate is that 2 million operations are unnecessary.

[5]Ann. Intern. Med. **78:**293, 1973.

[6]Conservative figures based on studies on overuse of antibiotics and tranquilizers, expenditures for useless over the counter drugs.

[7]Bureau of Radiological Health, FDA Statement on new X-ray Equipment Standards, July 30, 1974.

[8]Twin, E. H., and Fotcher, E. J.: Masters degree dissertation, M.I.T., 1973.

[9]Social Security Bulletin, Feb. 1974, p. 38. The actual figure for retentions (profit and operating expenses) is $5 billion. A conservative estimate of that portion representing profiteering is $3 billion.

in the health care system, he will have to give up 2 months' wages by 1979 or 1980 for the same coverage.

An example of the high level of costs concerns a member of our Auto Workers Union who was admitted to a hospital in Detroit for eye surgery. Within 24 hours he needed to have a lengthy emergency heart operation to save his life. But he died. The bill for 1 day's hospitalization was $7,271. The hospital bill of $3,588 included $900 for the operating room, $200 for the use of a heart-lung machine, $235 for laboratory fees, $727 for blood tests, and $320 for eight transfusion hook-ups—including the cost of 31 pints of blood. Some of the physicians' charges included $2,700 for a two-man surgical team, $500 for an anesthesiologist and $500 for a cardiac consultant. I am not suggesting that these charges are too high, only emphasizing that they are very high indeed.

Dr. Sidney Wolfe of the Public Citizens Health Research Group has developed the following table, Table 4, indicating the magnitude of wasted dollars in health care today.

Dr. Wolfe believes this estimate of $23.5 billion of waste per year is conservative, if per capita payments to all health care providers, relative to the same coverages, could be reduced to the level of per capita payments to prepaid group practice plans.

Not included in Dr. Wolfe's figures are additional savings possible from diminishing the profit element in health care delivery. Recent newspaper articles have pointed out the high administrative expenses of for-profit as compared to not-for-profit HMOs, the financial manipulation of Medicare and Medicaid by proprietary nursing homes to include the setting up of related corporations to sell facilities and services to themselves in order to jack up governmental reimbursement, and the higher costs and poorer quality of commercial, as compared with not-for-profit, independent laboratories.

Comparative health status

Americans must also ask what we are getting for our money. We have made major scientific advances in medicine. Yet when we examine the health status of Americans in the aggregate, it is obvious that we are being shortchanged. We are worse off today than 20 years ago compared to other countries, none of whom devotes as large a percentage of their national resources to health care as we do. In 1970, the United States ranked fifteenth in infant deaths during the first year of life, twelfth in life expectancy of females, and twentyseventh in life expectancy of males, just to mention a few commonly accepted indicators of health status. In 1972, regarding infant mortality, the U.S. rate improved from 19.8 per 1,000 live births to 18.5 but worsened relative to other countries, since we now rank 20th behind France, Ireland, and East Germany, among other countries.

The health status of blacks has continued to lag behind that of whites. White females born in 1971 can anticipate living 6.3 years longer than nonwhites born in 1971. White males born in 1971 can expect to live 7.1 years longer than their nonwhite brothers born the same year.[2] Poor health is not restricted to black Americans, for there are more than twice as many poor whites than poor nonwhites, and poverty breeds ill health regardless of race. Almost five times as many persons in low income families are confined to their homes with chronic diseases as are persons in moderate and high income families. Disabling heart conditions beset persons in poor families at five times the rate they occur in more affluent families. Poor families are over six times as likely to have a member afflicted by arthritis or rheumatism or handicapped by nervous or mental conditions, and they exhibit almost nine times the visual impairment of their more financially substantial brethren.

Delivery system

Why is it that we spend so much on health care and yet do not have meaningful enough results to show for it? Where is our money going? The obvious answer is that we are misusing our health resources in an inefficient, disorganized, and wasteful delivery system. There is maldistribution of physicians and other providers both geographically and by specialty. There are too many expensive acute care hospital beds and not enough primary services available. There are fewer primary care physicians per population than 40 years ago. As of 1972 there were 140 counties in the United States with no active physician providing patient care. These counties comprised 3.9% of the nation's land area and 0.2% of the population (200,000 people).[3] Many urban citizens must seek primary care in overcrowded hospital emergency rooms, which are not organized to provide such care but rather to deal with automobile accidents and other emergencies. Often, waits are over 2 hours in duration, the service is impersonal and undignified, referrals are made with inadequate explanation and follow-up, and charges are sky-high.

Illustrative of the problems of inadequate care is a physician's story described in a 1974 article in one of the medical journals. Three years earlier the physician wrote a best-seller for lay audiences about medical care. Now he was apologizing to general and family practitioners whom he had previously characterized as mother substitutes and dispensers of tender loving care and not very much else. The physician had had a heart attack. He had spent 2 weeks in a hospital where a team of cardiologists mismanaged his case. Following his discharge, he ran from specialist to specialist. Right after seeing the fifth specialist, he went into acute pulmonary edema. Then there were more complications and more superspecialists. Finally, a family friend, a general practitioner, visited him. The friend listened. He didn't give him short shrift. He examined him. He explained the probable course of the illness to the patient's wife. He took an interest in the patient as a human being. The patient subsequently made rapid medical and psychological progress to full recovery. Can you imagine, if a wealthy and knowledgeable physician encountered such difficulties, what the problems are for just ordinary human beings and their families?

Most sensitive physicians, concerned with the quality of care, readily acknowledge that among the essential components of quality medicine are the techniques of the physician, the comprehensiveness of services, and the "quality of caring." But when studies are made of the quality of personal health services, the "caring" component is generally omitted.

There is a lack of adequate mechanisms to guarantee the quality of medical care. Too many people are placed in the hospital unnecessarily. Some components of our health services system are overused, some are underused, and most are used inefficiently. Our spending for health ranks second only to that of national defense, but this huge system is operated essentially along the lines of the old corner grocery. We are dominated by fee-for-service, solo practice medicine with unevenly distributed and fragmented services. Moreover, too much emphasis is placed on provision of care by foreign medical graduates (about one fifth of the physicians in the United States), many of whom are more urgently needed in their home countries and some at least whose training is of questionable adequacy.

Lack of coverage

The private insurance industry has created a myth that almost all Americans already have health insurance that covers basic expenditures for care. The reality is that, even by the industry's own figures, the majority of Americans do not have adequate basic coverage. At least 40 million Americans had no health insurance at all in 1974. Half the population does not have coverage for such important basic services as visits to the physician's office. Half are not covered at all unless hospitalized, creating unnecessary hospitalization. Twenty-six percent of all full-time workers in private industry do not have group insurance. In particular, those 100-million-plus Americans who have commercial health insurance policies lack good basic protection. Many of the individual and family policies provide very low specified benefits, such as $10 a day for hospital daily service charges that are currently averaging $120 a day.

In 1974 and 1975 millions of workers lost their jobs. In addition to the loss of income they were forced to deal with the frightening reality of health care costs because of the termination of their employer-related private health insurance. Family illness of any length meant for most the expenditure of carefully husbanded savings or the demeaning prospects of "means tests," Medicaid, or both.

One thing we must recognize is that the practice of medicine is a social function. Physicians and other health providers deal with social units—individuals and communities. Surely by this time in our history, we realize that illness is not a private matter. I believe, along with the overwhelming majority of the American people, that access to good health services is a right of all Americans. It is a right that is of particular concern to workers and their families. They know from grim reality that they do not have substantial resources on which to rely. If they become ill or disabled for any period of time, particularly if they do not belong to a union that has negotiated good sickness and disability benefits, they quickly move from security to insecurity, from economic well-being to poverty.

Lack of consumer participation

American consumers—poor, worker, middle class, and upper class—want better personal health services for themselves and their families. In a voice louder and clearer, and at times more strident, than before, the consumer is saying "hear me—find a way of meeting my needs." Consumers, and this includes organized labor, are still largely excluded from the decision-making level of the health care system. Whether one looks at the advisory boards at the federal level, the Medicaid State Advisory Councils, the boards of directors of local hospitals, or almost any other segment of the health sector, consumers are on the outside looking in.

Consumers are insisting today that the payment of their premium monies and their tax dollars gives them the right to participate in the decision making process about the health care they receive. They believe that many of the problems between health care institutions and consumers and consumer groups derive from gaps created when agency boards are out of touch with the real life around them.

Consumers seek ways for their grievances about and their problems with health care institutions to be heard and acted on. Think of what happens to complaints from average citizens about the services they receive from physicians in solo practice or about the quality of care received. Where do average workers go to find remedies for what they believe to be callous treatment at the hands of hospital staff or nursing homes? Who gives them hearings? Or even more specifically, how often is it possible for them even to receive detailed bills?

Another aspect of consumer participation is the need to improve consumer health behavior and utilization of the system. This can happen with increased interaction between consumers and providers on a more equal basis. As medical economist Victor Fuchs has written, "the greatest potential for improving the health of the American people is . . . to be found in what people do and don't do, to and for themselves."[4] Improvements in what consumers do and don't do is obstructed by the current lack of dialogue between consumers and providers at the personal decision-making level as well as at the institutional level. For example, physicians, harried by crowded waiting rooms and outpatient departments, find it easier to merely prescribe pills than to take the time to listen to patients. Often the social milieus of the patients make it difficult for them to carry out their doctors' instructions, either because of the patients' lack of understanding of what is required on their part or because of social and psychological problems, which are unfortunately and unnecessarily overlooked.*

Ineffective regulations

Part of the problem in health care delivery is the lack of national and regional goals or objectives against which to measure the performance of the present system and of a system of incentives to influence health care providers to perform more effectively. Underlying the lack of performance in health care has been the complex but ineffective regulation of physicians and hospitals by the private insurance industry and by state governments. Presently, hospitals and physicians are often confronted by conflicting guidelines and duplicate reporting requirements. Provider accounting departments have quadrupled in size in responding to the demands of multiple carriers and agencies of government.

One hospital administrator complained recently that a 1 year count at his hospital revealed 105 separate required reports to, or inspections by, governmental agencies in addition to thirty-eight reports to voluntary bodies. Few, if any, other sectors of the United States have been subject to as much regulation. One analyst, Anne Somers, has written, "Hardly any aspect of hospital operation—from width of corridors and number of fire extinguishers to the method of cost finding and accounting and overtime pay—has not been subject to governmental scrutiny. Moreover, different government agencies are involved in the same regulatory activities. The present piecemeal uncoordinated system of regulation isn't working. The cost of care continues to rise, the quality of care makes no comparable advances, and care is unevenly distributed

*See, for example, Duff, R., and Hollingshead, A.: Sickness and society, New York, 1968, Harper & Row, Publishers, pp. 365-387.

so that millions of Americans do not receive minimally adequate medical services."

OBJECTIVES

I believe substantial progress can be made toward achieving the following health care goals for all Americans by the late 1970s:

1. Basic comprehensive health care available to all without economic deterrents to access
2. Medical care organizations and associations responsible for providing and arranging health care for all
3. A share of total health care resources allocated to improving the delivery system and the health status of all
4. An annual budget on total health care costs for basic comprehensive services
5. A system for involving consumers in the governance and operation of the delivery system, including the medical care process itself
6. A unified effective governmental regulatory system for holding providers accountable and for informing consumers of the performance of the delivery system

Available health care for all

Coverage must be universal with equal benefits assured for every American. There must be no categories, classifications, or other gimmicks to exclude or discriminate against members of society. Basic coverage includes physician, dentist, and hospital care. Ideally, skilled nursing home and mental health care should be included as well. Everyone has a right to basic health benefits as they have a right to elementary and secondary education.

Doctors and hospitals responsible for access

Health care coverage is not adequate and sufficient if millions of Americans are not able to obtain services when and where they need them. Physicians and hospitals in a geographic area must agree to contract for providing and arranging basic medical services for all Americans living there. This does not mean government medicine or denial of free choice of a physician. What it does mean is that physicians and hospitals must start being concerned with those who are now prevented from obtaining services and with those persons for whom physicians and hospitals have not been oriented to provide direct services. Rather than merely referring a patient to a hospital emergency room because the office is closed, general care physicians should be held responsible for seeing to it that their patients can get services at all hours, every day of the week. Obviously, this does not mean that each physician must provide all these medical care services, only that there will be established for all Americans a systematic plan for finding out how to get services at all hours and information as to whether services are needed. Part of our national budget for health services needs to be allocated for research and the development of pilot programs designed to improve our primary care system.

Allocation to improve the delivery system and health status

Billions of research dollars have been spent in the United States by our government to conquer disease, relatively little to improve the delivery of care to and the health status of all Americans.

This country needs a national health policy related to the multitude of existing and projected health programs. We need to establish some kind of priority system for governmental health expenditures, concentrating on important problems that we can do something about, for example, infant mortality. Today in Shanghai, according to American physicians who recently visited the Peoples' Republic of China, the infant mortality rate is less than half that of nonwhites in New York or Detroit and almost a third less than that of whites. The main reason for this low infant mortality rate in Shanghai, the physicians report, is good preventive medicine through intensive prenatal care.

We can lower American infant mortality if expenditures are allocated for these preventive services. The shockingly uneven level in the quality of medical care in the United States today results from failure to apply the lessons learned from medical research. We need an effective system for identifying areas in which special programs are needed and allocating funds for programs to alleviate problems in these areas.

In addition, health care literature is replete with articles on the importance of preventive services. But the private insurance system, with relatively few exceptions, does not pay for preventive services. Busy physicians and hospitals usually focus on caring for the ill and injured. As a result, except for those given by pediatricians, who only see a fraction of America's children, preventive services are neither given by providers nor received by consumers.

Controlling health care costs

Strong cost controls must be implemented, in particular, an annual budget ceiling on health care costs so that the present GNP devoted to health care will not expand.

There are many ways to control costs. We can control the supply of hospitals and physicians. But given the present system of health care delivery, controlling supply has resulted and will further result in price inflation and limited access to services. We can fix physicians' and hospitals' rates. But given the present delivery system this has resulted in and will result in further provision of an inflated number of services that are often unnecessary. However, once we control cost, by putting a lid on total costs, and set health care goals, physicians and hospitals will be encouraged to examine what services they are providing and to make reallocations of services so that these are more responsive to a population's needs.

Some propose the use of deductibles and coinsurance to control health care costs. I believe this to be counterproductive, since administrative costs then increase and utilization decreases, especially by lower income consumers. A Canadian province, Saskatchewan, provided a convincing demonstration of what happens when these provisions are introduced in health care insurance. In the first year, although the coinsurance amounts were small, utilization of health care services decreased. But most of the decrease was among the poor and the low-paid workers. Despite the coinsurance, utilization increased in the second year. By the third year of the program, costs rose to the same level as prior to the introduction of the deterrent payments. The deductibles and coinsurance were then, of course, eliminated by the provincial government.

Consumer involvement

I have assumed, in earlier comments on the reallocation of funds, that consumers will be organized and involved in decisions about resource allocation. Consumer participation must be encouraged at every level of administration of health care delivery, from governmental and institutional policy making to grievances against a physician, hospital, or government agency. Consumers must be involved in improving their own health and in using the system properly.

Effective governmental regulation

Some structure in society has to be charged with responsibility for formulating delivery system goals, holding the delivery system accountable for performance, and reporting such performance to the public.

The only structure in our society formally accountable to the people is government. We all know the limitations of governmental regulatory performance and of the people in holding government officials accountable. However, to paraphrase Winston Churchill, democratic government is the least bad alternative we have available to us.

Recent political movements in the United States are expanding consumer and legislative influence on governmental bureaucracies and offer hope that more effective government regulation can be accomplished in this decade. If not, we have no place else to turn. The accountability of government is a responsibility of all Americans, and we all should hold governmental officials accountable for the daily exercise of their bureaucratic duties by means of the ballot box, letters, visits, and criticism in the press.

NATIONAL HEALTH SECURITY: WE CAN GET FROM HERE TO THERE

At the end of 1968, an idea was conceived that has developed into the most broadly supported concept of what an effective, uniquely American, national health service program should look like and how it should operate. The program was developed by a team of professional and lay experts over a period of 18 months of study and analysis under the aegis of the Committee for National Health Insurance, of which I have been privileged to serve as Chairman. Since then CNHI and the companion Health Security Action Council have intensified their efforts to develop a grass roots health lobby that includes labor unions, educators, physicians and other health professionals, youth-serving agencies, senior citizens' groups, church and civic organizations, civil rights groups, and various social agencies. The Health Security Program is grounded on two basic principles: (1) that it should be part of the Social Security system to provide comprehensive health care for everyone living in the United States, and (2) that it should bring about major improvements in the organization, financing, and provision of health care.

The Health Security Act was introduced in the 92nd Congress by principal sponsors Senator Edward Kennedy and Representatives Martha Griffiths and James Corman and by 100 other members of Congress. Similar bills were introduced in the 94th Congress by principal sponsors Kennedy and Corman. The issue before the Congress is not the cost of competing national health insurance programs, since the various national proposals have similar effects on health care's share of the gross national product. The major issue concerns how the money is to be raised and how the money is to be spent to maintain and improve health services.

Other approaches to national health insurance propose no change in the health care delivery system and merely augment financing for certain services or for certain groups. One such approach suggests coverage of catastrophic expenses without recognizing that what is an ordinary expense for many of those suggesting such coverage may be a catastrophic expense for others using it. We are undoubtedly going to have national health insurance legislation in the not too distant future.

It is essential that we get the right kind of bill—one that meets health care goals set out in the next few pages.

Available health care for all

Under the Health Security Program, every individual residing in the United States will be eligible to receive benefits without economic deterrents to the receipt of care. With certain modest limitations, the program would provide comprehensive health benefits for every eligible person. The benefits available under the program would cover the entire range of personal health care services, including the prevention and early detection of disease, the care and treatment of illness, and medical rehabilitation. There are no cutoff dates, no coinsurance, no deductibles, and no waiting periods.

The four limitations in the otherwise unlimited scope of benefits are dictated by inadequacies in existing health resources or in management potentials. Skilled nursing home care is limited to 120 days per benefit period. Psychiatric hospitalization is limited to 45 consecutive days of active treatment during a benefit period. Dental care is restricted to children through age 15 at the outset, with the covered age group increasing annually until persons through age 25 are covered. Prescribed drugs are limited to those provided by hospitals or health maintenance organizations. For other patients, coverage extends only to drugs required for the treatment of chronic or long-term illness. These limitations could be liberalized by organized delivery programs like health maintenance organizations.

Since all Americans would be covered as a matter of right, the nation would not again be faced by the dilemma of millions of workers and their families suddenly cut off from health insurance benefits by reason of their loss of employment. Hospitals and other providers would be relieved of the worry of even greater deficits in a period of recession because of their inability to collect on bills incurred by workers' families who have no private insurance coverage. Only the Health Security Program protects against economic recession problems of this kind. Almost all the other national health insurance proposals before the Congress relate benefits to either employment or welfare status.

Physicians and hospitals responsible for access

The Health Security Program will provide incentives for health maintenance organizations and professional foundations, which are at present the only types of medical care organizations to assure responsibility for providing or arranging to provide basic comprehensive health services to all their members on a prepaid basis.

Incentives to these HMOs are built into the payment mechanism under which these organizations will be reimbursed (based largely on their present costs), while other providers, if they continue to increase the volume and price for their services, will receive only a percentage of a budget sum (based on past expenditures for their services). HMOs would also be enabled to use the economies resulting from prepaid group practice to improve benefits for members and augment incomes of their providers. HMOs will also benefit from allocations from the Resources Development Fund to be discussed.

Allocation to improve the delivery system and health status

An essential feature of the Health Security Program is the Resources Development Fund, which will come into operation 2 years before benefits begin. In the first year of this tooling-up period, about $200 million will be appropriated for the Fund; in the second year, $400 million will be made available. Once the program benefits begin, up to 5% of the trust fund—about $3 billion a year—will be set aside for resources development. These funds will be used to support innovative health care programs to improve the delivery of care. This means giving first priority to identification of the most acute shortages of personnel and facilities and the most serious deficiencies in organization and to means for the speedy alleviation of these shortcomings.

The Health Security Program includes various provisions to improve the quality of care. These include establishment of national standards for participating individual and institutional providers. Specialty services will be covered only if, upon referral, they are performed by qualified persons. The Commission on the Quality of Health Care will be established to develop parameters and standards for care of high quality and to promote their application in assessing and enhancing the quality of care furnished under the Health Security Act. In carrying out its duties, the Commission will give highest priority to care furnished for those illnesses and conditions that have relatively high incidence in the population and are relatively amenable to medical or other care.

Controlling health care costs

The essence of the payment mechanism and the central cost control feature of the program is that the health care system as a whole will be anchored to a closed-end budget established in advance. In no sense does the Health Security Program represent new money added to the existing system; rather, the Health Security Program simply redistributes the health care expenditures that are already being made. Even in the first year of the program, the comprehensive health services provided will be available for the same cost we would have paid for the partial and inefficient services of the existing system.

Each year the Health Security Board will make an advance estimate of the total amount needed to pay for health care services in the program. The Board will allocate funds to the several regions, and these allocations will be subdivided among categories of services in the health subareas. Advance estimates, constituting the program budgets, will be subject to adjustments according to program guidelines. The allocations to regions and to subareas will be guided initially by the available data on current levels of expenditure. Thereafter, they will be guided by the program's own experience in making expenditures and in assessing the need for equitable health care throughout the nation.

Some argue that the National Health Security Program will create a huge bureaucracy that will be costly and inflexible. This argument ignores the existence of an even larger, less effective commercial insurance company bureaucracy, since there are over 1,800 private insurance carriers who insure health care and serve as local intermediaries under Medicaid and Medicare. Each company has its own forms and procedures. In 1970, before the introduction of wage and price controls, the companies' administrative costs, including profits, were $1.5 billion. In 1973, after the institution of controls, their administrative costs, including profits, had increased to $3.3 billion—a rise of 120% over the 4-year period. The present system is one that almost by definition is duplicative and costly. Rather, we can build on the effective administrative system we now have in the Social Security Administration for the elderly and disabled. Canada, in its national health insurance program, changed, for reasons of economy and effectiveness, from relying in part on private carriers to a governmentally administered program. In the United States, the Social Security Administration already has relationships with physicians and hospitals under Medicare, which would facilitate any planned expansion.

Consumer involvement

Consumers will be involved in the Health Security Program in several ways. For example, HMOs, to qualify for participation in the program, must: (1) encourage health education of enrollees (including education in the appropriate use of health services), (2) make available to enrollees and to the public full information about services, (3) provide an opportunity for representatives of enrollees to participate effectively in the formulation of policies and in the evaluation of operations, and (4) provide fair and effective procedures for resolving disputes between enrollees and the HMO. Consumers are formally represented on all advisory councils of the program at the national, regional, and local levels. Also, four of the eleven members of the Commission on the Quality of Health Care established under the program are representatives of consumers. Of course, representatives of consumer groups, including the UAW, have been heavily involved in planning and drafting the Health Security Program itself.

Effective governmental regulation

The Health Security Program establishes a system of federal, regional, and local health planning and control to improve the performance of health care providers. The program makes the federal government the insurer for all Americans. This is essential in bringing about reforms in our health care system because such leverage is required to effectively control costs and improve the way health care is organized and delivered in the United States.

Under the program, a Health Security Board would be established, composed of five members to be appointed by the President, by and with the advice and consent of the Senate. The Board's duties would include evaluating the operation of the program, the adequacy and quality of services furnished under it, the adequacy of compensation to providers of services and of the costs of the services, and the effectiveness of measures to control the costs. The program will be administered by the Board through regions and within each region such health service areas as the Board may establish. Advisory councils would be established at national, regional, and local levels—composed of provider and consumer representatives for advice concerning goal formulation and implementation.

The Health Security Board will be able to make an agreement with any state that is able and willing to do so for determining whether providers of services meet or continue to meet the qualifications and requirements of the program. A state may also provide activities related to health education, the maintenance and improvement of the quality of covered services, the maintenance of effective utilization, the review or the better coordination of services of different kinds. The Health Security Board will also control providers in the event and to the extent that any state is unable or unwilling to do so at a level of inspection mandated by the program.

If nothing else, the establishment of national health care goals by the Health Security Board, as part of the annual planning and budgetary process, will improve the regulatory process dramatically by establishing standards against which the performance of local individual and institutional providers can be measured and regulated at the state level.

The Health Security approach replaces the historical pattern in the United States of tinkering with the financing of health care and keeping hands off the health delivery system itself. Our major thesis is that the federal government's leverage in using massive funds (premiums or taxes) will positively and effectively influence the behavior of health care providers. The opposite approach of adding financing of certain services for certain groups over time has had minimal influence over the past 20 years in improving health care delivery.

America has the knowledge and the capability—it is already making the expenditure—to achieve health care goals that will deal meaningfully with the problems in our health care system. While major changes such as I have described will not be achieved overnight, they can be accomplished through orderly evolution, if a comprehensive Health Security Plan is adopted for the nation.

REFERENCES

1. Roemer, M. I., and others: Health Insurance Effects Bureau of Public Health Economics Research Series No. 16, Ann Arbor, 1972, University of Michigan, School of Public Health.
2. Vital statistics of the United States. 1971, U.S. Department of Health, Education, and Welfare, Public Health Service, National Center for Health Statistics.
3. Committee on Ways and Means: National Health Insurance Resource Book, Apr. 11, 1974, Washington, D.C., 1974, U.S. Government Printing Office, p. 118.
4. Fuchs, Victor R.: Who Shall Live? Health, Economics and Social Choice, New York, 1974, Basic Books, Inc., Publishers.

4

Income and disease—the pathology of poverty

H. ASHLEY WEEKS

■ From 10% to 12% of the U.S. population lives in poverty. Recent studies have indicated that the poor have twice the infant mortality, 7 years less life expectancy, and significantly more bed-ridden disability days than the nonpoor in the U.S. population. Hypertension and heart disease are conditions related to poverty in both urban and rural settings, and perinatal abnormalities, parasitic diseases, and mental disorders are 1.5 to 5 times higher in black Americans and American Indians than in the white American population. Factors contributing to this cycle are income, race, education, distribution of physicians, and availability of health insurance. Poverty and illness form an ever widening dynamic circle in which poverty contributes to illness and illness brings about further poverty.

It is generally accepted by U.S. residents that it is possible to get the world's best medical care in the United States. Not only is it taken for granted here but there is evidence that in many other places knowledgeable persons look to the United States as providing the best obtainable medical care. U.S. newspapers frequently furnish examples of such evidence: a person of newsworthiness—a ruler, political figure, or wealthy individual—comes to the United States seeking care for a medical problem that apparently could not otherwise be helped. There seems to be no doubt that excellent medical care can be obtained here, particularly for those with the money to pay for it.

In view of such a claim, it seems a gross contradiction that when health statistics comparing various countries are compiled, the United States seldom stands at the top of the list. For example, fourteen or fifteen countries have lower infant mortality figures than does the United States. During the 1970s, there has been a worldwide decrease in infant mortality, but the United States has not gained in its relative position. Sweden, Norway, Finland, Japan, the Netherlands, Switzerland, France, Canada, the United Kingdom, Ireland, and the German Democratic Republic all had infant mortality in 1972 lower than that of the United States.[1] Although all the rates were somewhat higher, these same countries also had lower infant mortality than the United States in the years 1969 to 1971.

If medical care is reputed to be so excellent in the United States, why then is the maternal mortality also higher here than in many other countries? And why do some morbidity figures show unfavorable rates in the United States compared to other countries? Perhaps it is possible to get at least some suggested answers if the situation in various parts of the United States is examined. The fact is that none of these rates is uniform throughout the United States or, for that matter, within the same state. In every southern state the infant mortality is higher than that of the United States as a whole. This seems at least in part to be related to the fact that black babies are twice as likely to die within the first year after birth as white babies. The following figures show the infant mortality (per 1,000 live births) for ten southern states by race, for 1969 where available; when not available 1968 figures are shown. The rate in the United States as a whole for 1969 was 20.7 per 1,000 live births.

	White	**Black**
Arkansas	18.1	30.6
Florida	18.2	35.8
Georgia	17.3	34.6
Louisiana	18.3	35.1
Mississippi	22.6	47.4
N. Carolina	19.8	37.1
S. Carolina*	20.2	38.8
Tennessee*	19.7	35.7
Texas*	20.0	36.2
Virginia	18.8	36.9

*Figures shown are for 1968. From New South, vol. 26, no. 4, Fall 1971.

It is of interest that the white rates (except in Mississippi) are all somewhat lower than they are for the country as a whole.

The differential rates between nonwhites and whites are not just a phenomenon of the South, however. In a survey in California, the white infant mortality was found to be 40% higher than that in the population of Japanese descent. The rate for blacks was still higher than that for whites. One of the factors involved in these disparate figures seems to be the age of the mothers when they give birth. Nineteen percent of the Negro mothers were under 19 years of age, whereas only 2% of the Japanese-American and 2.5% of the Chinese-American mothers were this young. Ten percent of the white mothers were younger than 19.[2] Income level may be an associated variable in explaining this phenomenon, since mothers in low income families are generally younger than mothers in wealthier families. Infant mortality is high in

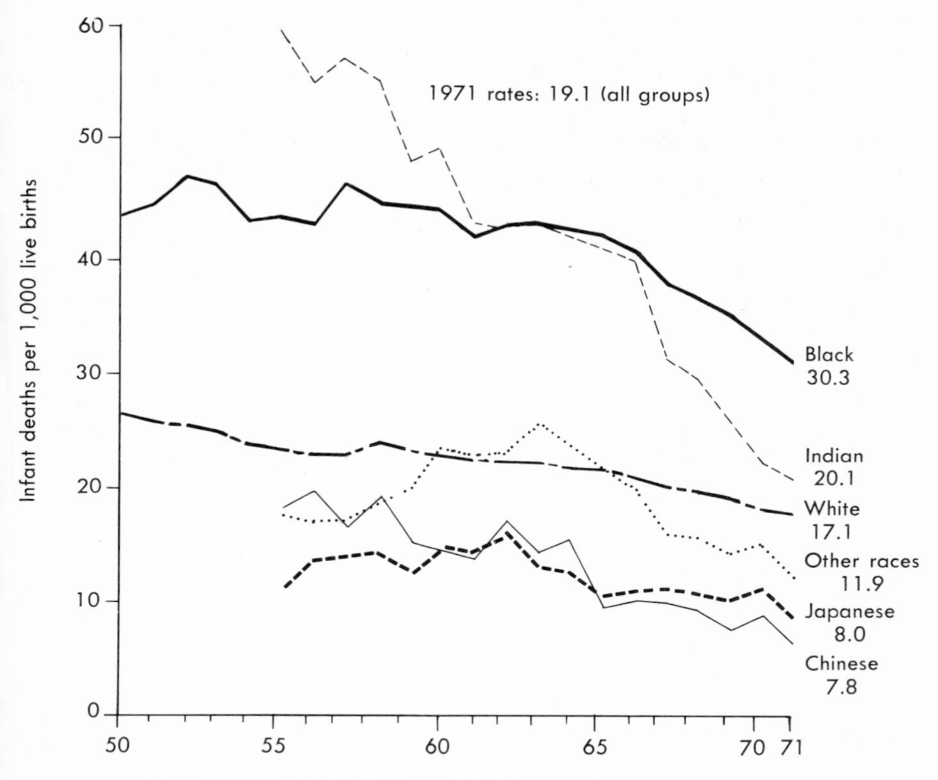

Fig. 5. Infant mortality by specified race, 1950-1971 (rates per 1,000 live births). (From Minority health chart book, 102nd Annual Meeting, New Orleans, La., Oct. 20-24, 1974, American Public Health Association.)

the slums of both urban areas and rural areas, with both Puerto Ricans and American Indians also having high infant and maternal mortality.[3] The adjusted death rates per 1,000 live births in New York City in 1968 were 22.6 infant deaths per 1,000 live births per year for infants of Puerto Rican mothers, compared to a rate of 12.6 for infants born to white, native born mothers.[4] Thus in 1968, deaths per 1,000 live births in New York City were 1.7 times higher in Puerto Rican children than in infants born to white Americans. This same increase in infant mortality was evident with American Indians, among whom the infant mortality is generally about 1.5 times that of the United States as a whole. Maternal mortality among Indians is about twice as high (Fig. 5) as in the United States as a whole.

This disparity between race, economic and educational status, and health is also reflected in life expectancy (Fig. 6). The life expectancy at birth of a nonwhite male in 1971 was 61.1 years compared to 67.6 in

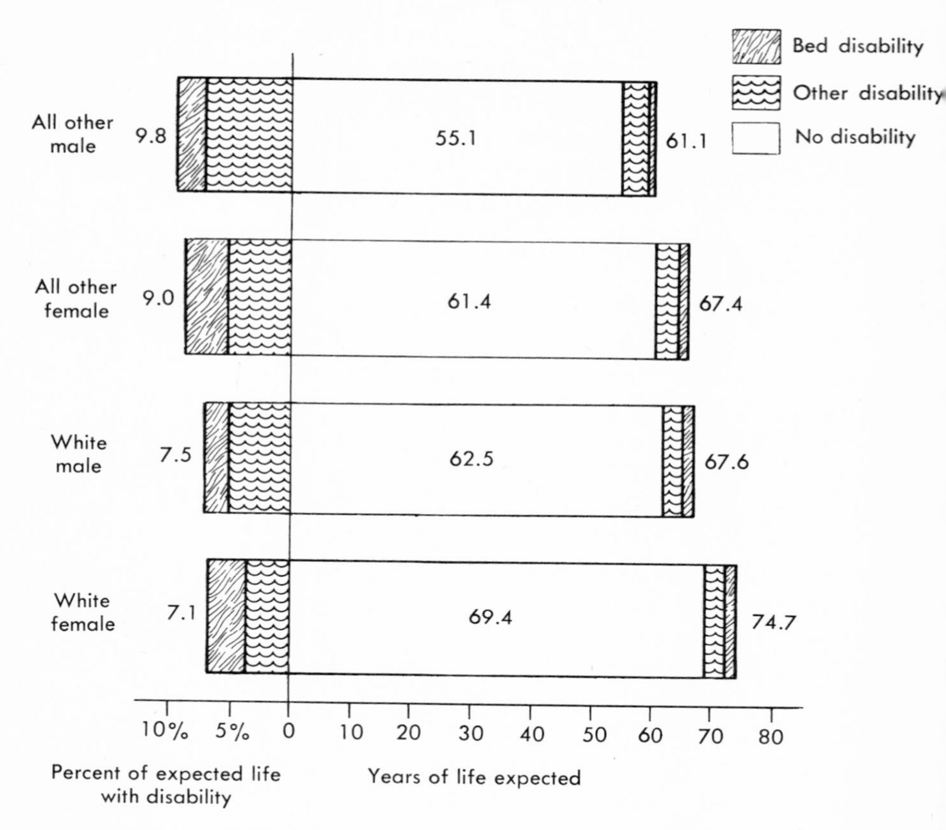

Fig. 6. Life expectancy at birth with or without specified degrees of disability, United States, 1960. (From Minority health chart book, 102nd Annual Meeting, New Orleans, La., Oct. 20-24, 1974, American Public Health Association.)

white males. This disparity also exists between white females and nonwhite females, 74.2 versus 67.4 years, respectively.

In addition to gross indices of the "quantity of life," the quality of health—that is, the percent of expected life with disability—is also influenced by these socioeconomic parameters. Both nonwhite males and females experience significantly more total disability and bedridden disability days than their white counterparts—9% of life expectancy compared to 7.7%, respectively.

That health care is not uniformly good throughout the United States is further exemplified by an examination of the relationship between poverty and disease rates. This relationship is well exemplified in the differentials in incidence rates found in hypertension. In most large cities, blacks have been found to have very high hypertension rates. Ten years ago a study of the aged in Detroit showed that the rate of hypertension for blacks (65 years of age and over) was higher than for their white counterparts; 36% of the blacks reported hypertension, whereas only 22% of the whites reported this difficulty. For both blacks and whites, a higher proportion of females than males reported this illness.[5] Recently more detailed studies of hypertension have found that while the blacks in the Detroit slum areas have unusually high incidence of hypertension, whites in these poor residential areas also have high hypertension rates. That hypertension is not just a problem of blacks is also borne out by a study of the Chinese-American community in Boston. High rates of hypertension, heart disease, and diabetes were found among the Chinese crowded together in the small Chinatown area in Boston.[6]

In general, persons living in slum areas appear to be much more likely to be subject to hypertension than those living elsewhere. But wherever persons live under stress in poverty conditions, high rates of hypertension are found. Dr. Jack Geiger, codirector of the Tufts-Delta Health Center in Mound Bayou, Mississippi, reported that not only was infant mortality at 60 per 1,000 live births and the maternal death rate at 15.3 per 1,000, but also that high blood pressure occurred in 23.8% of the families earning less than $2,000 per year, in contrast to only 3.9% among those who earned more than $7,000.[7]

Other examples of differentials in morbidity rates furnish additional evidence that all kinds of illnesses are distributed unevenly among contrasting economic groups. Deaths from mental illness were more than 4 times greater in American Indians and nearly 2.5 times greater in black Americans than in white Americans (Table 5). For over 25 years now, ever since Hollingshead published his studies in New Haven, it has been known that some mental illnesses are much more prevalent in city slum areas than in areas where the more affluent live. However, even in rural areas mental illness seems to be associated with poverty. One study reports that mental illness was present in twenty-six persons per 1,000 in families whose yearly income was under $2,000, but in only four persons per 1,000 in families whose income was more than $7,000.[8]

Undoubtedly many of these mental disturbances go back to the early lives of those adversely affected. In many poverty areas, lack of nourishment is a severe problem. In one study anthropometric measurements demonstrated that 27% of the children with food deficiencies had a bone age less than 75% of their chronological age. Malnutrition was so bad within the study populations that the physicians conducting the study often prescribed food.* Parents, fathers or mothers, came to

*This was an account of MAP—South: (The Memphis Area Project—South) carried on by a naturalized Dutchman, Dr. Paul Zee, at St. Jude Children's Research Hospital.[9]

Table 5. Deaths per 100,000 population by ethnic/racial groups and Caucasians in the United States—1971*

Disease categories	All races					
	Deaths/ 100,000	American Indian	Black American	Chinese-American	Japanese-American	White American
All causes		765.6	994.6	484.7	447.2	948.7
Circulatory system	508.7	209.0	437.4	219.6	214.7	522.2
Neoplasms	168.5	65.7	150.7	113.8	98.4	172.0
Accidents, poisonings, and violence	79.4	197.2	124.6	43.6	38.8	73.5
Respiratory system	53.2	53.3	53.8	27.3	30.6	53.3
Digestive system	36.5	67.7	41.1	26.2	16.8	36.0
Endocrine, nutritional, and metabolic diseases	22.7	28.2	30.2	16.7	12.7	21.8
Perinatal abnormalities	18.9	26.6	42.2	6.0	6.1	16.0
Genitourinary system	13.5	15.6	23.1	7.2	6.3	12.4
All defined conditions	13.0	32.3	34.9	3.5	2.5	10.3
Infective parasitic diseases	7.9	24.4	16.7	7.8	4.9	6.7
Nervous system	7.8	10.2	9.6	2.5	3.9	7.7
Congenital anomalies	7.8	11.0	9.5	6.0	4.8	7.6
Mental disorders	4.1	16.4	9.8	<1.0	1.1	3.4
Blood diseases	2.6	2.2	4.3	1.8	1.7	2.3
Muscular diseases	2.4	2.8	2.7	1.0	3.1	2.4
Skin diseases	0.9	1.4	1.8	<1.0	<1.0	<1.0
Complications of childbirth and pregnancy	0.3	1.4	1.2	<1.0	<1.0	<1.0

*Compiled from National Center for Health statistics.[11]

warehouses that had been set up as food centers and were given food to be used to supply adequate nourishment to growing infants and children. The study also indicated that food deprivation for 6 months seemed to permanently damage subsequent neurological development. Several years ago a national nutrition survey was started in ten states. While this survey was never completed, some of the preliminary findings indicated that malnutrition existed in a large proportion of the sample; for example, 25.9% of children living in poverty in Michigan were below the standard in growth percentiles.[10]

Whether it is a matter of poverty, insufficient education, or both, it is evident that the poor are not as likely to have as many physician visits as those with better incomes. In the southern United States, 34% of all the population and 41% of the nonwhite population reported no physician visits in 1967.[11] However, when these poor people become ill, they have the highest percentage with one or more chronic conditions, the highest percentage with activity limitation, the highest number of days of restricted activity per person, the highest number of bed disability days per person, and the greatest number of days lost from work per currently employed person of any group in the United States. In all age groups, average length of hospital stay is longer in the nonwhite than white population (Fig. 7).

A study of health care in infancy in a rural southern county also shows the relationships between some of these variables. The proportion of the total sample of 375 children who had no well-child care was 5%, but it was 17% for blacks and 21% in cases in which the mothers had only grade school education or less. It is of interest also that at the time of the study 57.5% of the sample either had not had complete immunizations or had not been given any immunizations. Of the babies who had been seen by a pediatrician, only 37% did not have complete immunizations, and all had had at least some immunizations completed during the first year of life. Mothers who took their babies to either a health department or a hospital clinic or both and had no private physician contact showed the worst records. Almost three out of four blacks (72%) used a combination of a health department and hospital clinic, and almost two out of three mothers (63%) with grade school education or under took their babies to such sources for care.[12]

All these morbidity and mortality rates are strongly related to at least five specific variables. These five factors, which in turn seem to be interrelated, are: poverty, race, education, distribution of physicians, and availability of health insurance.

While poverty or low income may be the predominant factor, since income is closely related to all the other items, it seems desirable to

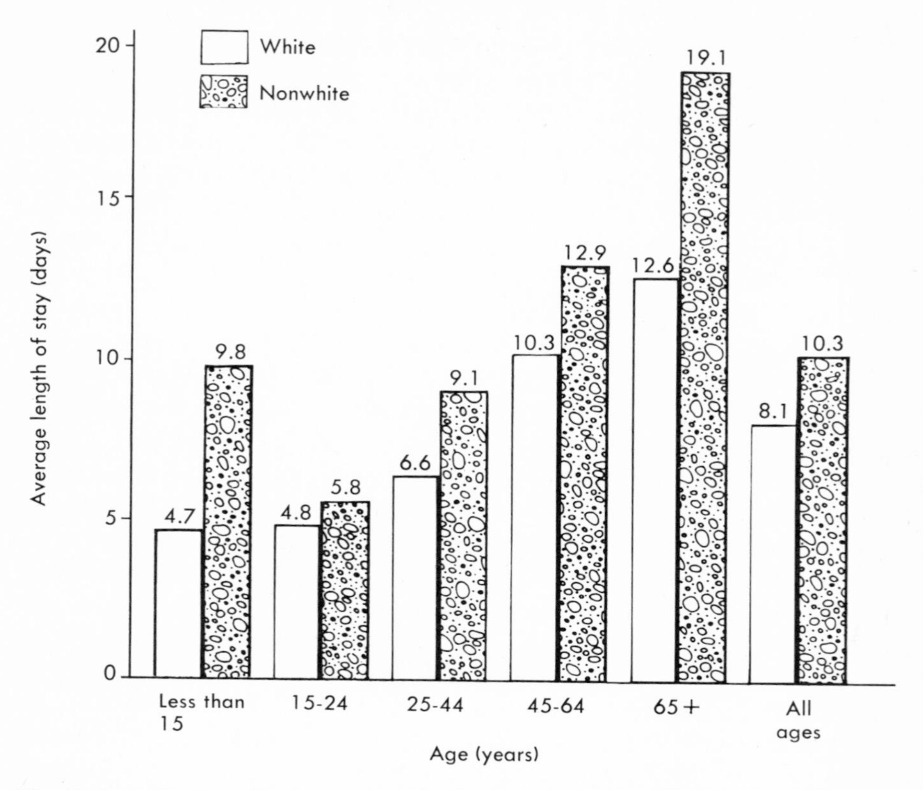

Fig. 7. Average length of stay per discharge from short-term hospitals by age and color, United States, 1972. (From Minority health chart book, 102nd Annual Meeting, New Orleans, La., Oct. 20-24, 1974, American Public Health Association.)

discuss each of these factors and attempt to illustrate how each affects the others.

When the Medicare and Medicaid programs were inaugurated, they were hailed as great social and humanitarian gains. Poverty as a bar to decent medical care was going to be banished. The aged, who had always had trouble meeting medical bills and of course often had more medical bills to meet, were now going to be protected.

Unfortunately, it has not turned out that way. The deductible has been increased and the coinsurance features of the bills have been raised. Persons with low incomes have not been able to purchase health insurance, and drastically raised premiums have made it difficult for even those who are employed to have adequate health insurance. Many economists are now pointing out how regressive the Social Security system is, including the provisions for medical care. Persons with less income pay the highest proportion for benefits, yet these benefits rarely cover any medical care expenses other than those encountered during hospitalization. Thus the brunt of these medical expenses must be paid by the group that has the least resources to pay them. It is estimated that only about a third of the poor is covered by any kind of health insurance. In some instances, if there is no health insurance, persons in need of medical care are not admitted to hospitals unless or until a substantial deposit is made. A pregnant 15-year-old girl waited over 12 hours to be seen and finally died because of lack of care.[10] This is not an isolated case.

It seems quite probable that lack of health insurance is closely related to high infant mortality and maternal mortality in the United States (see Chapter 14). Dr. Jack Geiger, cited before, claims that there is no doctor present at 48% of the births in the Mississippi Delta area.[11]

Not only do few of the poor have insurance, but even if they had it, they might find it difficult to get to or to see a physician. Not many physicians choose to settle in rural areas, where they often would be overworked, deprived of contact with their colleagues, and away from hospital facilities. Even when physicians are available, the medical care given may be inadequate.

There appears to be a possibility that physicians' isolation in rural areas can be helped by a reorganization of the medical care system. In one central Maine community, a group of physicians has established a group clinic, which is called Rural Health Associates. At present there are nine doctors, including two dentists, on the staff. There has been little problem in recruiting new staff when needed. This may be partly because of the fact that the physicians are all on salaries, so they do not hesitate to take regular days off. They know that their patients will receive good care. They do not have to worry about collecting fees, as would be the case in solo practice. The population with income below the poverty level is cared for on a per capita basis; those with higher incomes pay on a fee-for-service basis.

Since the clinic was first established, groups of the population in the various towns have worked to replace an old inadequate hospital with a new eighty room modern hospital plant, which has recently opened its doors. Although this hospital project had its birth pains, it now seems most pleasant and the physicians have a modern, up-to-date facility in which to practice. This type of rural health setting may be a model for attracting physicians and improving medical care and the health of rural residents.*

*The University of Michigan, Department of Medical Care Organization, School of Public Health, during the last 2 or 3 years has been studying health care in Franklin County, Maine, where the Rural Health Association Clinic is located, and is impressed with the medical service being given.

There are other hopeful signs. On the Papago Indian Reservation in the last several years there has been a significant expansion of health care. There is a fifty bed Public Health Service Indian Hospital at Sells, Arizona that provides medical and dental care. More and more the Indians on the reservation are becoming responsible for their own health care. The Papagos have organized an Executive Health Staff with the responsibility of coordinating all health care on the reservation, which has turned out to be extremely successful. Recently, they have been able, with federal assistance and powerful resources from scientists from NASA and Lockheed, to install an exciting telemedicine system. Not only can individuals coming to the hospital receive consultation via television from specialists located in Tucson or Phoenix, but Indians living in remote areas can, for the first time, secure excellent medical care with the aid of a completely equipped medical van with its own electric generator. The van can easily be driven to remote places where Indians may be seen by well trained physician assistants or paramedics. This van is equipped not only with the usual medical instruments but also with its own x-ray machine and television equipment, which allows it to have constant contact with the hospital at Sells or when necessary with hospitals at Tucson and/or Phoenix.

It is not easy, either, for the urban poor to get a physician because physicians are not likely to locate in the slums. When slum residents need medical care, it often means that they must plan days ahead to make arrangements for care of children and getting together enough money for transportation, to say nothing about the physician's fee.

Even when such residents go to a clinic in a general hospital for tests or relatively inexpensive care, it is a time-consuming trip, and they will lose their wages in addition to the cost involved in getting to the clinic and paying for the care. Residents in Watts used to be sent to the Los Angeles County Hospital. The bus fare alone was 65¢ each way, and those sent often lost their day's wages as well. Many who live in the Chicago area and make use of the Cook County Hospital have similar problems. The Wayne County General Hospital and the Detroit General Hospital involve long, time-consuming and expensive trips for many. It is no wonder that it is easier to put off needed medical care than to make the effort to get it.

As might be expected, where the educational level is low the morbidity rates are high. Whether this is the result of lack of knowledge or the concomitant factor of poverty is beside the point. Probably both contribute. In any case, many who have little schooling do not know what to do or where to go to get needed medical care. When problems associated with racial discrimination are added, the difficulties are compounded. Most studies show that among persons with low educational achievement there is very little prenatal care; mothers do not take children to well-baby clinics; there is a lack of immunization; and often a child does not get to a physician in 3 or 4 years and never gets to a dentist. It is known that among the poorly educated and the poor many of the usual recommendations are either not given or not carried out. All studies show a close correlation between high income and dental care.

There is no doubt that there are reciprocal relationships among all these factors. If income were more uniformly distributed and if all the population had equal access to medical care, there would not be such pronounced discrepancies in many of the morbidity rates discussed here.

When a large proportion of the population is ill with a contagious disease, it has always been up to society to segregate and care for the suffering. Society has made sure that water is reasonably pure. In many places individuals have voted for increased protection from dental caries by authorizing fluoridation of the water supply. Just as society must step in when adverse sanitary conditions threaten the population, it must step in when a person cannot pay for or get needed medical care. Such a situation is hardly a private affair. The evidence is overwhelming that some method of help to meet medical expenses must be established. The United States remains one of the few industrial countries that has not set up some such system. It seems odd that the problem has not been met when the United States often spends lavishly on other kinds of problems. Dr. Stanley Skillikorn, Santa Clara's Migrant Clinic director, observed that more money is spent conserving migrant birds than migrant workers. For years various health insurance proposals have been made, but no legislation has been passed and the health of the nation suffers. It seems most probable that many of the differentials discussed in this chapter would disappear if all had equal access to good medical care.

REFERENCES

1. Demographic Yearbook 1973, New York, 1975, United Nations.
2. Breslow, Lester, and Klein, Bonnie: Health and race in California, Am. Public Health Assoc. J. **61**:763-775, Apr. 1971.
3. Elling, Ray H., and Martin, Russell F.: Health and health care for the urban poor, Connecticut Health Services Research Series, no. 5, New Haven, Conn., 1974.
4. Kessner, David M.: Infant death: an analysis by maternal risk and health care, Washington, D.C., 1973, Institute of Medicine, p. 48.
5. Weeks, H. Ashley, and Darsky, Benjamin J.: The urban aged: race and medical care, Bureau of Public Health Economics, Research Series, no. 14, School of Public Health, University of Michigan, 1968, p. 22.

6. Frederick, P. L., Schlief, N. Young, Chung, Caroline J., and Gow, Albert C.: Health care for the Chinese community in Boston, Am. J. Public Health, vol. 62, Apr. 1972.
7. Geiger, Jack: Poor hungry babies, New South, vol. 26, Fall 1971.
8. New South notes, New South, vol. 26, no. 4, Fall 1971.
9. Poor hungry babies, New South, vol. 26, Fall 1971.
10. Anderson, Robert E.: Whatever happened to the national nutrition survey? New South, vol. 26, no. 4, Fall 1971.
11. Volume of physician's visits, United States, July 1966-June 1967, U.S. Department of Health, Education, and Welfare, Public Health Resources Administration, National Center for Health Statistics, series 10, no. 49, Rockville, Md., 1968.
12. Peters, A. D., and Chase, C. L.: Patterns of health care in infancy in a rural southern county, Am. J. Public Health **57**(3):409-422, Mar. 1967.

SELECTED READINGS

Anderson, Ronald, and Benham, Lee: Family income and medical care consumption preliminary data, Second Conference on the Economics of Health, Baltimore, Maryland, 1968.

Breslow, Lester, and Klein, Bonnie: Health and race in California, Am. Public Health Assoc. J. **61:**763-775, Apr. 1971.

Bullough, Bonnie: Poverty, ethnic identity and health care, New York, 1972, Appleton-Century-Crofts.

Elling, Ray, and Martin, Russell F.: Health and health care for the urban poor, Connecticut Health Services Research Series, no. 5, New Haven, Conn., 1974.

Ferman, Louis A.: Poverty in America, Ann Arbor, Mich., 1968, University of Michigan Press.

Foster, A.: Some socio-economic aspects of infant mortality, Intellect, vol. 103, Feb 1975.

Frederick, P. L., Schlief, N. Young, Chung, Caroline J., and Gow, Albert C.: Health care for the Chinese community in Boston, Am. J. Public Health, vol. 62, Apr. 1972.

Friedman, J. J.: Cultural constraints on community action: the case of infant mortality rates, Social Problems, vol. 21, Fall 1973.

Hurley, Rodger L.: Poverty and mental retardation, New York, 1969, Random House, Inc

Kosa, John: Poverty and Health, Cambridge, Mass. 1969, Harvard University Press.

Health characteristics by large, metropolitan areas and other places of residence, U.S Department of Health, Education, and Welfare, Public Health Resource Administration, National Center for Health Statistics, series 10, no. 89, Rockville, Md., 1974.

New South, vol. 26, no. 4, Fall 1971. This publication has many important articles dealing with the problems of this chapter. A few of the titles follow: Poor hungry babies Whatever happened to the national nutrition survey. Family planning in Louisiana Worms turn people off. Black lung and the tragedy of Appalachia.

Osborn, Richard Warren: Social and economic factors in reported chronic morbidity, J Gerontol., vol. 36, no. 2, April 1, 1971.

Peters, A. D., and Chase, C. L.: Patterns of health care in infancy in rural southern county Am. J. Public Health **57**(3):407-422, Mar. 1967.

Podell, Lawrence: Health care of pre-school children in families on welfare, N.Y. State J. Med., vol. 73, May 1, 1973.

Pratt, Lois: The relationship of socioeconomic status to health, Am. J. Public Health, vol 61, Feb. 1971.

Rahe, R. H., Gunderson, E. H., and Ransom, J. A.: Demographic and psychosocial factors in acute illness reporting, J. Chronic Dis., vol. 23, Oct. 1970.

Scott, Clarissa S.: Health and healing practices among five ethnic groups in Miami, Florida, Public Health Reports, **89**(6):524-532, Nov.-Dec. 1974.

Webber, Irving L., and Ritchey, Ferris: The West Alabama medical-care study, Sociological Studies no. 2, Bureau of Public Administration, University of Alabama, 1975.

Veeks, H. Ashley: Family spending patterns and health care, Cambridge, 1960, Harvard University Press.

Veeks, H. Ashley, and Darsky, Benjamin J.: The urban aged: race and medical care, Bureau of Public Health Economics, Research Series no. 14, School of Public Health, University of Michigan, 1968.

Vennburg, John, and Gittelsohn, Alan: Small area variations in health care delivery, Science, vol. 182, no. 417, Dec. 1973.

5

The elderly and disease—Medicare and Medicaid—help and hindrance

AGNES W. BREWSTER*

■ Another unmet need of our health delivery system is service to the elderly. Sharply rising costs, fragmentation of services, and unavailability of physicians, added to the lack of comprehensive health insurance, accentuate the problems of this ever increasing segment of the population. The elderly, who have the highest utilization of health services and are removed from the economic market, often have unique, long-term health problems and are paying for health services at ever higher proportions of their limited incomes. The guidelines of "prevailing and customary fee" are imprecise and, in the absence of a free market, are not susceptible to control (a feature of the health field). Because of gaps in coverage, deductibles, and coinsurance, Medicare covers only 40% of the total personal health expenditures of the elderly. Mrs. Brewster joins others in suggesting (1) expanding benefits under Medicare to include drugs, mental health care, appliances, and blood, (2) eliminating the deductible and coinsurance features of Title XVIII, (3) requiring standards for physician qualifications for such services as surgery, (4) changing Part B of Title XVIII to a program with fixed fees.

Medicare has been paying hospital insurance and supplementary medical insurance benefits for the nation's aged since July 1, 1966.

There are two basic components of Title XVIII of the Social Security Act. Part A, a compulsory hospital insurance (HI) plan, provides for inpatient diagnostic studies, hospital room and board costs, and extended care and/or home care services. Hospital insurance is provided to all persons aged 65 years and over entitled to monthly cash benefits under the Social Security or Railroad Retirement Acts. Excepted are federal employees not entitled to Social Security or Railroad Retirement benefits, aliens with less than 5 years of consecutive residence, and those who have been convicted of crimes against the security of the United States. The cost for the program is shared jointly by employees and employers through Social Security payroll taxes.

*Mrs. Brewster wishes to acknowledge with gratitude the role Barbara S. Cooper played in updating this chapter.

Part B, a voluntary supplementary medical insurance (SMI) program, is financed by monthly premium payments by each enrollee, matched by an equal sum from the general revenue fund of the federal government. This plan provides payment of physicians' and surgeons' fees, outpatient clinic and office visits, diagnostic x-ray studies and laboratory tests, some types of medical equipment such as wheelchairs, splints, and prostheses, and home health services. Under Part B, enrollees presently pay a monthly premium of $6.70. They also pay the first $60 of Part B expenses each year and 20% thereafter of the physician's "reasonable charge."

The law creating Medicare allowed the Social Security Administration less than a year to implement a massive program, the largest health insurance program in the world, and one fraught with new features and methods of reimbursing hospitals and physicians. Because of their experience, existing "fiscal intermediaries" (a term coined for the program) were used to administer the program. Thus Blue Cross and Blue Shield plans, private insurance corporations, and group practice plans determine rates of payment, disbursing of funds, and receiving and reviewing claims.

The providers of hospital insurance are reimbursed on a "reasonable charge" basis; that is, the rate must not be higher than that charged for a comparable service under comparable circumstances to a nonsubscribing member. Under SMI, the individual physician has the following alternatives in billing a patient:

1. The physician can bill the beneficiary for any amount he wishes. The patient must then pay the entire fee and file a claim for reimbursement. The patient will then receive 80% of the "reasonable charge," which may, of course, be considerably less than what the physician charged.
2. The physician can bill the government or the fiscal intermediary for 80% of the "reasonable charge" and the patient for the remaining 20%.

One feature of reimbursement under Part B, namely paying the physician's own "reasonable and customary" charges, was incorporated into the law in the mistaken belief that it had become a widespread practice among the insurance carriers. This turned out to be anything but a universal practice, and it has led to complications in the whole reimbursement process, causing delays and arguments and confusing the beneficiaries. Another untried practice (except in a limited way) was that of separating the services of radiologists, pathologists, anesthesiologists, and physiatrists from components of the inpatient hospital bill and putting them—for Medicare alone—under Part B, physicians' services.

EXPENDITURES UNDER MEDICARE

Governmental expenditures

Expenditures under both parts of the Medicare program have increased each year. Under the hospital insurance program (Part A), the total for the United States increased from $2.5 billion in the first year to $7.8 billion in the eighth year. The average cost per enrollee rose from $134 to $258 in calendar year 1971; rapid inflataion would make it considerably more than double today.

Reimbursements under the supplementary medical insurance program (Part B) more than doubled from $668 million in fiscal year 1967 to $1.6 billion in fiscal year 1969 and today are much much higher. The average SMI cost per enrollee rose from $38 initially to $100 in calendar year 1971.

In fiscal year 1966, just before the advent of Medicare, the elderly of the United States accounted for approximately 21% of the $36.8 billion paid for the health care costs of that year. A total of $7.8 billion was spent on the aged in fiscal year 1966, 69% from private sources and 31% from public funds. Seventeen percent of the aggregate was from state and local funds and 14% from federal funds.

The source of expenditures changed in character under Medicare. State and local expenditures for the aged dropped nearly $300 million and federal expenditures rose by $3.3 billion, thereby increasing by $3 billion the amount of tax money used to finance the aged's health needs. At the same time, private expenditures by and for the aged decreased by $1.7 billion. By fiscal year 1973, 82% of the money spent on behalf of the aged for hospital care came from tax sources. That only 12% of the combined expenditures for dentists, drugs, appliances, eyeglasses, and the like was met by tax monies in 1973 arises from the gaps in Medicare coverage.

Of the $80 billion spent on personal health care in the last fiscal year from which compiled data are available (1973), 28%, or $22.4 billion was for care of the aged. Some 64% of the expenditures for fiscal year 1973 were derived from public monies.

Additional evidence of changes in financial structure brought about by Medicare is that 57% of expenditures for nursing home care now comes from tax monies, whereas 38% came from tax monies in 1966 before Medicare.

The $14.5 billion expended for the aged under public programs in fiscal year 1973 were applied to Medicare (62%), public assistance vendor medical payments (23%), veterans' hospital and medical care (4%), other public hospital and medical care services (10%), and other programs (1%). Some 20% of total public expenditures for the aged are now derived from state and local funds; this proportion has risen from 17% since 1969.

Thus, although the federal Medicare program has replaced a large segment of private spending for the elderly's health care, 60% of their total health care expenditures are covered under other government programs (mostly Medicaid) or still remain a personal responsibility to be met out of Social Security cash benefits, other income, and assets and by relatives, friends, or private insurance.

Expenditures in personal terms

However significant and imposing the national statistics are, they must be translated into individual terms if we are to understand the grave medical cost problems facing millions of older Americans today.

The most striking attribute of the aged's medical care costs is their uneven distribution. The amount of hospital care required annually varies from none for 87% of the elderly to two or more stays for some of the elderly. Older persons with incomes of $10,000 or more used hospitals more heavily than the average person. Those with two or three hospital episodes required more than two or three times as many days of care as those hospitalized only once.

Visits to physicians vary by age, sex, and physical condition, as well as by city and income. Only 27% to 30% of the population aged 65 years and over go through a year without seeing a physician, and 7% see a physician thirteen or more times a year, or more than once a month. Thus costs can range from nothing to $400 or more just for physician visits outside the hospital.

Not surprisingly, prescribed drug usage varies widely; those with chronic illnesses require more than the average number of prescriptions. Since the purchase of prescribed drugs is not covered under the Medicare programs, sizable costs may accrue. Consequently, the cost of prescription drugs is the largest area of per capita private medical expenditure by the aged, averaging $55.35 in 1971, with 18% of the elderly spending $100 or more.

MEDICARE: THE BENEFITS, THE GAPS

Medicare pays a large portion of the hospital bills of the aged. The deductible of the first $104 of the hospital bill and the coinsurance in the later days of stays in the hospital and extended care facility do not affect many aged people in the course of a year. Under Part B of Medicare, however, enrollees pay not only $80.40 in annual premiums but also the first $60 of the insured services and 20% of the remainder of the charges. When a person sees a physician, quite often other charges, such as for laboratory work, prescriptions, and x-ray films, also are incurred Some or all of these charges represent gaps in Medicare coverage. Coverage of mental illness under Medicare is subject to special limitations on days of care (190 days in a lifetime) and on out-of-hospital treatment (50% coinsurance and a limit of $250 annually as well as the $60 deductible). Although 68% of all mental hospitals with 74% of all mental health beds participate in Medicare, the proportions vary by region of the country and by sponsorship. The problem was described by Dr. Robert W. Gibson, representing the American Psychiatric Association at United States Senate hearings in 1967:

> Under the supplementary medical insurance benefits for the aged, outpatient treatment may be paid for after a $50 deductible, with the patient paying 20 percent, and with no top limit. But, in the case of psychiatric treatment . . . there is a top limit of $250. This limitation seriously curtails outpatient psychiatric treatment for the aged patient. Many elderly patients can be successfully treated on an outpatient basis. *If such treatment is denied because of financial limitation, the inevitable result will be hospitalization. Such unwarranted hospitalization may not serve the best interests of patients, and will most certainly add to the cost of the hospital insurance program.*

Many physicians caring for Medicare patients will not accept assignment of the benefits. "Assignment of benefit" means that the aged person has instructed the Medicare fiscal intermediary to pay his physician directly (to assign his benefits to the physician). When a physician accepts assignment, he binds himself not to send a separate and additional bill directly to the elderly person; he collects 20% of the bill from the beneficiary and 80% from the trust fund via the fiscal intermediary. Surgeons, whose bills are usually larger than those of other physicians, show some willingness to accept assignment rather than to struggle to collect from patients, who may be able to pay only after receiving the claims payments themselves. But the proportion of bills paid by assignment has continually decreased.

The disadvantages of nonassignment are as follows:

1. The aged person must pay the physician's charges, whatever their level, without such deterrents as are imposed by having the fiscal intermediary screen for reasonableness and relationship to other physicians' charges.
2. The aged must themselves complete forms, submit claims, and pay the bills.
3. The higher charges soon become the accepted level of charges and are subsequently paid by the fiscal intermediary.
4. The dollar cost of the coinsurance of 20% mounts.
5. Workers pay more Social Security taxes as demands on the trust fund rise.

Certain types of health care—notably long-term nursing care for chronic illness, as distinct from posthospital extended care—are almost exclusively the domain of the aged. In Michigan, under Medicaid in 1969, nursing homes cost $420 a month on the average, or $5,040 a year. The current California charge is over $700 monthly. How can elderly people, who by definition are long since separated from the labor market and entitled in the main to the minimal Social Security cash benefit, afford the cost of nursing home care? The average extended care facility under Medicare costs more than $600 a month. Since Medicare coverage extends for only 100 days, personal income or other means must be used to pay for continued extended care, which often approaches $7,500 to $10,000 per year. Although Medicaid may pick up nursing home expenses, it may do so only after the patient has exhausted income and savings.

The lifetime of the program

Both the lack of coverage of many needed services that poor, ill people should have and the fragmentation in the delivery of the services that are provided are disturbing. All too often, when a question of funding comes up, cuts are made in Medicaid at the expense of the clients and not the providers.

Medicaid could be a useful vehicle for improving the delivery system for care of people were it not riddled with contradictory policies in its implementation in the various states.

CAN PRIVATE HEALTH INSURANCE HELP?

The Division of Research and Statistics of the Social Security Administration periodically reports on the extent of private insurance purchased by or on behalf of the United States population. According to this source, about half the aged population has supplemented its Medicare coverage with some form of private protection (see Table 6). The private policies are financed by the aged themselves or result from employee benefit provisions after retirement. Like private insurance generally, these policies vary widely in the scope of benefits and in the cost of premiums. Obviously, many aged cannot risk their meager cash resources on protection they may not find of much assistance.

Statistics prepared by the Blue Cross Association on just under 2 million such enrollees in twenty-eight Blue Cross plans showed that a total of 233 per 1,000 aged enrollees used the benefit in 1967. There was almost no need for full pay days (days beyond the Medicare benefit of 90 days)—only 5 days per 1,000 enrollees. The deductible and coinsurance benefit applied to 167 days per 1,000 enrollees. Since Medicare is used

Table 6. Percent of aged with private health insurance, by type, as of December 31, 1972*

Services	Percent covered†
Hospital care	53.2
Surgical services	46.3
Inhospital visits	38.5
X-ray and laboratory examinations	36.6
Office and home visits	20.5
Dental care	1.4
Prescribed drugs (out of hospital)	16.6
Private duty nursing	16.3
Visiting nurse service	21.2
Nursing home care	25.8

*From Social Security Bulletin **37**:21, Feb. 1974.
†"Covered" does not necessarily mean completely paid for.

at a rate of at least 3,100 days per 1,000 beneficiaries, the Blue Cross benefits are not heavily used except for meeting the initial deductible of $104 of the hospital bill.

Other insurance policies provide straight dollar indemnities for each day in the hospital, sometimes increasing the amounts at the sixty-first and ninetieth days. Usually incompletely, other cash indemnity plans may cover ambulatory care and include prescriptions, eye examinations, physical examinations, and other services that are excluded from Medicare. Prepaid group practice plans have worked out ways of dovetailing benefits so that their Medicare members can continue to receive routine physical examinations, eye examinations, prescribed drugs, and other services not included in Medicare's benefits.

Overall, however, it is apparent that many of the same reasons why voluntary health insurance could not provide the kind of protection the aged needed still hold. The sum of $13.40 monthly, or $160.80 annually, for a couple for Part B of Medicare, in addition to the deductibles and coinsurance under Parts A and B of Medicare that the beneficiary must meet and the expenses for drugs and the like, takes all their modest budget can manage.

IMPACT OF INFLATION ON MEDICAL COSTS

Health care expenditures per aged person in fiscal year 1969 averaged 3.3 times those of people under age 65 years. It becomes clear, then, that inflationary tendencies in the health field will have intense impact on care provided for the elderly and that public and private sources of this support are cetain to be strained during periods of dramatic cost increases.

During the period 1960 to 1965, when prices generally were rising less rapidly than at any time since 1946, the *Consumer Price Index* (CPI) showed a slowdown in the daily service charges of hospitals—from an annual 8.3% rise to a 6.3% rise. However, the deceleration stopped abruptly in 1966, when Medicare began in July of that year. In 1967 the index for semiprivate room charges rose by 17.3% and in 1968, by 15.9%. Physicians' fees rose 7.4% in 1967 and 6.1% in 1968. In the 8 year period from July 1966 to July 1974, hospital semiprivate room charges had risen 96% and physicians' fees, 46%. Overall, medical care services had risen 54%. A faster rate of inflation occurred after the period cited.

In the summer of 1965 the Social Security Administration arranged with the Bureau of Labor Statistics to collect prices for three surgical procedures (cholecystectomy, prostatectomy, and surgery on the fractured neck of the femur) and two in-hospital medical services (for myocardial infarction and cerebral hemorrhage) that are common among older persons, although not necessarily limited to them. Prices were collected for these five procedures but were not incorporated in the regular sample of the CPI. It was believed that fees for such services might be sensitive to the new Medicare program and hence would provide baseline data to assess the impact of the program on physicians' fees. These five special procedures are the reason for hospitalization for many elderly people. The average increase of 21% found for physicians' charges generally for the 36 months ending December 1968 compared closely with increases of 17% to 21% for the five procedures. No later data are yet available.

COSTS FOR THE ELDERLY

Although the CPI for drugs and prescriptions shows little change, there is a real question about whether or not the surrogate items priced for this index are in fact representative of the kinds of drug therapies the elderly require.

Although Medicare has generated powerful inflationary forces in the health care market, it can also be a force against runaway costs. The following excerpts from the first annual report of the Health Insurance Benefits Advisory Council of the United States Department of Health, Education, and Welfare give a balanced view of what may be possible in either direction:

> In its deliberations, and in drawing up its recommendations, the Council has tried to keep before it two major sets of facts about Medicare.
>
> On the one hand, this is an insurance program. It finances for older people, the purchase of services from the providers of health care, most of whom also supply services to all other age groups in the population. As a consequence, Medicare by itself cannot exercise a dominant influence over costs and stan-

dards in the health care field. At the same time in exercising its obligations t
beneficiaries in the provision of high-quality medical care and its obligation t
taxpayers in securing care at reasonable costs, Medicare can, in a limited bu
important way, indirectly affect the standards and costs of health care for th
population at large. . . .

While all third-party payers should have an important role to play in seekin
and applying cost restraints, this is particularly true of Medicare. The scope anc
coverage of the program are so large that what Medicare does may set a patter
for many other third-party payment programs.

One of the reasons that third parties have an important role to play i
controlling cost is that most of the forces of typical marketplace situation
which act to control costs for nonhealth services cannot perform effectively i
the health field. Cost reimbursement to hospitals offers no built-in incentives t
cost restraint. Charge reimbursement to doctors, as well, does not provide th
protection against increasing charges that are present in many other economi
areas.

The Council, in common with other parties, is concerned that medical car
expenditures and Medicare funds in particular should be spent most effectivel
in order to maximize the benefits received for the funds expended. The Counci
is very much aware that there are limits to the time during which medical cos
can continue to rise as rapidly as in recent years without creating serious issue
of the priority of allocation of further resources to medical care rather than t
housing in the inner city, to education or to the multitude of other demands no
now fully satisfied.

The ways that Medicare sets the amount it will pay for covered services ma
have very important effects on the entire health care industry.

The escalation of physicians' charges. The medical insurance program (Part
B) is designed to reimburse the beneficiary, or pay on his behalf, reasonable
charges incurred for physicians' services, and certain other medical services,
subject to applicable deductible and coinsurance amounts.

The law does not contemplate that reimbursement of physicians will be
based on a fee schedule. Nor was it expected that an individual's income would
determine the amount of the payment to be made. It is also clear, however, that
Congress did not contemplate reimbursement of physicians without controls of
any kind over the costs of the program or without limit to the liabilities it
assumed. The law thus provides that only reasonable charges will be reimbursed. To implement this reasonable charge limitation, the law calls for individual determinations or reasonable charges for specific services by the Medicare carrier which may not exceed the amount the carrier customarily pays under its own program under comparable situations and which take into account (1) the customary charges of the physician, and (2) the prevailing charges in the community. The concept of customary charges incorporates the idea that physican's fees to Medicare beneficiaries for a given service be no higher than his charges to other patients for the same service. As the program has developed, it has become clear that effective administration of this concept requires recognition of the idea that the physician's charges should not be higher than those that have been applicable in his practice for some time—in short, that customary fees should be those that have in fact been established by custom. The concept of prevailing charges incorporates the idea that a particular physician's fees to a Medicare beneficiary for a specific service should not be out of line with the level of fees generally charged in the locality.

The statute, therefore, is based upon the view that reasonable charges by hysicians and other persons under the program include only those which stay vithin the bounds marked out by the criteria of customary, prevailing, and omparability.

Enforcement of these concepts, under the Medicare program, is in the hands f the insurance carriers, operating within the regulations and under the supervision of the Social Security Administration. They are required to assure that he charges determined to be reasonable for Medicare meet the customary and revailing criteria. Comparison of individual charges with a profile of charges erived both from their Medicare records and the records relating to their own olicyholders and subscribers, and with other data on physicians' charges is the rimary means of determining that the Medicare reimbursement conforms to he statutory requirements.

ONTROLS UNDER MEDICARE AND MEDICAID

The Advisory Committee to the Senate Subcommittee on Health of he Elderly expressed grave doubts that in the absence of a free market, s is true in the health field, the concept of allowing the providers to ontrol their own reimbursement is susceptible to the imposition of ontrols. The terms "prevailing" and "customary" are imprecise and ardly made less so by setting the computer to record the seventy-fifth, nd eighty-third, or some other percentile. Limits on frequency of alowing individual physicians to raise a fee merely shift to the patient he amount denied and postpone for a period the day when the higher ee is recognized as the particular physician's customary one.

Efforts to find incentives that will induce hospitals to operate more conomically have so far produced few concrete savings. It is not ifficult to recognize the truth of the situation—that there is little reaon to control costs if your largest customer will pay costs, however njustified they actually are. Neither carrots nor clubs are effective for ong in such inflationary settings.

Standards for quality of care for physicians' services outside the ospital can be developed. New York City has done this and it must be one elsewhere. Those in the health field must be innovative and active n seeking ways to keep the cost to all—the aged, the remainder of the opulation, and public and private insurance programs—within ounds.

"CHEATING" UNDER MEDICARE AND MEDICAID

As the foregoing discussion suggests, there are serious voids in resent day cost controls under Medicare, and much more also must be one in the setting of standards for services rendered. The same is true f Medicaid also. It is equally true of other federal programs that purchase services, including the Civilian Health and Medical Program of he Uniformed Services (CHAMPUS).

There needs to be a reexamination of the role of fiscal agents and intermediaries in these programs from the point of view of their capability and willingness to promptly supply the data necessary to police the providers. There is a real or potential conflict of interest in expecting intermediaries to control utilization and costs in the public interest.

Whether the physicians' service review organizations (PSROs) will be of value is still in question. Will the main function of the PSRO be (1) to deter, similar to the policeman on patrol; (2) to have an impact on elevating the quality of care by reducing unnecessary procedures, such as surgery; (3) to increase the "visibility" of medical practice, such as in group practice plans; or (4) to be a gimmick that controls cost and nothing more?

DEFICIENCIES IN DELIVERY OF SERVICES

Medicare and Medicaid have helped to create inflationary pressures by raising new demands for medical services that were unavailable or in short supply. Thus deficiencies in the delivery system for health care services have played a direct role in creating the dollars and cents problems that elderly people who need medical care encounter.

Less apparent, but certainly of considerable impact, are other difficulties caused by faulty organization or nonexistence of services. Tables and statistics can tell only part of the story here.

The elderly, along with other age groups, suffer not only in terms of inconvenience but also in terms of direct dollar outlays because of irrational or outmoded delivery systems for medical care and services.

Ill, elderly persons usually have more than one ailment at a time. If they cannot get one-stop service for examinations or treatment, they become prime victims of a health care system recently described by Former Social Security Commissioner Robert Ball as "largely decentralized, largely uncoordinated, and largely voluntary." Former Surgeon General William H. Stewart called it a "nonsystem."

For the low income elderly, the problems can be even more intense, so much so that the health problems may reach the crisis stage before help is sought, thus increasing the dollar expenditure paid from public or private sources.

Use of health services for the aged increased significantly under Medicare, but utilization rates vary widely from state to state and area to area in a pattern that confirms the view that utilization of a particular service depends to a significant degree on its availability. In the case of hospitals, the variations in use, payments, and admission rates appear to be, in part, associated with the number of available hospital beds per 1,000 of the population.

Such factors as the availability of physicians in a community, their staff privileges, the geographical proximity of other health services, and local customs on use of extended care facilities and home health agencies (their uses vary widely) also must contribute to these variations in both the hospital and the medical insurance programs.

Home health agencies, in particular, offer uneven coverage: scattered among twenty-five states are ninety-nine counties with populations over 40,000 without a home health agency; in Rhode Island the "start of care" rate per 1,000 beneficiaries was 34.3, compared to 3.2 in Mississippi and 3.3 in North Carolina; and there are wide variations in the range of services offered.

Each organizational deficiency causes financial, social, and moral problems not only for governmental agencies but also for elderly individuals. Until the problems of persons needing direction, understanding, and treatment rather than delay, confusion, or indifference are resolved, the economic problems of the elderly will be needlessly intensified.

CONSIDERATIONS FOR FORMULATION OF PUBLIC POLICY

A comprehensive, compulsory health insurance program for all age groups—a program with built-in cost controls, standards for quality care, incentives for prepaid group practice, and other badly needed reforms—offers the best hope this nation has for living up to the often expressed declaration that good health care is the right of every man, woman, and child who lives in the United States.

As a vital prerequisite for establishment of a national health insurance program, and while there exists a dual system of financing through social insurance and by general revenues, public and private efforts should immediately be made to deal with demonstrated deficiencies in Medicare and Medicaid for the following reasons:

1. Health care problems of the elderly are still widespread, and they remain urgent.
2. The Medicare program has provided a valuable lesson in the operation of a major public health insurance program. The time has come to heed those lessons.
3. Current investigations into profiteering under Medicaid and Medicare have helped focus attention on the need for cost controls and establishment of uniform standards of care. Such reforms can have a beneficial effect on the entire health industry and can combat medical cost inflation.
4. Success in improving Medicare will lead to more general acceptance of steps necessary to provide higher quality health care to our entire population.
5. The lack of sufficient consumer representation in Medicare and its almost

total absence from state advisory committees for Medicaid is deplorable.*

The Advisory Committee to the Senate Subcommittee on Health of the Elderly concluded that Part B of Title XVIII should be recast to bring it under the Social Security payroll tax and do away with premium payments by the aged. This rearrangement would then make several simplifications of benefit administration possible, including (1) permitting capitation payments to group practice plans providing hospital and physician services and (2) fostering use of home health services without reference to coinsurance.

The Advisory Committee expressed the following beliefs:

1. Medicare benefits should be extended; it should include other services and supplies not now covered, and especially those drugs that are important for the treatment of the chronic diseases that commonly affect the aged. Eventually all prescribed drugs should be included. The deductible and coinsurance features of both Parts A and B should be eliminated.
2. The 3 pint deductible for blood and the "three days in the hospital" requirements for admission to an extended care facility and the lifetime limitation on the mental hospital benefit should be dropped.
3. Preventive and diagnostic services should be covered more fully, and eye and foot care should be included.
4. Medicare has established itself in the daily lives of millions of Americans; physicians should no longer be permitted to refuse to recognize it by not taking assignment of benefits.
5. Physicians' fees cannot remain subject to the whims of individual providers of service, if Medicare and Medicaid are to be fiscally predictable and gross abuses are to be stopped. The same is true of hospital costs.
6. Standards for physicians' qualifications should be promulgated by Medicare and be incorporated in Medicaid state plans to require that qualified surgeons alone be allowed to perform operations.
7. There should be more consumer participation in the decision making processes under Medicare and Medicaid.*

In February 1970 the Nixon Administration adopted in part the recommendations of the Advisory Committee and proposed to the Ninety-Second Congress the merging of Parts A and B of Medicare, with consequent elimination of the then monthly $5.60 patient payments for Part B premiums. Concurrently, as a cost savings measure, it suggested reducing the 60 day hospital period for which no copayments are necessary to a lesser number and increasing the Part B deductible.

The Administration also proposed the substitution for much, though

*Committee Print, 91st Congress, first session: Health aspect of the economics of aging prepared by an advisory committee of the Special Committee on Aging, United States Senate, July 1969, pp. 41, 42.

not all, of Medicaid by a new Family Health Insurance Plan with the federal government purchasing, through the private health insurance industry, a package of basic benefits.

It appears clear that the Medicaid and Medicare programs have constituted major advances in the assumption by the public sector of responsibility for payment of a large portion of the costs of medical care of the indigent and the aged.

The years immediately ahead should witness considerable changes in these programs in improvements in benefit coverages, the development of more effective cost and quality controls, and eventual integration of these innovative governmental activities into a broader and more comprehensive national health insurance plan for the United States.

Part two

ISSUES AND PROPOSED SOLUTIONS—ORGANIZATION OF HEALTH SERVICES

6

Primary care—definition and purpose

ALBERTA PARKER

■ In this provocative article, Dr. Parker outlines the ingredients of primary health care from an individual as well as a societal viewpoint. The minimum essential ingredients of primary care must include first-contact care with longitudinal and coordinated basic medical services. However, effective primary care should also coordinate the health of the individual with the health of the family. In addition, health promotion and maintenance are legitimate functions of primary care. To meet these standards, changes in the organizational patterns of medical care may be necessary.

THE NEED FOR A DEFINITION OF PRIMARY HEALTH CARE

The present attitude toward primary care in the United States can be characterized fairly as recognition without definition. In spite of the attention primary care has received, it is still difficult to know what is really meant when either of the terms "primary health care" or "primary medical care" is used. No description of the goals and objectives of primary care exists, nor of its nature, characteristics, and boundaries. No specific service can without equivocation be said to be a primary care service. For example, is a vasectomy a primary or secondary care service? Is the treatment of a recurrent attack of otitis media, whoever handles it, a part of primary care? And who practices primary care—the family practitioner, the pediatrician, and the internist? What about the obstetrician, the emergency room physician, the surgeon in a small town who spends half the day in family care, or the otolaryngologist who treats the otitis media mentioned above? And where do public health nurses fit into the picture? Or social workers, or mental health workers in crisis centers, or pharmacists dispensing over-the-counter drugs? And general dentists—are they also primary care practitioners?

Because assignments to the primary care level can be made only in an approximate fashion, we cannot obtain accurate counts of the primary health or medical care "visits" in the United States in a specific year, the number of "primary care physicians" available to the population, the number of organizations involved in primary care delivery, or the total costs of such care. More importantly, we have no generally accepted guiding principles on which to plan primary care programs, train personnel for them, or evaluate their performances.

In the first part of this chapter, I should like to consider some reasons for the lack of definite answers to these questions and to propose that this lack should spur the search for a clearer definition of primary care. In the second part of the chapter, I will present some of the questions that must be raised in the development of such a definition and some of the organizational and public policy implications that accompany them. Finally, I will present several methods that have been used to approach the definitional problem and outline the results of an enquiry using one particular method—a consensus of experts approach.

• • •

The deliberate creation of definitions for the systematic development of human services is unusual in actual practice. Planning, instead, emerges from the push and pull of conflicting philosophies, from ad hoc decisions taken to solve immediate problems, or from the efforts of special interest groups. This "disjointed incrementalism"[1] often leads to programs that are neither reflective of broadly based norms nor related closely to actual needs. Primary health care planning is an example of this process. Someone in a state or federal agency, for example, decides that certain home care services are not reimbursable. A group in the Office of Economic Opportunity decides that a comprehensive, integrative model of health care is needed and develops neighborhood health centers. In the educational sector, meanwhile, family practice, pediatric, and internal medicine departments are each defining the skills necessary for primary care practice. Thus are the boundaries arrived at—piecemeal and using vague and ill-formed parameters.

Why have we waited so long to define primary care more precisely? I would like to propose that there has been little need for clarity until quite recently. The needs on which primary care is based—the desire for a trusted healer who responds quickly to illness, pain, injury, and anxiety, and the need for support through life's crises at times of birth, death, and disease—are elemental and universal. So long as these needs are being met, however minimally, there is little reason to think further. Like the social concepts of family and marriage, the primary health care process needs little explicit definition until changes in society rupture its traditional form and throw its future form into doubt. Only when such a rupture happens is there a desire for an ordered explanation.

The last 50 years have witnessed changes both in the dominant types of health problems and in the responses provided by the health care system. At the same time, family and neighborhood life have changed enormously. Families are smaller, and members may be separated by the width of the continent. Urban living provides fewer support mechanisms for the ill, the aged, the dependent, the frightened, and the depressed. The need for a spectrum of services broader than medical care alone is increasing; but, at the same time, physicians are becoming more technically oriented, more specialized, and increasingly hard to reach.

Failures in the delivery of basic health services are often reported. To the common failures regarding quality, cost, and availability, we may add the predominance of the brief encounter, which provides little time for understanding the human needs that accompany illness, for the "talking out" of a problem, for the necessary attention to "anxiety," or for help during crisis periods. Second, the narrow focus on the physical aspects of health problems, often limited to one organ system or one condition, constitutes a primary care failure. Another is the fact that patient convenience is given little heed, facilitative services are rare, and the helping services that substitute for the family-provided services of years past are unavailable or can be obtained only in piecemeal fashion. Finally, our health care system has jeopardized the continuity and coordination of *individual* care by the distribution of different basic services among many providers, and it has failed to provide the continuity and coordination necessary for the whole *family's* care to be a coordinated reality.

Problems like these face the individual who is being served in the emergency room. They also face the clinic patient in the city outpatient department, the member of the large prepaid plan, and the patient of the highly trained internist in private practice.

The continuation of rapid social change and the increasing complexity of medical care organizations can only result in marked changes in primary care, and these changes will require a common base of understanding before rational policy decisions can be made about legitimate reimbursable costs, performance criteria, optimal organizational structures, and personnel distribution and utilization. Therefore, I believe, the time has come for us to define in more exact terms the parameters of primary care.

SIX QUESTIONS TO BE ANSWERED IN THE DEFINITION OF PRIMARY CARE

In approaching a definition of primary care, two different processes should be distinguished. The first process entails an outlining of the overall responsibilities and boundaries of the primary care process and an analysis of the unique functional and qualitative attributes that differentiate it from the rest of medical care. In the second process, particular services are assigned to the primary health care level. This assignment process is being tackled by various research efforts as well as residency programs, which are identifying the tasks appropriate to primary care through an analysis of the knowledge, skills, and experience necessary to perform them. It is the first process, the outlining of responsibilities and boundaries, that is dealt with in this chapter.

In clarifying these boundaries, six questions about primary care can be distinguished, each with its own unique organizational and policy implications:

1. What attributes characterize the delivery of primary care?
2. What should be the scope of this care?
3. Should a health orientation as well as a disease orientation be a part of primary care?
4. What should be the unit of attention—the individual or the family?
5. Should responsibility for health care for the individual or the patient group go beyond the patient-initiated contact?
6. Should interventive methods other than the delivery of personal health care services be used?

The attributes considered essential to primary health care

An analysis of the attributes of primary care must start, in my view, with health related conditions—both in planning specific programs and in developing more abstract conceptualizations. The system characteristics or qualities that differentiate primary care from delivery at other levels are determined by these conditions as are its services and functions.

An examination of the health conditions encountered by the general population allows us to distinguish three levels of care, customarily designated as primary, secondary, and tertiary levels, each assuming responsibility for a particular subset of conditions, and each having its uniquely important functions and qualities.

John Fry[2] first used this approach in the United Kingdom, examining the patterns of illness and resultant health needs in his own patient panel, and thereby defining the qualities of the primary level. Six aspects of general health conditions (and there may be others) can be used to differentiate the characteristics of the different levels of care[3]:

1. *Frequency of occurrence* is an aspect of health conditions relevant to levels of care. In any population certain disease states or conditions requiring health services will occur commonly, others only rarely. What is

rare and what is common will vary, of course, with the age and socioeconomic status of the group served and the environmental setting. Additionally, all populations, whatever their place in the world, share the need for health care for mothers and infants, health education, and attention to personal habits affecting health.

Commonly occurring conditions give rise to two system qualities that may be used to differentiate levels. First, the service system for common conditions needs to by physically close to the patient and easy to enter. Second, the service population can be small since frequently occurring conditions allow the provider—physician, physician's assistant, or village health aide—to serve a small population and still maintain the quality of care. This is not true of less common conditions. At the secondary and tertiary levels, which draw from a larger population, the uncommon becomes the common, and quality and service can be maintained.

2. A second characteristic working to create natural levels is the *nature of onset.* Those conditions that are acute in onset also need a close, easily accessible system. They require, in addition, a system capable of distinguishing rapidly between those diseases that are self-limited, or require only simple interventions, and the more serious conditions, which require complex, highly skilled, or intensive care.
3. *Duration* is also a factor. Some conditions are over quickly; others continue for long periods, perhaps throughout the remainder of life. Such chronic conditions require proximity of services plus continuity of providers, records, and patient care management.
4. Difference in the *technical complexity* of treatment can serve as a distinguishing criterion. Some conditions require the simplest of knowledge, skills, procedures, and equipment; others demand special equipment and training for effective intervention.
5. *Diversity* also plays a role. Common conditions, while they may be uncomplicated, involve every bodily system and every permutation of personal, family, or social relationships. Medical responses must be equally diverse. In addition, nonmedical responses, such as health education, assessment of the home, and provision of supportive relationships, are often required. This diversity requires generalists who are capable of handling multidimensional problems in a way quite different from the responses of specialists. For many, if not most, situations, it will require workers other than the physician—to work with the patient in the most favorable environment for patient compliance and behavioral change (often the home), to provide the skills and time often lacking when care is limited to the physician, and to allow for the delegation of certain tasks for optimal efficiency.[4]
6. *Changes in behavior* on the part of the patient may be required in many health conditions, particularly those conditions that can be prevented by changes in personal habits and patterns of living. To initiate and promote behavioral change requires time and interest on the part of providers. It also requires both an understanding of the patient's way of life and the existence of a relationship in which patient acceptance of the need for change can occur. A first imperative in building such a relationship is continuity between provider and patient; a second is mutual respect and trust.

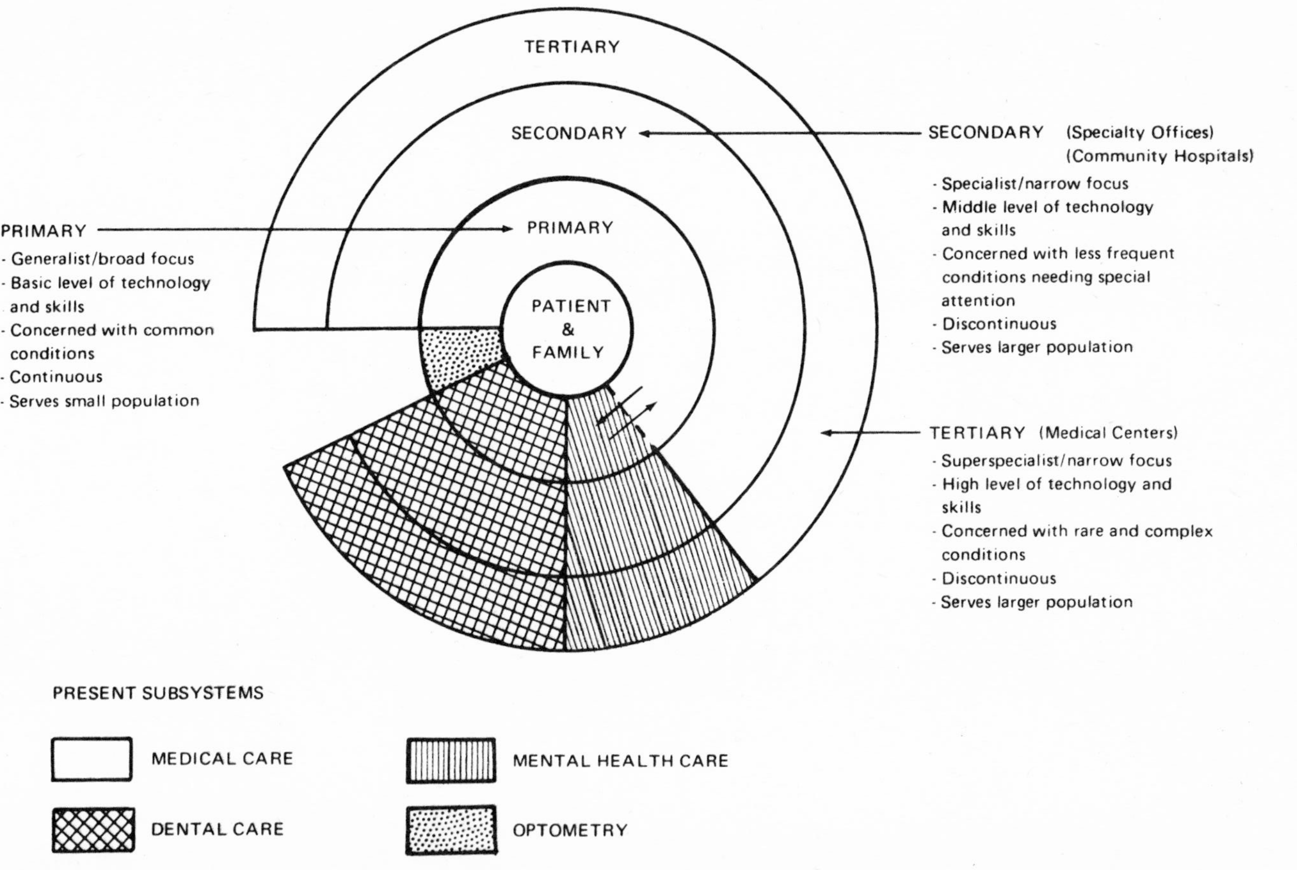

Fig. 8. Personal health care system: levels of care. (From Parker, A. W.: The dimensions of primary care; blueprints

In summary, by examining frequency of occurrence, character of onset, duration, complexity, diversity, and the possible need for behavioral change, it is possible to separate health care into different levels, each with its own attributes or qualities (Fig. 8). At the primary level, a small subset of patients can be served by a system that is:

Physically close to those served
Accessible and easily identifiable
Quick to respond
Able to filter out those problems needing referral
Able to provide technically noncomplex responses to widely different problems for those not needing referral
Continuous in its attention
Able to coordinate all facets of care
Able to develop a trusted and personal relationship with patients
Able to understand the total environment in which the patient lives

The higher levels of care, the secondary and tertiary levels, have system characteristics or qualities that are in direct contrast to those of primary care. The higher levels need to serve larger client groups and:

May be physically more distant from the home and the community
Need not be as accessible or easily identifiable
Need not respond quickly to all situations
Need to be more complex in approach
Provide a specialist response
May be noncontinuous
Are not required to coordinate all facets of care
May be psychologically more distant from the consumer with a less personal relationship

The scope of primary care

The scope of care appropriate to the primary level can be defined broadly or narrowly. In its narrowest sense, primary care can be seen as single unaugmented *subsystem care,* as, for example, primary medical or primary dental care. Primary medical care, in its simplest version, would simply be those services provided by a single physician (if a generalist) and his support staff. In a somewhat broader context, primary care can be expanded to what might be designated as *augmented medical care.* In this case, physician services would be enriched by those of other professionals able to provide the counseling, educational, promotive, preventive, supportive, and facilitative services that go beyond the physician's usual role. The broadest scope for primary care goes beyond both medical care and augmented medical care to primary *health care.* At this level, the primary delivery system becomes the coordinative and pivotal point at which all strands of basic health services are gathered together.*

Most primary care today is single subsystem care, tending to stay strictly within professionally defined boundaries and affording minimal relationship among subsystems (Fig. 8). In most cases it has little augmentation. Only in some outpatient departments, certain organized prepaid groups, and the comprehensive health centers does one find medical care augmented by the services of public health nurses, social workers, mental health workers, or health education personnel. And only in some of these same organizations, in particular the health centers, has integration of the subsystems been attempted.

A move for primary care organizations to assume responsibility for the coordination of *all* health services would require the formation of new organizational structures and new coordinative mechanisms and the training of physicians to work as peers with other health professionals. To develop augmented medical care would also require considerable change in this direction. I predict that we will continue in the near future with the primary medical care model, moving, possibly, in a gradual way toward augmented medical care.

What will be the functions of primary medical care or its augmented variant, and what implications do these functions have for the types of services that will be included?† Three key functions for primary *medicine* have been proposed by Alpert and Charney.[5] The first is *the provision of "first contact" care.* This provision has a wider meaning than simple entry to a system; it also includes the responsibilities of reaching out actively to patients, informing them about services, helping define when care is appropriate, and following up when necessary. To this list I would like to add the subfunction of serving as a competent filter between primary care and other levels—retaining those appropriately handled at the primary level, but not overlooking those who should be referred. The other functions proposed by Alpert and Charney are *the assumption of longitudinal responsibility for patient care,* implicit in which is the acknowledgment that provider responsibility is ongoing and does not end

**Health care* used in this sense begs the issue as to whether or not this care has a disease or a health orientation. I shall return to this point in a later section.

†As noted previously, services, like qualities, develop naturally from the health care conditions of the population served. Organizational functions derive from them. In a previous paper,[3] I outlined the categories of services that I believe are necessary to meet health care needs at the primary care level. They are: outreach, triage, and referral; patient care management and coordination; facilitative services and a range of basic health services, including education; supportive and all clinical-technical services. In this chapter, I will not discuss these services in greater detail but will move directly from them to suggested functions, since such functions presume implicitly an underlying pattern of services.

Table 7. Estimated primary physician visits by selected organizational modes,* United States—1969 (in millions)

Private office based practitioners (a)	442
Hospital outpatient departments (b)	61
Emergency rooms (c)	40
Prepaid group practices (d)	21
Neighborhood health centers (e)	2
Free clinics (f)	1
TOTAL	567

*Based on an estimated total of 740 million nonfederal, nonhospital physician visits, excluding 100 million telephone contacts. Assumes that the "specialty" visits of general practitioners, all internists, and all pediatricians correspond in quantity with "primary" visits of specialists. From Parker, A. W.: The dimensions of primary care: blueprints for change. In Andreopoulos, S., editor: Primary care: where medicine fails, New York, 1974, John Wiley & Sons, Inc., p. 27.

(a) National Center for Health Statistics: Physician visits—volume and interval since last visit, United States, 1969, Vital and Health Statistics, Series 10, Number 75, Washington, D.C., July, 1972, U.S. Department of Health, Education, and Welfare. (Figure represents office and home visits of all internists, all pediatricians, and general practitioners minus the estimated primary visits to prepaid groups.)

(b) Piore, N., Lewis, D., and Seeliger, J.: A statistical profile of hospital outpatient services in the United States, New York, August, 1971, Association for the Aid of Crippled Children. (Figure represents outpatient visits to community hospitals minus 40 million emergency room visits, minus an estimated 25% specialty visits.)

(c) National Center for Health Statistics: Health resources statistics, health manpower and health facilities, 1971, Rockville, Maryland, 1972, Department of Health, Education, and Welfare.

(d) Estimated on the basis of seven million members each with four visits per year, three of which we assign to the primary level using the primary specialty ratio of office practice.

(e) Piore, Nora, *et al.: op. cit.*

(f) National Free Clinic Council.

with one episode of illness, and *serving as the "integrationist" for patient care,* that is, taking responsibility for the management of the physical, social, and psychological aspects of care, as well as coordinating the care of different providers and different levels of service. This latter function serves to discover service gaps and to uncover antithetical therapies and creates, out of the jigsaw of health services, one coherent pattern.

I would like to add two further functions that I consider unique and essential for full care at the primary level. First is *the assumption of responsibility* for human supportive services required at times of physical or emotional crisis. When the "caring" function of medicine is discussed, the affective relationship between patient and provider, potentially so important in the therapeutic process, is usually meant. I speak of a function that can be identified as "caring" but that goes beyond the affective relationship to the provision of actual supportive assistance to individuals and families. It is the active manifestation of the underlying

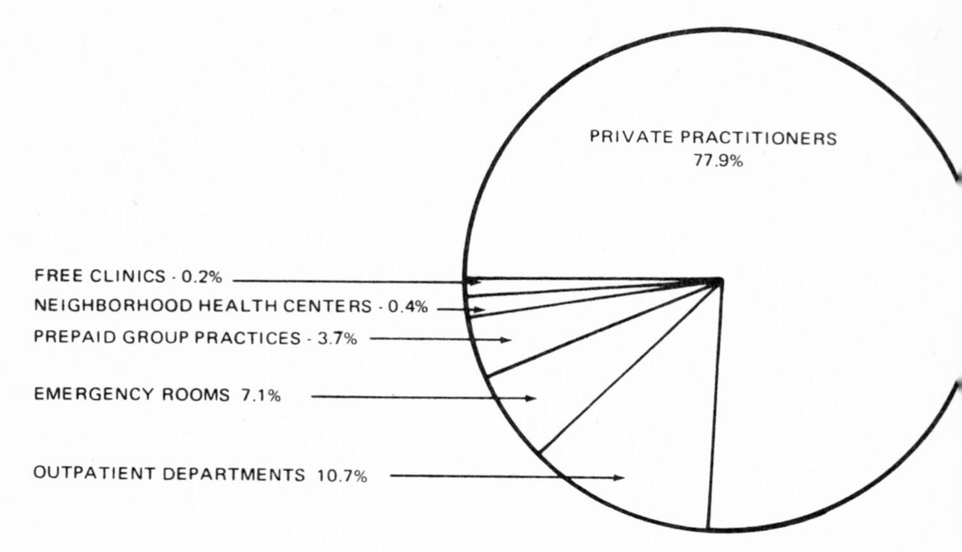

Fig. 9. Estimated percent distribution of nonfederal primary physician visits by selected organizational modes, United States, 1969. (From Parker, A. W.: The dimensions of primary care: blueprints for change. In Andreopoulos, S., editor: Primary care: where medicine fails, New York, 1974, John Wiley and Sons, p. 28.)

"caring." Finally, I should like to add *the provision of all basic health and health-related services* needed for the prevention and treatment of commonly occurring health conditions and for the utilization of these same services.

How close are we in the United States to including these functions and their underlying services in our requirements for primary health care delivery? It has been estimated that in 1969, 77.9% of all physician visits were made to private office-based practices (both solo and group), 10.7% to hospital-based outpatient departments, 7.1% to emergency rooms, 3.7% to prepaid group practices, 0.4% to comprehensive health centers, and 0.2% to free clinics (Table 7 and Fig. 9).[3] For the 7% or more of primary visits that are made to emergency rooms,* there is little opportunity for expression of these functions. There is no maintenance at the primary level, and therefore there is no guarantee of longitudinal responsibility for management and integration, little human support, and no comprehensiveness in the sense of availability of facilitative, supportive, educational, or follow-up services. Access, in this case, is only to minimal, episodic services, not the kind of first entry

*Between 1969 and 1974 visits to emergency rooms rose from 40 million to 61 million.[6]

care described by Alpert and Charney. This is, of course, the extreme situation. For those attending outpatient departments, comprehensiveness of services is improved, but longitudinal management of patient care and the integrationist function receive little attention. For the majority of visits, the approximately 80% of visits made to private office based practices, entry and continuity for medical care are often greatly improved. However, for the most part, patient care management remains confined to the clinical-technical sphere. Services beyond these are rarely provided, precluded by payment mechanisms, organizational structure, and the dearth of workers other than physicians. The limited time available for most patient-physician contacts and the paucity of other workers also combine to block the "integrationist" and supportive functions from full development.

Thus, the majority of the population of the United States does not have access to service systems ensuring the full realization of the functions of primary care as outlined previously. For patients to receive such care, shifts in medical care organization, manpower deployment, payment mechanisms, and attitudes of health providers and public policy makers must occur.

Should a health orientation be added to the present disease orientation?

Another facet of the issue of scope is whether or not primary care should be assigned a role beyond the prevention and cure of disease and injury and the alleviation of the resultant pain, disability, and dysfunction. Should it advance to the very different task of *health promotion* and *maintenance?* After the constant rhetoric about health maintenance in recent years, this may seem to be a nonsensical question, but in fact few health-directed activities are part of the present health care system. Most promotive and preventive actions are directed toward disease prevention, not toward enhancement of the coping and rallying forces of the human body and mind. If health and disease are separate phenomena and not conceptually the two ends of the same spectrum, health-oriented interventions may turn out to be quite different from disease-oriented interventions. Unfortunately, knowledge about health creation and the techniques to be applied in its achievement are still minimal. As knowledge and technology improve, however, health care systems will need to decide where they fit in. Logically, the primary care level is the one most concerned, since hospitals and medical specialists, perforce, deal with the already ill.[11] What will eventually be included in primary health care will depend, perhaps, on the type of intervention in question. If a particular intervention can be administered by an accepted health care professional, primary care will no doubt claim it. If, on the other hand, it requires group techniques or activities going beyond personal health care or is seen, like exercise or meditation, as something entirely different from other medical care services, it may fall outside of the umbrella of primary health care services.

The unit of attention appropriate to primary care

Whatever the scope of primary care, what should be its unit of attention? Should it be the individual or the family? On this dimension, three levels of practice can be distinguished.

1. *Care can be totally directed to the individual.* Health problems can be diagnosed and treated with little regard for the other aspects of life influencing health status and health outcomes—in particular the family situation, the most important environment for most people.
2. *Care can be family oriented,* that is, the individual can be treated with consideration of the family milieu and its effects on his or her health. This requires, as a minimum, a way to collect and maintain an adequate data base of family information and the ability to relate to other members of the family about the patient's care, when appropriate.
3. Finally, *care can be coordinated family care.* In this case, the whole family (or household or living group) is considered the unit of care; each member's care is coordinated with that of the others to create an optimal outcome for the unit as a whole.

Even if primary care should stay strictly medical in scope, a decision to change the focus of care from the individual to the family unit would require changes in organizational patterns. In 1973 to 1974, the National Drug and Therapeutic Index (NDTI) estimated that of the total of 1,659,513,000 visits (by diagnosis count) made to 177,318 physicians in private, office-based practices in all specialties, 938,945,000 were made to generalists,* 40% to pediatricians and internists, and 60% to general-family practitioners[7] (Table 8).

We do not have much information about how many family members are cared for by the average generalist.† However, it is obvious that practitioners who care for all ages are *potentially* in a better position than the age-related "specialoid" to institute both *family-oriented care* and *coordinated family care* in its broadest meaning, if the family or living unit includes both adults and children. Whether or not such care is given depends not only on the physician's interest and belief in its importance but also on the time available and type of assisting staff.

*Arbitrarily, for this purpose, I am defining primary care as services provided by generalists—that is, family or general practitioners and the age-bound generalists—pediatricians, and internists.

†One study in upstate New York, for example, reported that 78% of the patients seen by general practitioners were members of families where other members were cared for by the same physician.[8]

Table 8. Visits to private, office based physicians (general practitioners, pediatricians, and internists)*

Type of practitioners	July 1973 to June 1974 all diagnoses, number of visits (in millions)	Percent of all primary care visits
General-family practitioner	564.695	60
Internist	241.895	26
Pediatrician	132.355	14
Total primary care visits	938.945	100
(Total visits to all types of physicians)	(1,659.513)	

*Adapted from National Disease and Therapeutic Index: NDTI Review, Ambler, Pa., 1974, IMS America Ltd., p. 3.

For the 40% of visits made to pediatricians and internists (and this percentage is increasing as the percentage of non–age restricted generalists decreases[3]) *family oriented care,* though fully possible, is often curtailed by the previously mentioned factors. Caring for the family as a whole unit, however (again, speaking of families that include children), can exist, in my opinion, only when the internist and pediatrician work together as a dyad, having access to each other's records and sharing a common group of patients. For the internist or pediatrician in solo or in single specialty group practice, the achievement of *coordinated family care* by these criteria becomes, therefore, an impossibility. The internist-pediatrician partnership and the small multispecialty group practice in which internists and pediatricians work as de facto teams caring for a common group of families are conspicuous by their rarity. The health center, the outpatient department, and the large multispecialty group (whether prepaid or fee-for-service) are organizationally capable of forming teams but, except for the health centers, have rarely chosen to do so. In these health care settings, the scatter of families among many practitioners and the problems inherent in maintaining and using family records make coordinated family care extremely difficult and unlikely. Even when such teams have been formed, the experience of the health centers tells us of the many organizational and process difficulties to be overcome before teams, and especially dyad teams, can successfully deliver family care.[9]

If coordinated family care, accommodating all ages, were to become a key element in the definition of primary care, health care organizations would have to shift their staffing toward family practitioners or would have to develop pediatrician-internist teams working with common groups of families and able to share in usable family record systems.

The extent of responsibility of primary care

How far should the responsibility of the primary care system extend? Should it go beyond the patient/family-initiated contact? If so, an implicit or explicit contractual arrangement between patient and provider is necessary in order to set the boundaries of the relationship. This can be limited—for example, it can formalize a relationship in which the provider takes responsibility only for patients already under care, ensuring appropriate follow-up, notifying patients about needed immunizations or screening examinations, and creating the environment and facilities for education. The contract can also be set in a larger context, covering full responsibility for a defined patient group, whether it be identified by enrollment, registration, utilization, or geographic site.

Kerr White's[10] conceptualization of the way adults make use of the health care system is helpful in gaining perspective about these issues (Fig. 10). Should the health care system (and only primary care would be able to go beyond traditional responses in this regard) be responsible only for the 250 seeking the attention of a physician, or the 750 with illness or injury not seeking assistance, or the 250 still well? The well and the ill, the utilizer and nonutilizer—how far should its responsibilities reach?

If responsibility is to be extended to the group, can the service system predict expected needs in the population served? Can it, for example, predict the number of cervical cancers expected in a year from the age, race, and socioeconomic status of the women under care? Can it reach out to the individuals at risk with effective case-finding methods, provide the needed care, and monitor the outcomes? And if the answer is yes, who should manage this new type of patient care? Should the primary physician be responsible for a panel of patients, as is possible with patient panels in the United Kingdom, or should the physician follow the Kaiser model of assuming responsibility for medical care only, remaining apart from the management of care for an assigned sector?

Responsibility for *individual* care beyond the patient-initiated visit is already a reality with many physicians. In order for more physicians to practice in this manner, attitudes about the appropriate role of medical care must change and a way must be found to provide and pay for the time and staff for follow-up and educational services. Responsibility applied to a *group,* however, requires much more than this. It requires the identification of the group by an enrollment process in order for outreach, surveillance, and education to take place, and it requires shifts in patient attitudes, provider organization patterns, and

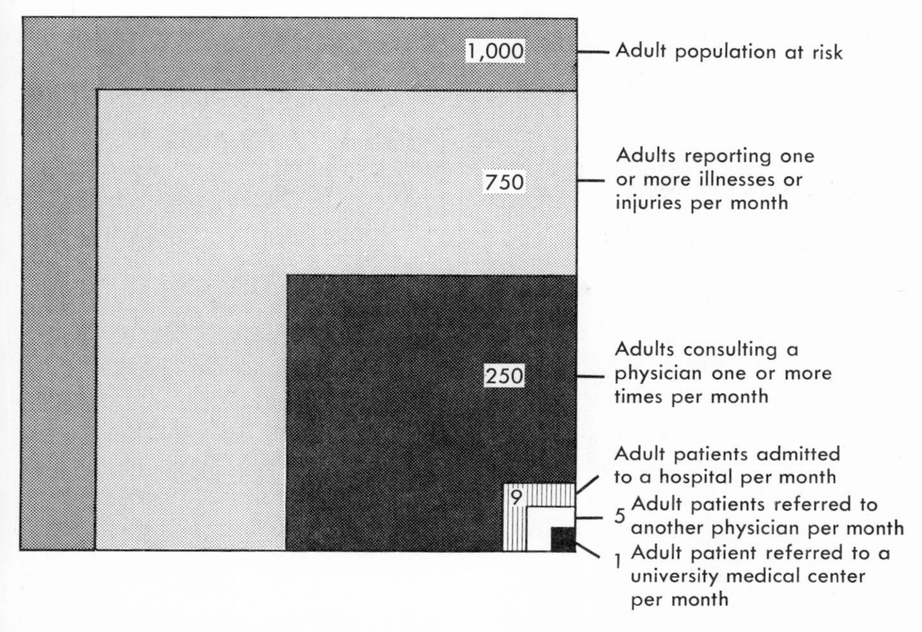

Fig. 10. Estimates of monthly prevalence of illness in the community and the role of physicians, hospitals, and university medical centers in the provision of medical care (adults 16 years of age and over). (From White, K. L., Williams, T. F., Greenberg, B.: The ecology of medical care, N. Engl. J. Med. **265:**885, 1961.)

payment mechanisms. The most drastic change would be if a shift were to occur in the physician's role—from individual provider to team leader, responsible for the entire management of care for a patient panel. For this to happen, medical education would have to move beyond its focus on the management of individual clinical care and would have to train physicians in the specific methodologies required for patient care management in groups.

Interventions other than personal health care

Should primary care move beyond the delivery of personal health care services provided to the individual or the family toward the interventive methods more commonly associated with health departments or voluntary agencies? There are many ways in which primary health systems could act to decrease the risk of disease and injury in the population served. These have been well tested. Educational programs can be developed; patient groups can be organized to overcome serious health hazards, and programs can be created for special risk groups. Health centers under the Office of Economic Opportunity (OEO) were mandated in this direction—to provide services impinging on poor housing, inadequate nutrition, or polluted water and to organize groups to take greater responsibility for their own health problems.[11–13] If primary health care organizations were to be given a similar mandate in the future, rather than remain confined to the delivery of personal care, patient groups would have to be defined by enrollment or geography, and new types of professionals would have to be added to the primary health care organization.

APPROACHES TO THE DEFINITION OF PRIMARY CARE

If the development of definitional boundaries is to precede the coherent advance of primary care planning and evaluation, we need to examine how such boundaries can be determined. Two approaches have been used in the past. The products of both in final analysis have been normative in derivation, strongly influenced by what exists and by what powerful persons and groups believe. Neither, in my opinion, has been adequate for planning and evaluation purposes. In the future, the closer we are able to move toward an empirically based definition, the closer the primary care service system will approximate actual "need."[14]

The first approach is descriptive. In its most common form, primary care is defined by a single benchmark. For example, it may be defined by referring to a past time, "Primary care is what the family physician used to do"; or by referring to what it is not, "Primary care is nonspecialist or nonhospital care"; or by describing its most common denominator, as "Primary care is basic health services." Most characteristic is the tendency to use the phrase "primary care" and assume everyone knows its meaning. Clearly this benchmark method is oversimplistic, imprecise, and inadequate for planning or evaluation.

A more elaborate description derives from defining primary care by the status quo, that is, by using the functions and qualities of an arbitrarily determined type of practitioner or organization as the definitional standard—for example, examining what a pediatrician, internist, or general practitioner actually does. This method locks primary care into the present, and if patient needs are presently unmet, as I believe them to be, this definitional process will not help to meet them.

A second approach has been through the use of the judgments of knowledgeable individuals or professional bodies. Generally, such definitions have described primary care as the sum of its essential functions and qualities, as in the definition by Alpert and Charney that I have quoted previously.[5] Two other examples of this kind follow:

> . . . primary health care is what most people use most of the time for most of their health problems. Primary care is *majority* care. It describes a range of

services adequate for meeting the great majority of daily personal health needs. This majority includes the need for preventive health maintenance and for the evaluation and management on a continuing basis of general discomfort, early complaints, symptoms, problems, and chronic intractable aspect of disease . . . primary health care describes a focus which should serve the patient as an entry point into a comprehensive health care system . . . responsible for assuring continuity for all the care the patient may subsequently need.[5]

Primary medical care . . . refers to first-contact care. It is "care" in the sense of "caring about" and "caring for"; it is the care the patient receives when he first approaches the health-services system or formally participates in the process of medical care.[16]

This second method, no matter how thoughtful, has been up to the present limited in the breadth of the opinion represented.

A CONSENSUAL DEFINITION OF PRIMARY CARE

In recent research by the Primary Health Care Study Program,* we have taken the judgmental approach a step further by surveying a large number of persons widely acknowledged to be "experts" in the fields of primary health care planning, development, administration, education, or research. In this research, 333 important statements concerning the attributes of primary care were generated by a nominal group process[17] with three panels of respondents.[14] The first panel consisted of "experts," most of whom were physicians. The second panel, representing a broad range of race, age, sex, and socioeconomic status, consisted of consumers who had been active in the planning, development, and management of health programs. The third consisted of public health nurses and social workers who had worked for at least 5 years in community health programs.

The 333 statements were reduced to ninety-two unduplicated statements, all concerned with the functions and qualities of primary care. Each statement was placed on a card, and a packet of ninety-two cards was sent to 125 "experts" who were asked to separate them into five categories ranging from "most important" to "least important."

The same priority-setting procedure was conducted with the experienced consumers, public health social workers, and nurses who had been part of the generational panel and, in addition, with a randomly selected sample of primary care practitioners (general pediatricians, general internists, and general-family practitioners) practicing in the San Francisco Bay counties of Alameda and Contra Costa.

*This was done as part of a larger study by the Primary Health Care Study Program, University of California, Berkeley, which is examining the relationship of performance in primary care to organizational structure and context. The "most important" attributes will serve as criteria on which to judge performance.

Table 9. Fifteen highest ranking statements of "expert" group by percent in categories "most important" and "second most important" (1 and 2)*

	Percent placed in categories 1 and 2
Statements concerned with functions of primary care	
1. Identifies problems that cannot be handled appropriately at the primary level and makes appropriate referrals.	98
2. Identifies problems that can be handled appropriately at the primary level, avoiding unnecessary referral.	90
3. Assumes ongoing responsibility for individual patient care and patient care management and coordination.	90
4. Provides preventive intervention for those diseases which can be prevented.	90
5. Ensures that immediate emergency care for physical disease and trauma is available for patients served.	88
6. Provides basic health services for minor/acute illnesses and for chronic health problems, whether physical or emotional.	87
7. Provides a supportive and caring relationship as an integral part of the treatment process, especially in times of emotional or physical crises.	86
8. Provides crisis intervention for mental health problems.	84
9. Coordinates primary care services with the secondary and tertiary services received by the patient.	82
10. Ensures that critical information relevant to ongoing patient care is recorded and easily available.	81
Statements concerned with quality of primary care	
11. Responds to patients as human beings, not as depersonalized numbers.	86
12. Gives care with dignity. Respects all patients including those on welfare and those with alternative lifestyles.	84
13. Provides the best possible service to those needing care regardless of any personal characteristics (e.g., race, socioeconomic position).	83
14. Focus on causes (physical, social, environmental, or psychological) as well as on symptoms when prescribing care.	81
15. Is concerned with the whole person and all his health problems in the context of the total life situation—his family, community, social setting, and past history.	80

*From Parker, A. W., Walsh, J. M., and Coon, M.: The normative approach to the definition of primary care, Milbank Quarterly Series, Fall 1976.

All the results were analyzed by the percent of respondents who placed each statement in one of the two highest categories of importance. For example, the statement ranked highest by the "experts" was placed in the highest or next highest category by 98% of these respondents; the statement ranked lowest was placed in one of these two categories by only 6%. The corresponding range of percentages for the primary care practitioners was 95% and 6%. Table 9 presents the

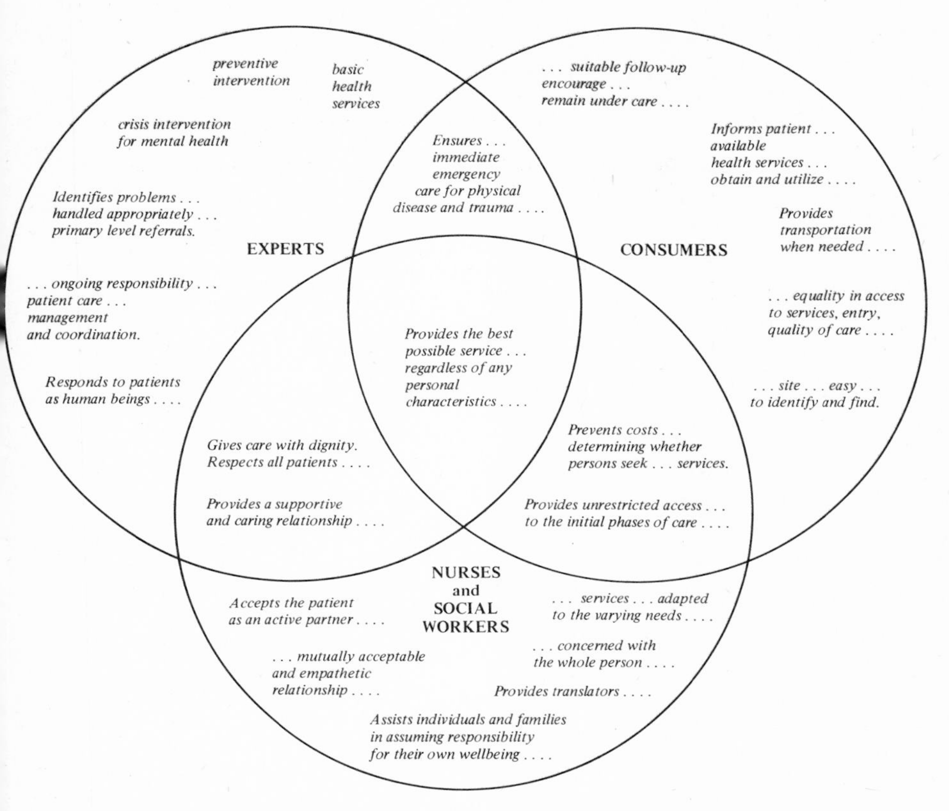

Fig. 11. Statements ranked highest by experts, consumers, and public health nurses/social workers. (From Parker, A. W., Walsh, Jane M., Koon, Merl: The normative approach to the definition of primary care, Milbank Mem. Fund Q., 1976.)

fifteen statements ranked highest by the experts, all of which were placed in one of the two high categories by more than 80%.

Together these statements by the experts create a description of primary care that is very close in content to previous definitions of primary care—not surprisingly, since they tap into the same opinion pool. This set of statements is primarily oriented toward the traditional *functions* of primary care, the *qualities* associated with how patients are treated, and *equity*. The statements ranked highest by the primary care practitioners were remarkably similar in content. In fact, thirteen of the fifteen statements in Table 9 were ranked high by 75% or more of the practitioners. On the other hand, quite different sets of statements were ranked high by the consumer panel and by the public health workers panel. Figure 11 compares the statements ranked highest by each panel. Consumers were almost solely concerned with issues of access. Like the

Table 10. Functional areas by order of importance as ranked by experts and practitioners*

Functional areas	Number of statements included	Mean percentage by experts (and range of percent)	Mean percentage by practitioners (and range of percent)
First entry (includes access to entry, triage and referral, immediate care)	5	86 (72-98)	80 (61-89)
Provision of comprehensive basic services	4	83 (78-90)	76 (66-84)
Longitudinal management of care	3	83 (78-90)	75 (69-80)
Coordination of care	3	77 (74-82)	71 (67-77)
Family oriented care	2	72 (63-80)	72 (69-76)
Responsibility for individual beyond patient-initiated contact†	1	64 (64)	42 (42)
Coordination of care other than medical	3	61 (57-64)	46 (43-50)
Incorporates medical, dental, mental health and social services into care	1	59 (59)	28 (28)
Concern with accessibility and convenience	11	57 (46-72)	41 (28-56)
Responsibility for group‡	3	50 (43-59)	15 (12-21)
Provision of facilitative services	4	41 (31-59)	14 (7-19)
Functions beyond delivery of personal health care§	5	22 (16-31)	22 (10-32)
TOTAL	45		

*In column two the percentage of experts ranking each statement high in each of these clusters has been averaged across all the statements making up each cluster. (For example, the statements referring to first entry were ranked high by an average 86% of the experts.) The figures immediately to the right of each percent indicate the range of placement of the different statements in each cluster—for example, for first entry the statements ranked by the experts ranged between 72% and 98%. The figures in column three give the corresponding averages and ranges for the primary care practitioner group. In Appendixes A and B, three of these clusters have been broken down into the original statements to give the reader an indication of the types of statements making up a functional area.

†See Appendix A for a breakdown of the cluster by statements.

‡See Appendix B for a breakdown of the cluster by statements.

§See Appendix C for a breakdown of the cluster by statements.

consumers, the public health nurses and social workers placed access statements high. They also stressed two additional areas—the quality of the affective relationship between providers and patients and the act of assisting the patients in taking responsibility for their own well-being as well as the recognition of the patients as active partners in the treatment process.

In Table 10 forty-five of the ninety-two statements have been clustered into twelve functional areas corresponding to certain of the questions posed earlier in the chapter.* By examining the relative placement of these functional clusters as well as the highest ranking statements (Table 9) we are afforded a view of expert and practitioner opinions about primary care. One can hypothesize that these views indicate the direction decisions would take if these respondents were responsible for setting program priorities or for the allocation of money and staff in primary care programs.

The most telling indicator would seem to be the acceptance by both groups of the present medical care model for the delivery of primary health care as evidenced by the emphasis placed on the medical care process itself and by the lack of emphasis placed on measures that move primary care delivery away from "traditional medical care." Both groups, however, fully support the care functions cited earlier in this chapter—first entry, assumption of continuing responsibility, the coordinative role, and the provision of basic medical care services.

Although neither shows strong support for measures that go beyond traditional responses, differences in the attitudes of the two groups are detectable—the experts being more favorably inclined than the practitioners toward innovative change. This is true when one considers concern for patient convenience and ease of access to services, integration of other health care services with primary care, making primary care the pivotal point of broad coordinative efforts, the assumption of responsibility for groups of patients, and the provision of such facilitative services as transportation, translators, and babysitters. Both are in close agreement, however, that methods other than services provided to the individual are not important functions of primary care.

• • •

In summary, if one uses the placement of statements and statement clusters by our respondents as indicators of their views about primary care and if they can be considered representative of the expert and practitioner groups as a whole, we may be permitted two inferences about future directions in primary care. First, their agreement about the essential ingredients of primary care provides a firm foundation for building a primary care system that ensures first contact care, with longitudinal and coordinative aspects of basic medical services, a goal still far from reality for many persons in the United States. Second, their lack of enthusiasm for major innovation suggests that there will be little change in overall direction, certainly no move toward systems with the characteristics of the health centers of the 1960s.

*Appendixes A, B, and C provide a breakdown of the actual statements included in three of the functional clusters.

Whether more radical change in the organization and function of primary care is desirable or not is, of course, a matter of personal opinion. If new directions are to be undertaken in the future, however, the influence of other participants in the system, the emergence of a new generation of experts and practitioners with different viewpoints, or the development of new methods of relating health care needs of populations to primary health care service systems may be required.

REFERENCES

1. Blum, Henrik L., and others: Health planning: notes on comprehensive planning for health. San Francisco, American Public Health Association, Western Regional Office, 1969.
2. Fry, J.: Profiles of disease: a study of the natural history of common diseases, London, 1966, E. & S. Livingstone, Ltd.
3. Parker, A. W.: The dimensions of primary care: blueprints for change. In primary care: Andreopoulos, S., editor: Where Medicine Fails, New York, 1974, John Wiley & Sons, Inc.
4. Parker, A. W.: The team approach to primary health care. Neighborhood Health Center Seminar Program, Monograph series no. 3, Berkeley, Calif., Jan. 1972, University of California.
5. Alpert, J. J., and Charney, E.: The education of physicians for primary care. U.S. Department of Health, Education, and Welfare, Public Health Service Health Resources Administration, Bureau of Health Services Research, DHEW Pub. No. (HRA) 74-3113, 1973.
6. Hospital statistics: 1973 data from the American Hospital Association Annual Survey, 1974, American Hospital Association.
7. National Disease and Therapeutic Index, NDTI Review, Ambler, Pa., 1974, IMS America Ltd.
8. Riley, G. J., Wille, C. R., and Haggerty, R. J.: A study of family medicine in upstate New York, J.A.M.A. **208:**2307-2314, 1969.
9. Wise, H., Beckhard, R., Rubin, I., and Kyte, A. L.: Making health teams work, Cambridge, Mass., 1974, Ballinger Publishing Co.
10. White, K. L., Williams, T. F., and Greenberg, B.: The ecology of medical care, N. Engl. J. Med. **265:**18, 1961.
11. The Comprehensive Neighborhood Health Services Program—Guidelines, Washington, D.C., 1968, Health Services Office, Community Action Program, Office of Economic Opportunity.
12. The Dr. Martin Luther King, Jr. Health Center Fourth Annual Report, New York, Jan.-Dec. 1970, Report of the Community Health Advocacy Department, pp. 123-150, 231-248.
13. The Dr. Martin Luther King, Jr. Health Center Fifth Annual Report, New York, Jan.-Dec. 1971, Department of Community Health Advocacy, pp. 195-272.
14. Parker, A. W., Walsh, J., and Coon M.: The normative approach to the definition of primary care, Milbank Quarterly Series, 1976.
15. A conceptual model of organized primary care and comprehensive community health services, Division of Health Care Services, Community Health Service, U.S. Public Health Service, Department of Health, Education and Welfare, 1970.
16. White, K. L.: Primary medical care for families—organization and evaluation, N. Engl. J. Med. **277:**847-852, 1967.
17. Delbecq, A. L., Van deVen, A. H., and Gustafson, D. H.: Group techniques for program planning: a guide to nominal group and delphi processes, Glenview, Ill., 1975, Scott, Foresman and Co.

APPENDIX A

Percent of respondents placing statements concerned with responsibility for the group in categories 1 and 2

Statements	*Experts (percent)*	*Primary care practitioners (percent)*
Assumes responsibility for a defined population (geographic or enrolled). Such responsibility extends to well and ill, utilizers and nonutilizers."	59	12
Is concerned with the consumer before he enters the system—reaching out to assist those not receiving services."	47	12
Carries out surveillance on the health states, health needs, and health priorities of the population served."	43	21
Average of means	49.6	15

APPENDIX B

Percent of respondents placing statements concerned with functions beyond the delivery of personal health care in categories 1 and 2

Statements	*Mean percentage of experts*	*Mean percentage of primary care practitioners*
"Develops services for special needs of the groups served—for example, adolescent care, alcoholism services."	31	26
"Takes responsibility in the community for the mobilization of needed and unavailable personal health care services."	24	24
"Provides leadership in the community for health-related issues: makes recommendations to groups having influence over environmental, economic and political factors that may contribute to poor physical or mental health."	21	32
"Intervenes when necessary to improve the community's health in ways other than delivery of personal health care (for example, housing, water, waste disposal)."	18	10
"Provides educational services for the community in order to create an awareness of health, health needs and health services."	16	17
Average of means	22	21.8

APPENDIX C

Percent of respondents placing statements concerned with responsibility beyond patient-initiated contact in categories 1 and 2

Statements	*Experts (percent)*	*Primary care practitioners (percent)*
"Maintains continuous 'contact' (formal or informal) for health care with patient and/or family, independent of the presence or absence of disease."	64	42
Average of means	64	42

7

Ṫhe hospital—its role and limitation n the health care system

OHN D. THOMPSON

Professor Thompson identifies four major social groups to which the ommunity hospital must respond: (1) providers of medical care, (2) community lients of the hospital, (3) third-party payers, and (4) governmental rganizations. Each of these groups has different and often conflicting ideas oncerning the best means of organizing and even the proper goals of the ommunity hospital. The problems of the allocation of hospital costs, the ıability to appraise the quality of medical care, and the need to provide ersonalized but efficient medical services are discussed within this social ·amework. The author offers a solution to these problems based on viewing he hospital's role in the context of a larger health care system—a system ased on progressive patient care. This patient care concept must extend utside the hospital's walls and requires a change in the hospital's traditional oncern toward its four major constituencies. It must be actively involved ı the organization of the total medical care spectrum of a comprehensive ealth care system.

The community hospital today is responding in different ways and vith varying success to the pressures of four identifiable social groups vithin the pluralistic society it serves. The first such group consists f the providers of medical care, primarily the physicians, who compose he medical staff of the hospital but who, with a few exceptions, carry ıo responsibility for its management. The community clients of the ıospital form the second group. Although not as formally organized as he first group, they apply direct pressure on the hospital by their lemand for services. More often than not, they make their wishes ːnown indirectly through the medical staff or through the board of rustees of the hospital. Specific minority groups have begun to express heir desires for the services of the hospital as well. Although a subset f the community clients, these groups are requesting that, in addition o patient care services, the added dimensions of employee training ınd educational and economic opportunities be made more available by hospitals to specific sections of the community. The third group includes private, governmental, and quasi-public organizations, which are the third-party payers for hospital services. Finally, there are the federal and state governments and their surrogates that are attempting to exert the pressures of society as a whole on the hospital.

The requests of each of these groups may lack internal consistency. These four groups also have different views of the role of the hospital and consequently often apply pressures in opposing directions. One group's concerns may conflict with those of another. The providers and clients of the hospital may, for example, be interested in expanded medical services, whereas some of the governmental agencies and third-party payers are more concerned about the escalation of hospital costs and, therefore, may wish to constrain or control these same services.

Various kinds of hospitals may be subject to different combinations of these pressures. Teaching hospitals that view their service mission as the training of physicians may be more responsive to the wants of a special kind of provider, the physician member of the medical school faculty, and consequently may be less responsive to the desires of community factions unless they are needed for teaching and research programs. Urban hospitals faced with the emigration of their original clients are beginning to redefine their role in relation to the needs of the core city and often have to do so with a depleted or disinterested medical staff.

When coupled with the absence of a national health policy, resulting in the lack of an overall medical care delivery system and a prescribed role of the hospital within that system, these varying pressures are major factors contributing to the two primary problems facing the American hospital today—rising costs and depersonalization of services.

PROVIDER INTERESTS

The provider groups, which have until this time initiated most hospital planning and program development, have been dominated by the physicians as the members of the medical staff who are primarily concerned with the "scientific excellence" of the hospital and the translation of recent medical advances into services for the treatment of their patients. Never before have medical staff members had such dramatic opportunities to save or prolong life. Physicians consider themselves the primary developers and users of innovative services and are quite likely to wish them available regardless of their cost or the probability of their use over a period of time. Examples of these new services are the various kinds of "special care" units that have resulted in decreases in the mortality from selected diseases[1] and the diseases of early infancy.[2] In the latter case there is a serious question of whether every hospital "needs" to have such a unit. Both kinds of units are characterized by having random input and rather unpredictable peak demands. As a consequence, they are often occupied by very few patients, are expensive to construct and staff, and, even more importantly, represent new services added to existing services, which themselves may not be needed.[3] Such units are usually operated under the supervision of highly paid professional and technical personnel. Indeed, the number of hospital-based full-time physicians, including radiologists, pathologists, anesthesiologists, and cardiologists, is increasing as these or other programs are developed. This development may well increase the pressure exerted on the hospital by a more involved medical staff concerning the definition of the hospital's role and the allocation of its resources.

COMMUNITY CLIENT INTERESTS

Unfortunately, the concerns of the community clients of the hospitals are usually only indirectly applied to the institution, although in many communities patients "vote with their feet," by coming to the hospital's emergency room in ever-increasing numbers.[4] This trend is transforming this former "accident service" to a primary general medical care facility. The exact reasons for the increase in utilization of the emergency service are not clear. Many articles point out that such factors as the unavailability of a private physician, the lack of a family physician, or actual referrals by private physicians to this source of care are contributing to this pattern of use.

The effects of the Medicare and Medicaid programs are just now becoming evident on those parts of the hospital where patients also have direct access to services, such as the outpatient department. What seems to be happening is that Medicare patients apparently are finding the offices of private physicians open to them and are, therefore, underrepresented in the clinic population. Medicaid patients, on the other hand, still comprise a very high percentage of the hospital's outpatient clientele. In urban centers where these patients are found in the greatest number, the clients often view the hospital as "their doctor." It is rather difficult for any patient to make use of the services of a hospital other than the emergency service and the outpatient department without a physician's intervention.[5] Thus community pressures on the inpatient services are then translated by the medical staff to the hospital in the name of the patient.

Perhaps just as important are the informal social demands of selected segments of the community on "their" hospitals.[6] Demands for patient ombudsmen in hospital emergency rooms and outpatient departments are fairly common now on the part of blacks and Spanish-American groups in larger cities. The makeup of the boards of trustees is being questioned and minority representation is being requested. Some black organizations are considering total takeover at the policy level of hospitals within their communities or are agitating for some way of negotiating community demands outside formal administrative channels.[7] Above all, they want hospitals to be responsive to their concerns as they perceive them. This must be recognized as a change in the demand for equal treatment. Programs specifically responding to minority needs, such as concerning lead poisoning screening, are now being requested.

The hospital has historically provided an educational opportunity resulting in upward mobility in both a social and an economic sense. Formal educational programs such as nursing schools, radiology and laboratory technician programs, as well as various in-service training programs for less defined technical groups such as medical stenographers and nurses' aides have in the past offered the opportunity for minority groups to move into various technical, semiprofessional, and professional strata. This educational effort is expensive if it is more than an apprentice program. There are very real questions as to whether the patient should be charged for these costs[8] or whether the community should assume the financial responsibility for these educational programs as it has for other programs within the formal school and college systems. But whoever provides them, the minority groups want in.

INTERESTS OF THIRD-PARTY PAYERS

The third-party payers are strangely powerless in their interaction with hospitals. True, they control vast amounts of the monies used to pay for hospital services under contracts usually negotiated each year, and it is also evident that in many states they are under some pressure from their respective insurance commissioners to de-escalate hospital costs every time they request a new increase in their own premiums. What is not so obvious is that these insurance schemes are merely payers for care; they are not buyers of care. They can not direct their enrollees to the cheapest hospital—in fact, they can exert very little pressure on their subscribers to influence any choice for care. There are also the factors of internal competition between the various components of these payers, which often center around such issues as community versus experience rating and the provision of services versus cash benefits, as well as the use of contract limitations such as deductibles, coinsurance, and selected riders as features of their policies. The relative influence of these payer agencies does not even increase when the federal and state governments assume the role of payers under Medicare and Medicaid.

Occasionally, there are exceptions to this general state of powerlessness on the part of third-party payers. By indirectly influencing the providers through the support of voluntary planning efforts, these agencies provide the impetus for shared services between hospitals as well as the prevention of unnecessary duplication of services among them. A few of these third-party payers began to put financial teeth into the recommendations of these voluntary planning agencies by creating different payment rates to those hospitals that participated in such voluntary regional planning and accreditation programs. One Blue Cross plan actually implemented a voluntary concurrent utilization review program involving most of its hospitals.[9] But, for the most part, such attempts are short-lived, and their effect on cost and utilization of services is minimal.

SOCIETAL REQUIREMENTS

In various ways society is refashioning the hospital as an instrument of its own policy. Through the formal channels of governmental regulations, recent legislation of federal and state governments has attempted both to broaden the role of the hospital and to reshape its social responsibility. Unfortunately, it is difficult to determine just how these governmental bodies are going to bring about this broadening and reshaping.

As confused and inconsistent as are the positions of the first three constituencies concerning the role of the hospital within a restructured health services delivery system, they are models of shining clarity when compared with the policies of the governmental bodies. If ever the federal government spoke with a forked tongue, it was in the two major pieces of legislation that were to prepare the way for change—the Heart, Stroke, and Cancer and the Comprehensive Health Planning Acts. To state, as does the latter (Public Law 89-749), that a citizen's right to health or that the organization of regional health services must be constrained by the issue of whether or not it interferes "with existing patterns of private practice of medicine, dentistry and related healing arts" is to give with one hand and deny with the other. A series of hastily conceived programs were mounted within 4 or 5 years—all attempting mainly to influence the institutional medical care delivery system, though some efforts were directed toward private office practice. Most of these programs, such as the Regional Medical Program Experimental Health Delivery Systems, and Experimental Medical Care Review Organizations, are dead or dying, killed as much by internecine warfare among the agencies as by their lack of success in influencing the care system.

Hospitals were particularly affected by the Medicare legislation. If ever there was a gap between intent and results, it was in this most complex and optimistic program. Medicare and Medicaid were intended to be more than the designation of fiscal relationships between hospitals and federal and state governments. Unfortunately, these attempts to add some measure of public accountability and control over hospitals and other kinds of medical care institutions ended in costly failures and in no way retarded the inflationary influence of the "reasonable cost" reimbursement base. The Medicare and Medicaid utilization review requirement was never effectively implemented and soon required replacement by the legislatively mandated professional service review organizations (PSROs). Hospitals under the extended care transfer agreements were notified that close formal relationships between various components of the institutional medical care delivery system must be implemented. This too often resulted in institutional links about as strong as the paper the agreements were written on. More specifically, hospitals were affected by the hospital-based specialist payment policy in Medicare. Instead of building toward a comprehensive health care system, this arbitrary splitting of the radiology charge, for example, into a professional component covered under Part B and a hospital service charge under Part A has been characterized as "the dominant disturbing factor in implementation of the program and a disruptive influence throughout the health care field."[10]

The influence of all these federal efforts can best be crystallized in the section entitled Findings and Purpose of the National Health Planning and Resources Development Act, Public Act 93-641, which states, "The massive infusion of federal funds into the existing health care system has contributed to inflationary increases in the cost of health care and failed to produce an adequate supply and distribution of health resources and consequently has not made possible equal access for everyone to such resources."

State governments, which for the most part were passive recipients of these federal monies and programs, became alarmed at their inflationary effect on hospital costs. Many seized on the public utility model to control these costs, and a few, as will be elaborated, began to fashion their own public policies on health,[11] most of which resulted in another set of pressures on the hospitals.

THE HOSPITAL'S RESPONSE

The governing body of a hospital (the board of trustees in a voluntary nonprofit hospital) must allocate the institution's finite resources of money, manpower, and materials in response to these various pressures while under the constraint of preserving the viability of the institution. Since an allocation process based on responses to various inconsistent pressures is essentially political rather than rational and defensive rather than positive, the main concern of the governing bodies is often directed toward careful control, by maintaining a delicate balance of the various pressure groups. Changes in such a situation are difficult to institute, particularly when the hospital's internal organization is under stress.[12]

Both professional and technical hospital employees have begun demanding, often through unionization, that their wages and perquisites be raised to the level of those employed in industry and comparable service organizations outside the medical orbit. Since hospitals are a "labor-laden" industry (about 70% of hospital expenses are labor costs), these pressures also contribute to the escalation of the cost of the hospitals' "units of service," that is, the costs per patient day.

The community hospital lacks both the internal resources and the supportive external constituency to enable it to address the two particular concerns that are most threatening to its survival—increased costs and the decisions pertaining to the types and sizes of institutions that can be most responsive to the needs of patients and specific communities. The real questions, then, are who can meet these challenges if the hospitals no longer can, and what configuration of institutions and programs will deliver the medical care of the future? Before exploring the answers to these two questions, it is necessary to explore further the cost and size-accessibility problems.

HOSPITAL COSTS

The national expenses per patient day and per patient stay in hospitals are shown in Table 11.

These data clearly show both the rise of two service unit costs over a 20 year period (beginning in 1954) and the change in these expenses around the time of the implementation of Medicare (July 1, 1966). During the first decade, costs per day increased 78.8% and costs per stay by a slightly lower rate of 76.5%. Over the next 10 years, during which Medicare went into operation, costs per day increased by 175.8% and costs per stay by 179.4%. Another way of stating the findings is that it took 11 years for the per diem costs to double, 4 years for them to triple, 2 more years to quadruple, and 2 years later they were five times the

Table 11. Absolute value of total expenses per patient day and per patient stay in nonfederal short-term general and other special hospitals, United States, 1954-1973*

Year	Cost per patient day	Relative increase (1954 base)	Relative increase (1964 base)	Cost per patient stay	Relative increase (1954 base)	Relative increase (1964 base)
1954	21.76	100.0		169.76	100.0	
1955	23.12	106.3		179.77	105.8	
1956	24.15	111.0		186.11	109.6	
1957	26.02	119.6		198.13	116.7	
1958	28.27	129.9		214.67	126.5	
1959	30.19	138.7		235.66	138.8	
1960	32.23	148.1		244.53	144.0	
1961	34.98	160.8		267.37	157.4	
1962	36.83	169.3		279.91	164.9	
1963	38.91	178.8		299.61	176.5	
1964	41.58	191.1	100.0	320.17	188.6	100.0
1965	44.98	206.7	108.1	346.94	204.4	108.4
1966	48.15	221.3	115.8	380.39	224.1	118.8
1967	54.08	248.5	130.1	448.64	264.3	140.1
1968	61.38	282.1	147.6	515.59	303.7	161.0
1969	70.03	321.8	168.4	581.25	342.4	181.5
1970	81.01	372.3	194.8	668.42	393.7	208.8
1971	92.31	424.2	220.0	738.48	435.0	230.7
1972	105.21	483.5	253.0	831.16	489.6	259.6
1973	114.69	527.1	275.8	894.58	527.0	279.4

*Data reported with permission from Hospitals Journal of the American Hospital Association, Aug. guide issues: Hospital Statistics 1954-1973.

Table 12. Private consumer expenditures for health and medical care, United States, selected years 1969, 1970, and 1971 (in millions)*

Type of expenditure	1969			1970			1971			Percent increase per capita 1969-1971
	Total	Percent	Per capita	Total	Percent	Per capita	Total	Percent	Per capita	
Hospital care	$10,378	30.5	$50.56	$12,964	33.4	$62.51	$14,472	34.1	$69.08	37
Physicians' services	8,877	26.1	43.25	9,690	24.9	46.42	10,688	25.2	51.02	18
Dentists' services	3,589	10.5	14.48	4,041	10.4	19.41	4,400	10.3	21.00	45
Drugs and appliances	7,819	23.0	38.09	8,319	21.4	40.11	8,779	20.7	41.90	10
Nursing home care	742	2.2	3.61	1,186	3.1	5.72	1,314	3.1	6.27	74
Other expenditures	2,652	7.7	12.92	2,650	6.8	12.78	2,824	6.6	13.48	4
TOTAL†	$34,057		$165.92	$38,850		$185.65	$42,477		$202.75	22.2

*Adapted from Rice, Dorothy P., and Cooper, Barbara S.: National Health Expenditures, 1929-71, Social Security Bulletin, Jan. 1972.
†May not total because of rounding.

1954 figure. Costs per stay followed somewhat the same pattern during the first 11 years, but they tripled only 3 years after doubling and quadrupled 3 years later. The increase in length of stay from 7.9 days in 1966 to 8.3 in 1967 and 8.4 in 1968, again around the time of Medicare, meant that two inflationary pressures—cost per day and the number of days within an average stay—were both increasing at the same time.

In Table 12 the relative increases of expenditures for hospital care are shown and compared with total medical care expenditures. The cost trends illustrated in these two tables are dramatic evidence of a significant rise in real expenses per unit of hospital service whether measured by expenses per day, expenses per average length of stay, or relative expenditures for this component of total medical care expenditures. They fail, however, to answer the question of how much of this cost rise results from expansion of scientific medical care, increased salaries for employees, new personnel, "inefficient" internal operation, or finally, the faults within the total institutional care system, which dictates inefficient and ineffective use of hospital beds.

Specific aspects of increasing costs

With the focus on the expense of providing a day of inpatient hospital care, the experience of one state with a sophisticated accounting cost system might offer some insights and in this way permit hospitals to focus their attention on the real issues.

The trends, from 1960 to 1973, of Connecticut's thirty-five short-term hospitals (Table 13) seem to indicate that the Medicare bulge is over; costs have been increasing at a slower rate for the nonmaternity patient day in 1972 to 1973. Whether these costs, as well as those for maternity and newborn days, would have dropped so dramatically without the actions of the Cost of Living Council is unsubstantiated.

Matching these cost figures with utilization data adds another dimension to the problem of rising hospital costs. Not only has the cost of the service unit (per nonmaternity patient day) increased by 248.5% in the 13 years under study, but also the units of service used have increased by 38% over that same period (Table 14). Since the population served increased by only 22.5% over the same number of years, this means that each 1,000 citizens of the state used 104 more hospital days per year in 1973 than in 1960. Here the effect of Medicare is less obvious; although there was a 5.2% increase in 1967 over 1966, there was a similar increase in 1963 over 1962 without Medicare.

Maternity days, on the other hand, revealed a decrease both in days of care given and in days per unit of population used—a decrease of 58 days per 1,000 of the population per year. Maternity beds in the state

Table 13. Average cost per nonmaternity, maternity, and newborn patient days, Connecticut hospitals, 1960-1973*

Year	Average cost per nonmaternity patient day	Relative increase (1960 base)	Percent yearly increase	Average cost per maternity patient day	Relative increase (1960 base)	Percent yearly increase	Average cost per newborn patient day	Relative increase (1960 base)	Percent yearly increase
1960	$ 34.93†	100.0	0.0	$ 36.51‡	100.0	0.0	$12.60	100.0	0.0
1961	35.99	104.5	4.5	37.76	103.4	3.4	13.33	105.8	5.8
1962	38.40	111.5	6.7	42.43	116.2	12.4	14.99	118.9	12.5
1963	40.45	117.5	5.3	45.45	124.5	7.1	16.16	128.3	7.8
1964	43.13	125.3	6.6	48.44	132.7	6.6	17.21	136.6	6.5
1965	46.33	134.5	7.4	52.30	143.2	8.0	18.61	147.6	8.1
1966	50.66	147.1	9.4	57.84§	158.4	10.6	21.28	168.8	14.4
1967	57.06	165.7	12.6	67.10	183.8	16.0	25.03	198.6	17.6
1968	65.41	190.0	14.7	77.94	213.5	16.2	28.90	229.3	15.5
1969	74.61	216.7	14.1	86.33	236.4	10.8	32.65	259.0	13.0
1970	85.38	248.0	14.5	97.97	268.3	13.5	37.56	298.0	15.0
1971	98.43	285.9	15.3	113.80	311.7	16.2	44.04	347.5	17.3
1972	109.98	314.9	11.7	130.28	356.8	14.5	54.08	429.2	22.8
1973	121.74	348.5	10.7	139.71	382.7	7.2	55.93	443.9	3.4

*From Connecticut Hospital Association annual cost analyses, New Haven, Conn., 1960-1973, Connecticut Hospital Association.
†Thirty-five Hospitals.
‡Thirty-four Hospitals.
§Thirty-three Hospitals.

Table 14. Percent increase or decrease in population, nonmaternity and maternity beds, and nonmaternity and maternity patient days, Connecticut, 1960-1973*

		Nonmaternity						Maternity					
Year	Population	Beds	Relative increase (60 base)	Percent year increase	Patient days	Relative increase (60 base)	Percent year increase	Beds	Relative increase (60 base)	Percent year increase	Patient days	Relative increase (60 base)	Percent year increase
1960	2,535,234	6,806	100.0	0.0	2,084,822	100.0	0.0	1,154	100.0	0.0	265,145	100.0	0.0
1961		6,997	102.8	2.8	2,122,258	101.7	1.7	1,150	99.7	−0.3	266,218	100.4	0.4
1962		7,140	104.9	2.0	2,188,967	104.9	3.1	1,161	100.6	1.0	250,183	94.3	(6.0)
1963		7,404	108.8	3.7	2,300,793	110.3	5.1	1,157	100.3	−0.3	252,926	95.3	1.0
1964		7,616	111.9	2.9	2,386,035	114.4	3.7	1,156	100.2	−0.1	250,268	94.3	−1.0
1965		7,871	115.7	3.4	2,443,621	117.2	2.4	1,125	97.5	−2.7	240,374	90.6	−3.9
1966		7,973	117.2	1.3	2,507,331	120.2	2.6	1,110	96.2	−1.3	227,971	85.9	−5.2
1967		8,324	122.3	4.4	2,637,401	126.5	5.2	1,082	93.8	−2.5	212,255	80.0	−6.9
1968		8,479	124.6	1.9	2,710,226	129.9	2.8	1,034	89.6	−4.4	200,874	75.7	−5.4
1969		8,915	131.0	5.1	2,775,330	133.1	2.4	952	82.5	−7.9	199,670	75.3	−0.6
1970	3,031,709	9,081	133.4	1.9	2,819,970	135.2	1.6	915	79.3	−3.9	198,605	74.9	−0.5
1971		9,197	135.1	1.3	2,846,594	136.5	0.9	928	80.4	1.4	181,612	68.4	−8.6
1972	3,078,400	9,498	139.6	3.3	2,865,596	137.5	0.6	903	78.3	−2.7	157,006	59.2	−8.6
1973		9,564	140.5	0.6	2,877,883	138.0	0.4	818	70.9	−9.4	144,743	54.6	−7.8

*From The Connecticut Hospital Association annual cost analyses, New Haven, Conn., 1960-1973, Connecticut Hospital Association.

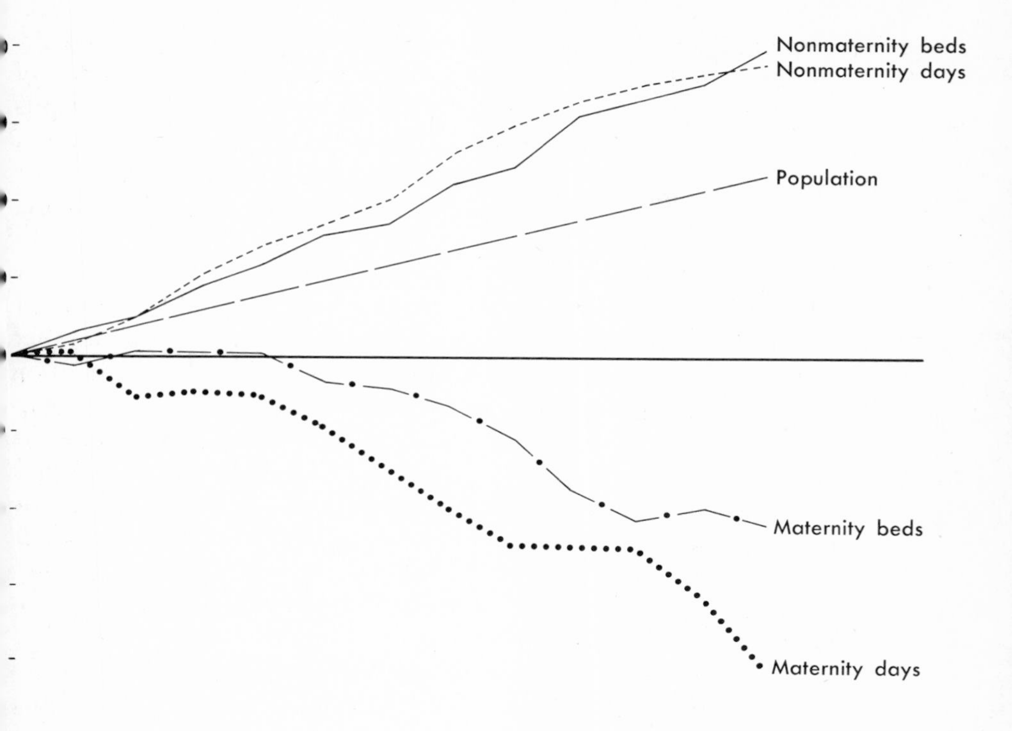

Fig. 12. Percent increase or decrease in population: nonmaternity beds and nonmaternity patient days, maternity beds and maternity patient days in Connecticut, 1960-1972. (From Connecticut Hospital Association Reports, New Haven, Conn.) 1960-1973.

did not adjust to this decreased demand (see Fig. 12). The patterns of costs for these maternity and newborn days exhibit quite a bit of difference when compared to the nonmaternity costs. A sizable portion of the increased cost was caused by maintenance of a separate staff to handle these beds, according to state law, even though occupancy of the beds was lower. Both facilities and staff also had to be large enough to respond to sudden peaks in the random independent input.[3] This increased cost problem is obviously an *internal* one, primarily the result of the way the hospital assigns its resources. Economies of scale are not being realized. The solution is obviously one of merging underutilized services into regional units rather than multiple small units. Such a scheme has been recommended.[13]

The nonmaternity utilization data, on the other hand, illustrate the other facet of the cost problem—the climbing number of hospital days unrelated to the size of the population served. Fig. 12 indicates that satisfied demand (nonmaternity hospital days) is increasing at a faster rate than the population and seems to be related more to the number of beds available than to the population served or to payment programs such as Medicare and Medicaid. This experience seems to be a reaffirmation of "Roemer's law,"[14] which purports that the greatest indication for treatment in the hospital is the existence of an available hospital bed.

It is obvious, when the rate of increase in nonmaternity days is compared to the population growth, that the cost of hospitalization for a given population would still rise as a result of the increasing number of hospital days used by that population. This increase in utilization would have occurred even if costs per hospital day had remained constant. This increased demand is generated *outside* the hospital, and it is probably true that the hospital is used because often there is no other way for the patient to receive certain kinds of medical care. Hospitals have no other choice, then, but to begin to control the demand for their inpatient days by promoting the development of medical care delivery systems inside and outside their walls, so that their own inpatient facilities will be used more effectively.

There are two ways to approach a solution to this problem of increasing hospital costs: either attempt to lower the cost of the product or plan to buy fewer units of the product. Although the possible effects of the former approach should not be discounted, now is the time to decrease inpatient hospital days by examining the total system of delivering medical care.

THE PROBLEM OF SIZE

Another trend, one affecting the organization of hospital services, is interhospital mergers, which might offer both economic and quality advantages. This pattern reflects similar trends in nonmedical service and manufacturing industries. There are some indications that merging these hospital services into larger institutions might obviate the uneconomical duplication of hospital services characteristic of many communities.[15]

The new technology also has contributed to this trend toward mergers, since rapid processing of such information as laboratory test results makes the location of each type of laboratory in every hospital less critical. Another contributor to this trend is the disconcerting, but unverified, feeling that there are real differences in the quality of care delivered in varying size institutions—that larger hospitals,[15] through either more stringent professional standards or the greater availability of sophisticated support services, are able to do a better job in patient care than are smaller institutions with more limited resources. Discussion of shared services of various kinds, both in logistic support and in professional skills, reflects this desire for increasingly larger institutions with a centralized administrative bureaucracy.

It may be that there are some payoffs in large-scale institutions. However, it also may be that the most economical size might lead to further impersonalization of patient care.[5] Hannah Arendt wrote in another context:

> The disintegration process, which has become so manifest in recent years, the decay of many public services, of schools and police, of mail delivery and transportation, the death rate on the highways and the traffic problems in the cities—concern everything designed to serve mass society. Bigness is afflicted with vulnerability, and while no one can say with assurance where and when the breaking point has been reached, we can observe, almost to the point of measuring it, how strength and resiliency are insidiously destroyed, leaking as it were drop by drop from our institutions.*

Hospitals are not free from this danger; in fact, they are probably more vulnerable because of their intensely personal services, involving decisions of multiple professional, administrative, and service personnel. Nor is the problem solely one of the administrative span of control; equally important is the community's span of concern.

These classic problems of centralization and decentralization are being considered at a time when there is no doubt that monitoring and controlling the quality of medical care in the hospitals of this country is becoming one of the primary concerns of all groups of society, and this concern is reflected in the PSRO legislation.[17]

What little quality control and monitoring are now taking place in the medical care field are occurring mainly within the walls of the hospitals. Comparative performance data between hospitals, outside of those subscribing to the Professional Activity Service of Ann Arbor, Michigan, are, however, simply not available. Even these data, unless they are linked to some measurement of institutional resource use, cannot provide the quality-cost link necessary for effectiveness comparisons.

THE HOSPITAL'S ROLE IN AN INSTITUTIONAL MEDICAL CARE SYSTEM

How can hospitals deal with the following problems: (1) the increasing costs of hospital services, (2) the inability to appraise satisfactorily the quality of patient care, and (3) the need to provide medical care institutions of the types and sizes designed to meet patient and community needs? The hospital cannot solve these problems alone. They can be

*Arendt, H.: Reflections on violence, New York Review of Books, Feb. 27, 1969, p. 24.

attacked only through a total systems approach, involving all components of the institutional medical care system. Such a system must first be considered conceptually as being regional, rational, responsible, and responsive, and it should then be legally instituted as a *social utility system.*

The words "social utility" have been used rather than the term "public utility" in order to reflect the unique social role of this system. In a comprehensive review of the problem of regulating one component of this sytem—the hospital—Anne Somers points out that "hospitals do share several characteristics with industries that have been declared public utilities," including some aspects of monopolies, the provision of a basic needs, the lack of the ability of the consumer to judge the quality of the services, and the unreliability of competition to automatically provide some degree of public protection.[18] To these characteristics Klarman adds the "widespread agreement that the number of hospital beds must be limited" by somebody and the relatively high capital investment required to provide hospital beds.[19] Both authorities, however, state that the usual public utility model should not be applied to hospitals.

Rather than having as its primary concern financial control and public safety, which characterize the public utility model, the social utility concept must push the development of new services and new systems for the delivery of those services. The term "social utility" implies a more active participation in the management of the system than exists in the public utility model, which, in essence, has a more passive role, responding to and approving programs submitted to it by the electric, water, and transportation services. This means that the social utility must then have surveillance over the planning efforts in the state.

One of the most important factors in applying a public utility model in the medical arena is the fact that unlike gallons of water or kilowatt hours of electricity, medical care is not delivered in standardized units of services, all uniform and measurable, the quality of which is easily assessable.[20] The exactitude with which service costs can be controlled is not, then, the central charge of the social utility's charter.

Regionalization is basic to any public utility model, whether over power sources, water, or transportation. This characteristic would apply also to the social utility that is building on existing, and for the most part ineffectual, regionalization legislation.

The rationale on which the social utility is structured should be the needs of the patients. The needs of the patients are conceived as being multiple, varying in complexity, and requiring different levels of service at different times. This service must be rendered effectively and efficiently.

Progressive patient care

One such scheme based on the principles just mentioned is the concept of progressive patient care. If there is one phrase that could be used to describe the rationale of the future design of institutional medical care systems, their planning, design, operation, and management, it would be "progressive patient care writ large."

Following are the principles basic to the concept of progressive patient care: (1) the patient will be admitted to the appropriate facility; (2) the patient will be transferred to other types of facilities as required; and (3) each facility or "care zone" will be designed, equipped, and staffed for patients with similar needs.

As it was originally conceived, the system called for three zones of care to be available within the hospital walls: intensive care for the very ill, intermediate care (closely resembling the usual inpatient unit), and self-care for the ambulatory patient in the beginning or end of a hospital stay. Some time later three additional elements were added: a long-term care zone, an organized home care department, and an outpatient department—all still operating in, or emanating from, the hospital.[21]

The phrase "writ large" means the further expansion of the progressive patient care concept in two ways: through an increase in the number of "care elements" to be considered, and, even more importantly, through a change from thinking in terms of a progressive patient care *hospital* to thinking in terms of a comprehensive progressive patient care *system* of hospitals and other kinds of medical care institutions and programs.

In actuality, very few hospitals can hope to achieve the goal of comprehensive medical care solely within the walls of the single institution. The problem areas are at both ends of the care spectrum, that is, in primary patient care (the physician's office type of ambulatory patient care) and in long-term care.

It is extremely difficult to offer high-quality primary care in a hospital setting such as the outpatient department. The hospital outpatient department is, on the other hand, eminently suitable as an ambulatory referral center for complicated diagnostic treatment procedures or consultations by superspecialists who require extensive equipment or a large patient base for effective practice. This arrangement maximizes the use of such expensive ancillary services as x-rays, radiotherapy, and laboratories, since the use of the outpatient department is not dictated by the number of beds filled at a given time. Formal cooperative ar-

Services:		Options: I	II	III	IV	V	VI
Ambulatory care	Primary care	×					×
	Secondary specialist care	×	×				
	Tertiary specialist care	×	×	×			
	Emergency care	×	±	±			×
Support services	Routine ancillary services	×	±				
	Special ancillary services	×	×	×	×		
	Inpatient care	×	×	×	×	×	×
Continuing care	Rehabilitation	±	±	±		±	
	Long-term care	±	±			±	
	Home care	±	±			±	

Fig. 13. Hospital-health maintenance organization relationship options.

rangements for these services with primary care organizations would make it unnecessary for health centers, group practice clinics, or groups of private physicians to duplicate these expensive facilities or add these superspecialists to their own staffs.

The hospital, indeed, is faced with a variety of options in its relationship to primary care ranging from ownership and operation of a primary care center through a series of contracts covering secondary and tertiary care or the simple provision of inpatient care only. Fig. 13 illustrates these options and the resources required for the hospital to implement them.[22]

However, these relationships with the primary (noninstitutional) medical care system are critical to the problems of cost and quality outlined previously. Many studies have identified the effect of the organization of the primary medical care system on the requirements for hospital care.[23] In effect, the private practice of medicine in the community controls the inputs to the institutional system, consequently affecting the very basis of its economic and service pattern. From the experience of prepaid group practices—from the oldest to the most recent—one can anticipate at least a 30% decrease in hospital days used per 1,000 of the population per year. It is doubtful that the cost per patient day can be reduced by such an amount.

The long-term care zone within the progressive patient care scheme must soon expand into hospital-related extended care, that is, nursing home care[24] and social care. The only new kind of continuing care facility, known as a social care institution, is a foster home with nursing supervision. Patients who are, for the most part, ambulatory, who are fragile rather than ill, and who require some kind of treatment or medical or dietary maintenance can be cared for in these institutions at considerably less cost than in nursing homes.

It is easy to see, then, why the emphasis of progressive patient care has switched from a single progressive patient care hospital to a progressive care system of institutions. What is now required is to strengthen the arrangements and monitor the boundaries between these different kinds of institutions and programs so that the patients will receive the right treatment and be in the right bed at the right time and for the right period of time.

Utilization review

The social utility cannot perform effectively, however, unless patients' conditions and, consequently, their needs in terms of resources required are closely monitored. Determinations as to the appropriateness of care being receiving and the probability of progress through the system are imperative. These require an expansion of the concept of utilization review, transferring it from a monitoring technique to a planning and operational tool. Such monitoring can best be accomplished through a multipurpose, regional medical information system.[25]

This regional medical care information system must include patient-centered and institution-centered cost information along with sufficient patient-centered medical information abstracted from the charts so that cost effectiveness studies that include quality measurements can be mounted. Public accountability for the expenditure of the community's resources can then be viewed with the amount and quality of the "product" processed by these resources.[26]

A regional medical care information system should certainly provide patient-centered statistics, reflecting the utilization of facilities, that is, how well demand within the region is being satisfied. Such information is central to the planning of programs and institutions.

At the same time these institutions must be so operated as to maximize their responsiveness to the specific needs of their communities. This is somewhat implied in the concepts of regionalization and of responsibility for public accountability, but these two characteristics must be buttressed by the added dimension of community representation at the policy-making level. Ways must be found to include representatives of various community groups on the policy-making boards of these medical care institutions. Such representation should not be confused with the one-man, one-vote concept since these are executive boards, not legislative bodies. It does, however, mean that there must be better channels of communication and increased awareness of, and involvement in, both the planning and operational levels by various community groups.

The exact mechanism of bringing this about is undetermined. Community participation is complicated by the fact that there are different kinds of ownership by the various hospitals and medical care institutions involved. Proprietary hospitals do not have any community boards, for example. However complex, this problem must be attacked patiently but thoroughly if, indeed, the institutional medical care system is to work in the United States. The social utility model does offer a responsible alternative, whether conceived as a state health commission, as recommended by the American Hospital Association's Ameriplan, or primarily as a consumer-dominated body.

Implementing change in the hospital's role

It must be noted, however, that little effective concern has been expressed by any of the four social groups on the central question of the role of the hospital in the total medical care delivery system. In fact, the effect—deliberate and incidental—of many of these group pressures is to prevent the development of such a role definition.

The provider group, particularly the medical staff, continues to be quite fearful of the extension of the hospital's involvement to either end of the comprehensive care spectrum, that is, to primary care or to post-hospitalization follow-up care.

Even those programs where success is central to the survival of the present system—such as the Professional Service Review Organizations—have not received the full endorsement and cooperation of organized medicine. The threat of the extension of utilization review from a retrospective to a concurrent basis for Medicaid patients resulted in a lawsuit, which still beclouds the role of the PSROs.[27]

Organized medicine has labeled institutional incursions into these areas as the "corporate practice of medicine." Since support for this position has been built into many state laws, their defensive strategy has been most effective. It is most unlikely, then, that the hospital's medical staff would direct its influence toward extending the hospital's service role outside its walls. The reaction of organized medicine to the proposals that attempt to alter the organization of medical care delivery has, in all too many instances, been negative.

Oddly enough, the pressure of client-consumer groups for a change is not as identifiably consistent as one would expect in these days of ferment. Only organized labor has attempted to change the system. Union-operated health center–hospitals have been established in some parts of the country; new, more cooperative health insurance benefits have been negotiated; cooperative ventures with other community groups have been mounted in selected cities to establish group practice units; and much staff time has been contributed in the effort to obtain compulsory health coverage for all. Other consumer groups, on the other hand, tend to respond to local problems. Some of the local solutions, though temporarily increasing consumer input into the design and operation of innovative approaches, soon foundered with the withdrawal of federal or philanthropic funds. The required base of service funds derived from operations was not enough to continue the programs. There simply is no widely based patient hospital association as exists in the education arena with the Parent Teacher Association.

It is unreal to expect a clear indication from the various minority groups on desirable characteristics of a medical care system since they have had little success in effecting their perceived needs in any single component of that system, and they, too, have been primarily concerned until now with local issues. Even the most articulate statement of these needs by the National Welfare Rights Organization, although specific in its views of how the hospital should react with the community, really does not address itself to the restructuring of the entire health care delivery system and the consequent clarification of the role of the hospital within that system.[7]

In at least one state third-party payers have been thrust, however reluctantly, into acting as a change agent in redirecting hospitals' concerns to the broader arena of medical care. The state of Pennsylvania, with the appointment of a charismatic, unorthodox, and publicity-wise insurance commissioner, adopted the approach of including many control measures in the contract between the five Blue Cross plans within the state and their participating hospitals. The latest "guidelines" proposed by the Pennsylvania Insurance Department list sixty-seven suggestions, including the possibility of transferring costs of house staff to the attending physicians, assurance of consumer representation on Blue Cross boards and hospital boards, open-door privileges for all physicians in all hospitals, stepped-up utilization review, participation in hospital statistical services, and a moratorium on all hospital construction.

It is important to note that the state department of health was not involved in these contract negotiations; the insurance commissioner was. The commissioner sets the guidelines* and must eventually approve or disapprove the contracts negotiated on these guidelines.

*Statement by Herbert S. Denenburg, Pennsylvania Insurance Commissioner, at the opening of negotiation sessions between Blue Cross of Greater Philadelphia and the Delaware County Hospital Council, Mar. 1973 (mimeo).

Formal governmental attempts to change and control the larger medical care system are presently characterized by conflicts between federal and state programs[28] and the dispersion of the three basic responsibilities required to implement the social utility model directed to the assessment of the cost, quality, and accessibility of that care.

A review and analysis of present and proposed state public utility legislation suggest that their development will involve four different stages of control and monitoring. For a time these stages will be implemented consecutively; though as experience is gathered, the total model may be legislated at one time.

The first stage is control of the units of production through certificate-of-need legislation. The granting of such a certificate, though declared unconsitutional in North Carolina, is now required under recent federal amendments for Medicare reimbursement. At the present time, twenty-five states and the District of Columbia have enacted such legislation and an additional four are considering such a step.[29] All but fourteen states have signed contracts with the federal government to implement the review and approval of facilities mandated under Section 1122 of the Social Security Act.

The second increment of state control—adopted in eight states, pending in sixteen, and being considered by four others[30]—is the review, approval, or setting of charges for institutional services. The new Federal Planning Act (P.L. 93-641) will select six states to act as sites for the future development of this increment. This function is now assumed by a federal program (P.L. 93-641).

The third stage is the review and monitoring of the quality of institutional care. Though measurement techniques are part of some state bills, the paucity of such techniques applicable to a state or regional frame renders the enforcement of this criterion ineffectual. There is some potential for conflict in these provisions with the function of the PSRO agencies mandated by federal legislation.

The last step in the model is review and monitoring of the effectiveness of that portion of the medical delivery system under the purview of the state. Again, this stage, like the quality stage above, is implied rather than programmed at this time. The word "effectiveness" is, however, contained in most of the laws that have been reviewed. It is obvious that unless firm measurements of cost, quality, and utilization are available, the assessment of cost effectiveness cannot be grasped. A further extension, and a most important one, involves cost benefit measurement, which would involve the previously mentioned factors, established on a population basis.

The conflict between state and federal programs is obviously not limited to the PSRO area of quality measurement. Why is the federal government going to study six out of sixteen state cost control agencies under P.L. 93-641? What about the conflict between state certificate-of-need legislation, the Social Security amendments, and the function of the Health Services Agencies in the new planning act? When you add to this the fact that these three functions may be in three different settings within one state, who is responsible for the trade-offs among cost, quality, and accessibility?

The basic problem facing the American hospital today is deceptively simple to pose, that is, how the hospital can optimize its contribution to a rationally integrated, comprehensive medical care delivery system. The solutions to the problem are, however, anything but simple, although some characteristics of that solution do emerge. The role of the hospital within the system must be fashioned not to the interests of the providers of medical care but to the needs of the community of patients it serves. The hospital must be prepared to change its present role and style from a concern with the delicate balance of its four constituencies to one of active involvement in the organization of the total medical care spectrum of institutions and agencies comprising a comprehensive health care system. The reality is that one can see little constructive assistance to the hospital in achieving this integration on the part of its medical staff, its community, its payers, or its governments.

REFERENCES

1. Church, G., and Biern, R. O.: Intensive coronary care—a practical system for a small hospital without house staff, N. Engl. J. Med. **281:**1155-1159, 1969.
2. Gluck, L.: Newborn special care unit, facility for a large center, Hosp. Pract. **3:**33-39, Jan. 1968.
3. Fetter, R. B., and Thompson, J. D.: The economics of the maternity service, Yale J. Biol. Med. **36:**91-103, Aug. 1963.
4. Thompson, J. D., and Webb, S. B., Jr.: The effect of the emergency department on the hospital inpatient service: a statewide analysis, Inquiry **10**(2):19-26, June 1973.
5. Duff, R. S., and Hollingshead, A. B.: Sickness and society, New York, 1968, Harper and Row, Publishers.
6. The American health empire: power, profits and politics, a report from the Health Policy Advisory Center (Health-PAC), New York, 1970, Random House, Inc.
7. National Welfare Rights Organization vs. The American Hospital Association: an indictment, Washington, D.C., 1967, The National Welfare Rights Organization.
8. Governor's Committee on Hospital Costs, a report, New York, Dec. 15, 1965.
9. Riedel, D. C., and Bailey, D. R.: Recertification and length of stay: the impact of AID in New Jersey hospitals, Blue Cross Reports, vol. 6, no. 3, Chicago, July-Sept. 1968.
10. Somers, H. N., and Somers, A. R.: Medicare and hospitals, Washington, D.C., 1967, Brookings Institute.
11. Toward a state policy in health delivery, the report of the Health Care Study Committee, Connecticut State Legislature, Mar. 1971. Prepared by the Section of Health Services Administration, Yale University Department of Epidemiology and Public Health, 1971.

12. Thompson, J. D.: Strong triumverate fragmentizes system, Hosp. Progr., **52:**38-41, 1971.
13. Obstetrical services in Connecticut, Branford, Conn., 1970, Connecticut Hospital Planning Commission.
14. Roemer, M. I., and Shain, M.: Hospitalization under insurance, American Hospital Association Monograph no. 6, Chicago, 1969, American Hospital Association.
15. Brown, L.: Hospital management systems, Germantown, Md., 1976. Aspen Syrkrus Corporation.
16. Mellins, S., and Fritch, H. M.: Connecticut perinatal mortality by size of hospital of birth, Conn. Health Bull. **38:**154-157, May 1969.
17. Decker, B., and Bonner, P. L.: P.S.R.O.: organization for regional peer review, Cambridge, Mass., 1973, Ballinger Publishing Co.
18. Somers, A. R.: Hospital regulation—The dilemma of public policy, Industrial Relations Section, Princeton University, 1969.
19. Klarman, H. E.: The economics of health, New York, 1965, Columbia University Press.
20. Donabedian, A.: Promoting quality through evaluating the process of patient care, Med. Care **6:**181-202, May-June 1968.
21. Fetter, R. B., and Thompson, J. D.: A decision model for the design and operation of a progressive patient care hospital, Med. Care **7:**450-462, Nov.-Dec., 1969.
22. Thompson, J. D.: Alternative patterns in relationships between an academic medical center and an HMO, J. Med. Educ. **48**(4, 2):60-66, Apr. 1973.
23. MacColl, W. A.: Group practice and prepayment of medical care, Washington, D.C., 1966, Public Affairs Press.
24. Jones, E. W., and others: Patient classification for long-term care: users manual, Department of Health, Education, and Welfare Publication no. HRA 74-3107, December, 1973.
25. Thompson, J. D.: A comprehensive utilization and patient information statistical system, Proceedings of Conference Workshop on Regional Medical Programs, vol. 2, Washington, D.C., Jan. 17-19, 1968.
26. Thompson, J. D., Mross, C. D., and Fetter, R. B.: Case mix and resource use, Yale University Institution for Social and Policy Studies, Center for the Study of Health Services, Working Paper No. 33, June 1974.
27. Burford, R. B., Crompton, D. E., Frizd, T. G., Sasportes, M., and Thompson, J. D.: P.S.R.O.s present status and future prospects. A report to the Subcommittee on Oversight and Investigations of the Committee on Interstate and Foreign Commerce, Washington, D.C., 1976, House of Representatives.
28. Thompson, J. D.: Comment: state vs. federal health policy, Inquiry **10**(Suppl.)(1):78-83, Mar. 1973.
29. Summary of enacted state certification-of-need legislation as of June 1974, The American Hospital Association, Chicago.
30. Summary of enacted state rate review legislation as of May 1974, American Hospital Association, Chicago.

8

Health maintenance organizations

ROBERT E. SCHLENKER

■ Although the term "health maintenance organization" (HMO) is new, its underlying concepts are not. Such organizations have been in operation for many years. Two developments, however, are new. One is the federal government's strategy (begun in 1970) to encourage HMO development. The other is the recent, rapid proliferation of HMOs. Although these two phenomena are interrelated, they are not as closely linked as they seem at first glance. Ironically, although recently passed federal laws are intended to encourage HMO development, they may actually have an inhibiting effect on HMO growth and development. These new federal laws as well as the various patterns of organizational structures of HMOs are discussed.

The key principles of a health maintenance organization (HMO) are:

It accepts the responsibility to deliver comprehensive medical care to its members

Its members enroll voluntarily and pay a fixed amount periodically, regardless of the amount of services they actually receive

Although the term "HMO" is new, the concepts underlying it are not. Organizations of this type have been in existence for many years. The largest and probably best known is the Kaiser Foundation Health Plan, established in California in the late 1930s, and now operating in five states with over 2 million enrollees.

To many, the major appeal of the HMO is its cost containment potential. We will, therefore, first examine this potential in more detail and describe how this led to the awakening of the federal government's interest in HMOs around 1970.

HMOs' cost containment potential stems from what happens to provider's incentives in HMOs. Since the HMO obtains a fixed sum of money from each member, and since it has the responsibility to provide comprehensive medical care within that revenue constraint, HMO providers, especially physicians, must be concerned not only with the quality of care but also with its total cost. This differs markedly from fee-for-service medical care, especially with regard to hospital care. If the patient is heavily insured for hospitalization, then neither he nor his physician need be concerned with hospital costs. While this is fine for the individual patient, it is disastrous for the aggregate. When costs are disregarded, they escalate rapidly, as evidenced by the rapid escalation in medical care costs in the United States during the 1960s because of the expansion of private health insurance and public health care financing programs (Medicare and Medicaid).

Physicians in an HMO have strong incentives to provide the necessary care in the most efficient and economical way possible. Ways to do this include reducing the lengths of hospital stay, performing more tests and even surgery on an outpatient basis, and stressing preventive services and early disease detection. The HMO also has the incentive as well as the capability to maintain accurate and complete medical records on its members, and this also contributes to improved and more efficient care.

The above are potential advantages of HMO members, but HMOs can, through example and competititve pressure, also benefit non-HMO members. If enough HMOs exist to create competition over benefits and prices between HMOs and non-HMO providers, then consumers will be able to choose the type of medical care delivery system they prefer. Even if most do not choose the HMO, this competition should force non-HMO providers to monitor their own cost performance more closely.

Unfortunately, there is also a potential risk. Competitive pressures could spur HMOs to cut costs by cutting services. Yet, although this and other potential dangers cannot be ignored, evidence from well-established HMOs indicates that they have successfully provided high-quality medical care at lower cost than does the conventional system.[1] This evidence, in the face of the rapid rise, in the late 1960s, in medical care costs generally and in those borne by the federal government particularly, aroused the federal government's interest in HMOs.

THE FEDERAL HMO STRATEGY

By 1970, medical care costs were of major concern to the federal government; consequently, the potential cost containment advantages of HMOs became quite appealing. The result was a federal HMO strategy, which was officially unveiled in a March 1970 statement by Robert F. Finch, then Secretary of HEW,[2] and was reinforced by President Nixon's February 1971 "Health Message to Congress" and a subsequent HEW White Paper calling for a national goal of 1,700 HMOs to be in operation by 1980.

The health maintenance strategy eventually gained bipartisan congressional support, and major legislation on HMOs was enacted in both 1972 and 1973. In 1972, the Social Security Act was amended to include changes in the way HMOs could participate in the Medicare program. The major action in 1973 was the passage of the Health Maintenance Organization Act (P.L. 93-222), signed in December 1973. The act provides financial assistance to developing HMOs, overrides certain restrictive state laws standing in the way of HMO development, and requires that most employers give their employees the option of applying employer health benefit contributions toward HMO premiums. Ironically, while these legislative actions were intended to foster HMO development and competition between HMOs and other providers, they may in fact have the opposite effect. The fact that HMOs themselves were forming and growing quite rapidly without the benefit of either new laws or substantial federal government aid while the federal legislative debate over HMOs was underway heightens this irony.

DEMOGRAPHIC TRENDS IN HMOs

According to information collected periodically by InterStudy's HMO Studies Group, the number of HMOs has grown dramatically since 1970. At the start of the decade, fewer than forty such organizations existed; 5 years later, their number had risen to over 180, with almost 7 million enrollees. Over 100 HMOs formed in 1973 and 1974 alone.

The federal government's role in this growth was not, however, important. Direct federal assistance to HMOs was minimal. Although the strong interest in HMOs demonstrated by the federal government undoubtedly encouraged the organization and development of some HMOs, recent government report indicates that only thirty-nine of the HMOs operational by the end of 1974 had obtained any federal financial or technical assistance.[3]

At the present, HMOs provide only a small fraction of the health care services in the United States. Enrollments in HMOs are still quite small; half the HMOs have fewer than 5,000 members each; nearly half of all HMO members are in the six regional Kaiser Foundation Health Plans in northern and southern California, Colorado, Oregon, Hawaii, and Ohio. In addition, geographic variations in the number of HMOs also exist.

California dominates the HMO picture, with around 40% of both HMO organizations and HMO enrollees in the country being located in California. While the large number of enrollees is due primarily to the presence of the Kaiser System, the large number of HMOs in the state probably stems from state legislation that allows Medicaid recipients to obtain care from health maintenance organizations, legislation most other states have not enacted. Many California HMOs, therefore, rely heavily on Medi-Cal, as the Medicaid program is called in California, for their enrollment. A January 1975 InterStudy survey indicates that about two thirds of the responding California HMOs had Medi-Cal members; more striking, 70% of these HMOs with Medi-Cal members obtained over three quarters of their entire enrollment from the program. While Medi-Cal has thus obviously stimulated HMO formation, considerable controversy surrounds the program, with opponents alleging improper marketing and service of poor quality, and defenders claiming it is providing needed and high-quality care to Medi-Cal recipients at lower cost to the state than fee-for-service providers. At this time, the issue remains unresolved.[4]

Although California dominates the HMO picture, all but six states had some HMO development activity at the start of 1975. By the beginning of 1975, HMOs were operational in thirty-two additional states and the District of Columbia. In addition HMO planning activity was underway in nearly all other states (Table 15).

At this time, HMOs are largely an urban phenomenon. Ninety percent of HMOs operational at the start of 1975 were located in urban areas, that is, in standard metropolitan statistical areas (SMSAs). HMOs also tended to cluster in the larger SMSAs; 75% of urban HMOs were located in SMSAs with populations of over 1 million. In fact, sixty-four of the 166 urban HMOs were located within the Los Angeles, San Francisco, and San Diego metropolitan areas, with Los Angeles having the most with forty-three HMOs and San Francisco having the second largest number with nine. Other metropolitan areas have far fewer HMOs.

Many urban regions are still, however, without HMOs. Only one fifth of the 300 SMSAs in the country had HMOs at the start of 1975, and, as noted, these tended to be the larger SMSAs. Recently, however, HMOs have moved into more and smaller urban areas. In 1973 and 1974 new HMOs formed in forty-one SMSAs; twenty-three of these SMSAs had populations of less than 1 million, and twenty-six had no previous HMO. Inroads are now being made in the formation of HMOs in rural areas. At the beginning of 1975, seventeen rural HMOs were located in fourteen states. In addition, the number of rural-based HMOs is growing more rapidly than the number of urban ones: 35% of the rural HMOs became operational during 1974, compared to 25% of the urban HMOs. This trend may intensify in the future, since the federal HMO Act promises preferential treatment to grant and loan applicants in medically underserved areas, many of which are rural.

Table 15. HMOs by state, Jan. 1, 1975

	Operational HMOs	Formational/ Planning HMOs		Operational HMOs	Formational/ Planning HMOs
Alabama	—	3	Missouri	4	5
Alaska	1	1	Montana	—	—
Arizona	4	—	Nebraska	1	4
Arkansas	—	1	Nevada	1	1
California	81	69	New Hampshire	1	—
Colorado	4	1	New Jersey	1	17
Connecticut	2	5	New Mexico	2	—
Delaware	—	1	New York	6	23
District of Columbia	3	5	North Carolina	—	2
			North Dakota	—	2
Florida	4	12	Ohio	3	8
Georgia	—	3	Oklahoma	—	1
Hawaii	3	3	Oregon	3	4
Idaho	—	3	Pennsylvania	7	10
Illinois	7	9	Rhode Island	2	1
Indiana	1	3	South Carolina	—	3
Iowa	—	1	South Dakota	—	—
Kansas	2	1	Tennessee	—	8
Kentucky	4	4	Texas	2	18
Louisiana	—	3	Utah	1	3
Maine	2	—	Vermont	—	1
Maryland	3	7	Virginia	—	2
Massachusetts	4	8	Washington	5*	5
Michigan	4	13	West Virginia	1	5
Minnesota	8	12	Wisconsin	6*	4
Mississippi	—	1	Wyoming	—	1
			TOTAL	183	297

*Using different criteria, one of the HMOs in each of these states can also be regarded as a loose confederation of several separate HMOs.

ORGANIZATIONAL PATTERNS

While the type of medical services and method of consumer payment of most HMOs are similar, large organizational diversities exist among HMOs. The two main organizational categories are the prepaid group practice (PGP) and the individual practice association (IPA). In PGPs, participating physicians are usually part of a multispecialty group practice and are paid on a salary or capitation basis. In IPAs, physicians are most often in solo practice or small group settings and are reimbursed for care to HMO members on a modified fee-for-service basis. Part of the IPA physician's fee is put in a reserve to be disbursed if the HMO's overall costs are within some previously agreed upon limits. The Kaiser organization exemplifies the PGP model, while the San Joaquin Foundation for Medical Care in Stockton, California embodies the IPA approach.

HMOs are, however, far more diverse than this simple PGP-IPA distinction implies. For example, the portion of a physician's total income obtained from care rendered to HMO members varies greatly among HMOs. In some HMOs all physicians are full-time HMO physicians; in others, only a small fraction of their practice involves HMO members. Another source of variation is the degree to which physicians are actually financially "at risk" in the HMO. In some HMOs, physicians share directly in the financial gains or losses resulting from care rendered by the HMO, including, particularly, hospital care. In other HMOs, no such risk sharing is involved. Finally, as noted in the PGP-IPA comparison, physicians may be paid on a fee-for-service basis or on a salary-related or capitation basis.

Network arrangements represent another form of HMOs; these usually operate from a central location and contract for health care with several provider groups throughout a wide geographic area. Examples are Communicare of Los Angeles and Co-Care of Chicago, both of which are sponsored by Blue Cross. Intergroup Prepaid Health Services, Inc. of Chicago is an insurance-sponsored network, and the Family Health Program of Southern California in Long Beach, is an independent plan. Sometimes more than one network uses the same provider group(s), as do Co-Care and Intergroup in Chicago.

Organizational diversity is also prevalent in the arrangements HMOs make to provide hospital care. Some of the larger HMOs own or control their hospital, while at the other extreme, a few HMOs are part of and are controlled by a hospital. However, most of the newer, smaller HMOs make arrangements to purchase care from a local hospital or hospitals. In some cases, hospitals accept some of the financial risk associated with providing care to HMO members. In most cases, though, no such risk-taking is involved, and the HMO purchases care from the hospital just as any other customer or third-party payer.

One important advantage of all this diversity is that it creates a "natural laboratory" in which to examine the effects on health care delivery of a wide variety of organizational linkages and incentive arrangements among health care managers, physicians, and hospitals. The lessons thus learned should be of great value in the design of future health delivery systems and government programs.

CURRENT FEDERAL POLICIES

The major new federal laws affecting HMOs were the 1972 Social Security Act amendments and the 1973 HMO Act. However, as a result of delays in implementing these laws, all the HMOs in operation by the beginning of 1975 were all formed before the major 1972 and 1973 federal legislation affecting HMOs was in effect. In fact, these new federal laws may turn out to be more of a hindrance than a help to the development of HMOs as an alternative delivery system available to American consumers. One minor and short run problem associated with the 1972 and 1973 federal HMO legislation has been the time lag in implementation. Neither the 1972 amendments nor the 1973 Act were fully implemented as of the beginning of 1975. The resulting uncertainties inhibit those interested either in starting HMOs or in purchasing HMO services. This problem should, however, be of relatively short duration.

Other and more serious problems are embodied in the legislation. Although the subsequent discussion will concentrate on the HMO Act, a few comments on the Social Security amendments will help broaden the perspective on the current policy situation.

Prior to the 1972 amendments, HMOs that provided care to Medicare recipients were reimbursed on essentially a cost-reimbursement basis. This method ignored HMOs' built-in efficiency incentives because it linked reimbursement directly to costs and thereby neither rewarded cost savings nor penalized excessive costs. The amendments introduced a new "risk-sharing" payment method for HMOs to remedy this defect. Unfortunately, few HMOs will be able to qualify for participation under this arrangement in the near future. The law requires that to be eligible for a risk-sharing contract an urban HMO must have an enrollment of 25,000 members and have had an enrollment of at least 8,000 for each of the 2 preceding years. For rural HMOs the enrollment must be 5,000 and have exceeded 1,500 for each of the preceding 3 years. HMOs not meeting these requirements will have to use a cost-reimbursement method similar to the one already in effect. Most HMOs will thus be compelled to use cost-reimbursement, since they are still far too small to meet the risk-sharing requirements.

Even those that could qualify for risk-sharing will have little financial incentive to do so. Under risk-sharing, any losses must be borne totally by the HMO, while any savings will be split between the HMO and the Medicare Trust Funds, with savings beyond 20% of costs going entirely to the Medicare Trust Funds. Thus, given the eligibility problems of the risk-sharing mechanism and the small potential for financial reward it offers, I expect few HMOs to participate with Medicare in a risk-sharing relationship.

The unattractiveness of risk-sharing under Medicare is evident in an InterStudy survey of July 1974. Fifty-two responding HMOs enrolled some Medicare beneficiaries, and thirty-six more intended to do so by July 1975. Yet of all eighty-eight, only *two* indicated they would attempt to enter into a risk-sharing contract with Medicare. Thus, it does not appear that the new amendments will change the basically cost-reimbursement nature of HMO participation with Medicare.

Will the HMO Act provide more encouragement to HMOs? This, too, is uncertain. While the Act will provide grants and loans to developing HMOs, will override certain state laws thought to impede HMO development, and will require employers to offer employees the option of joining a qualified HMO (called the "dual choice" option), the Act also includes many potentially inhibiting provisions.

To understand this, it must first be noted that only "certified" or "qualified" HMOs can obtain the Act's benefits, and second, that the certification requirements are extensive and therefore costly. For example:

1. A certified HMO is required to make its services *accessible and available* to enrollees. When medically necessary, services must be available and accessible 24 hours a day, 7 days a week.
2. Certified HMOs are also required to have a *fiscally sound operation* and adequate provision against insolvency satisfactory to the Secretary of HEW. In addition, certified HMOs must have grievance mechanisms for enrollees and are not allowed to expell an enrollee for reasons of health status.
3. Certified HMOs must have a *quality assurance system* and must report pertinent data to the Department of Health, Education, and Welfare.
4. Perhaps one of the most powerful and yet simple safeguards in the Act *prohibits an HMO from enrolling more than 75% of its enrollees from a medically underserved population* (where the underserved are defined to include Medicare and Medicaid enrollees). This provision will prevent HMOs from enrolling large numbers of the underserved unless the HMO has also been successful in attracting other enrollees.

These requirements, while perhaps somewhat burdensome to fledgling HMOs, appear quite reasonable as measures to protect the HMO consumers. Other requirements, however, create more serious problems. Some of these are:

1. *An extensive basic benefit package.* The HMO Act not only requires the generally recognized minimum essential benefits of preventive and therapeutic physician services, emergency and inpatient hospital services, diagnostic x-ray and laboratory services, and out-of-area emergency coverage, but also requires that HMOs offer many other services such as short-term mental health, alcoholism, and drug abuse services. Seventy-one percent of the HMOs responding to our survey in May 1974 said they could not meet these requirements without increasing their present benefit package and, hence, their premium.
2. *Permanent regulation.* The Act gives the Secretary of HEW permanent regulatory power over certified HMOs. No time limit or escape clause is provided whereby HMOs can remove themselves from such regulation.

3. *Open enrollment.* The Act requires that a certified HMO have an open enrollment period of not less than 30 days a year during which it accepts individuals up to its capacity in the order in which they apply without regard to health status.
4. *Community rate rating.* Except for some allowance for administrative cost differences, HMOs are to charge the same premiums to all their members. Obviously, this means low users of services "subsidize" high users.

While these requirements appear laudable on the surface, the problem is that they will be *unilaterally* imposed on HMOs. Other insurers and providers must not meet the same requirements as to benefits, open enrollment, community rating, and so forth. Unfortunately, HMOs must *compete* with other insurers and providers for members, and the premium levels necessary to meet the various requirements of the HMO Act may make HMOs unattractive alternatives to the conventional system.

Of course, HMOs could choose to operate outside the umbrella of the HMO Act. This, however, raises a crucial dilemma. The dual choice provision of the Act may, in effect, compel HMOs to seek certification. Dual choice will require employers to offer their employees the option of joining an available certified HMO and of applying toward the HMO premium the employer's usual health benefit contribution. Since offering a noncertified HMO would not meet this requirement and would probably create additional administrative costs for the employer, noncertified HMOs are likely to have considerable difficulty gaining access to employed groups in areas with certified or potentially certified HMOs. HMOs may thus feel compelled to seek certification, even though certification is likely to increase their costs, possibly to uncompetitive levels. The HMO Act could thereby stifle competition by forcing the majority of HMOs to become high-priced "Cadillac" HMOs.

The ultimate impact of all these elements of the HMO Act is thus quite uncertain. In the short run, the Act appears to have retarded HMO development. Delays in preparing regulations, especially on dual choice, have resulted in employers holding back on offering an HMO option to their employees, and this has impeded the growth of existing HMOs as well as the formation of new ones. Presumably, these hurdles will soon be overcome. Then, the longer run issues discussed above will become dominant.

THE FUTURE

Although the number of HMOs has grown rapidly in the past few years, recent federal legislation has changed the rules of the game. Ironically, the new federal laws intended to encourage HMOs may actually inhibit their growth as effective competitors in health care delivery.

Yet even the present situation is temporary. The HMO Act is now being amended and made more flexible. In addition some form of national health insurance appears inevitable in the foreseeable future. If this results in the uniform application to all health care insurers and providers of similar requirements regarding benefit packages, quality assurance, open enrollment, and community rating as will be applied to HMOs under the HMO Act, then the rules of the competitive game will be more equitable, and HMOs may then do quite well. If they do, the ultimate beneficiary of the resulting competition among various forms of health care delivery will be the consumer.

REFERENCES

1. Roemer, M. I., and Shonick, W.: HMO performance: the recent evidence, Milbank Mem. Fund Q. **51**:271-317, 1973.
2. Lavin, J. H.: HEW's new drive to change health care delivery, Medical Economics, May 25, 1970.
3. U.S. Department of Health, Education, and Welfare, Health Services Administration: Health maintenance organization program status report October 1974, DHEW Publication (HSA) 75-13022, Washington, D.C., 1975, U.S. Government Printing Office.
4. U.S. General Accounting Office: Better controls needed for health maintenance organizations under Medicaid in California, Report B-164031(3), Washington, D.C., 1974, U.S. Government Printing Office.

9

Community mental health centers—impact and analyses

LORRIN M. KORAN
BERTRAM S. BROWN
FRANK M. OCHBERG

■ One of the successful models of integrated health services is the community mental health center. These centers now offer inpatient, outpatient, emergency, consultative, and educational services to nearly 40% of the U.S. population. Recent amendments to the Community Mental Health Centers Act require community mental health centers to provide additional services, such as screening for referral to state mental hospitals and follow-up care through community residences and halfway houses to persons discharged from these institutions. While recent legislation has created challenges for the planners of mental health services, the overall effect of the community mental health centers has been positive.

The centers have resulted in increased usage of mental health services by communities, extension of psychiatric services into general community hospitals, and changes in the patterns of treatment of mental disorders, including greater reliance on partial hospitalization and family crisis intervention. In addition to direct treatment of patients, the centers have offered consultation, education, and training in the area of mental health to other care providers. They have also been responsible for greater interest and involvement in community mental health among community residents.

The decade of the 1960s was characterized by increasing awareness of the need for a responsible federal role in the provision of health services. For mental health, passage of the Community Mental Health Centers Act in 1963 initiated an active federal partnership in the development of community-based mental health service systems. By setting up criteria for comprehensive service programs available to all residents of designated geographical areas and by awarding construction and staffing grants on a matching basis to state and local agencies—both public and private nonprofit—to meet those criteria, the National Institute of Mental Health has profoundly altered the structure and goals of service delivery organizations. Concepts such as continuity of care, accessibility in cultural as well as physical terms, and responsiveness to community needs, now regarded as truisms in theory if not always realized in practice, received major impetus from the experience of these local programs over the past 10 years.

The first community mental health center built under the Act became operative in July 1966. Since then, more than 540 centers have become fully operational and are offering services to a population of approximately 77 million people. In 1974 over 1.7 million patients received treatment from these centers. In former years some of these patients would have had no psychiatric services available to them; a large number would have received fragmented, uncoordinated services from separate agencies; and many would have been sent for prolonged periods to distant, overcrowded state hospitals, which often offer little hope of recovery.

Community mental health centers are intended both to serve mentally ill patients and to raise the level of general mental health in their communities. Centers are designed, for example, to provide psychotic patients with inpatient care and with partial hospitalization and outpatient care as needed. They offer treatment to elderly patients with organic brain syndromes and to young children who have school phobia or persistent temper tantrums. They offer 24-hour emergency services to the suicidally depressed and to adolescents and others suffering from drug-induced "bad trips." Center staff utilize many kinds of therapy including family crisis intervention, group psychotherapy, individual psychotherapy, drug dispensing, milieu therapy, and other interventions that benefit mentally disturbed individuals. In attempting to raise the level of general mental health in their communities, centers offer consultation and education services to the general public and to care-giving groups such as schools, public health programs, police, courts and probation systems, and welfare agencies.

The program's ultimate goal is to develop effective networks of comprehensive mental health services in all of the 1,500 catchment areas in the United States. Some of these areas have been able to develop adequate service programs without federal assistance. When all of the centers that were awarded grants prior to June 30, 1975 (a total of 603) have reached full operational status, about 40% of the goal will have been achieved.

HISTORY

The community mental health center concept had one of its roots in a 1952 report of the World Health Organization Expert Committee on Mental Health.[1] The report recommended that facilities be built to offer a wide range of coordinated services, including inpatient care, outpatient care, part-time hospitalization, rehabilitation, research, and community education. The idea that one facility should offer a range of coordinated services was translated into the idea that centers should provide comprehensive services. In order to qualify for federal funds, centers were required to offer five essential services: inpatient care, outpatient care, partial hospitalization, 24-hour emergency service, and consultation and education. Five additional services were recommended to constitute a more fully comprehensive program: diagnosis, rehabilitation, precare and aftercare for state hospital patients, training, and research, including program evaluation.

A second root of the mental health center concept was the conviction based on research and clinical experience that mental health services should be in large measure community-based rather than state hospital–based. The desire for community-based services was sparked first by the introduction of tranquilizing drugs, which allowed thousands of patients to leave state hospitals and return to their communities. Their return created both an awareness that they could be treated in their communities and a demand for such services at the community level. The need for community-based services was also stressed by the Joint Commission on Mental Illness and Health created by Congress in 1955. The Commission consisted of representatives of thirty-six organizations and agencies and had as its mission analyzing and evaluating the needs and resources of the mentally ill in the United States. In addition to recommending more support for research and training, the Commission's 1961 report, *Action for Mental Health,* recommended a major overhaul of many parts of the mental health care delivery system and particularly emphasized developing community-based services.[2]

Responding to the Commission's report, President John F. Kennedy appointed a cabinet-level committee to suggest possible courses of action. At the same time, he appointed a parallel committee on mental retardation. The recommendations of these two committees were analyzed and integrated by the White House staff in late 1962 and resulted in President Kennedy's message to Congress in February 1963—the first Presidential message Congress had ever received on behalf of the mentally ill and the mentally retarded. In this message, the President called for "a bold new approach" to the needs of the mentally disturbed. "We need a new type of health facility;" he said, "one which will return mental health care to the mainstream of American medicine, and at the same time upgrade mental health services." As the key to this bold new approach, the National Institute of Mental Health proposed the development of community mental health centers in all parts of the country.

Congress responded to President Kennedy's message by enacting the Mental Retardation Facilities and Community Mental Health Centers Construction Act of 1963 (P.L. 88-164). Title II of this act authorized federal matching funds of $150 million over a 3-year period for construction of community mental health centers. Congress subsequently appropriated $135 million of these authorized funds to the National Institute of Mental Health for the launching of the centers program. In 1965 Congress supplemented the 1963 act with the Mental Retardation Facilities and Community Mental Health Centers Construction Act Amendments of 1965 (P.L. 89-105), which authorized $73.5 million over 3 years to assist in meeting the initial costs of staffing centers.

In 1967 and again in 1970 Congress authorized and appropriated additional funds to support the centers program. In 1968 Congress began amending the Community Mental Health Centers Act to include additional services. The 1968 amendments included facilities within centers for the prevention and treatment of alcoholism and narcotic addiction. The 1970 amendments authorized funds for special facilities and services for children and addressed themselves to several of the financial problems that had been affecting centers. First, the amendments increased the duration of staffing grants from 51 months to 8 years to compensate for the slower-than-expected growth of nonfederal sources of support. Second, rural and urban poverty areas were granted a higher percentage of costs than nonpoverty areas. Finally, staffing funds were made available to support technical personnel, such as accountants, medical transcribers, and dietary personnel, whose services were needed to operate a center. Legislation passed in 1972 mandated treatment services for drug abusers in all centers located in areas where such services are not otherwise available. This legislation also authorized additional staffing funds and provided for confidentiality of patient records.

GOALS

Beyond making mental health services available to all Americans, the centers program has a number of goals: to reduce the incidence, prevalence, and degree of disability associated with mental illnesses; to keep mentally ill patients living and functioning in their own communities, where they have the support of their families and friends; to increase community understanding, acceptance, and support for mentally ill individuals; and to raise community levels of general mental health. In pursuing these ultimate goals, centers work toward a number of intermediate objectives,[3] which include providing a range of coordinated preventive, treatment, and rehabilitative services; ensuring that all members of the community have access to the center's services; increasing the quantity of services in the community; increasing the ability of nonpsychiatric physicians to help patients who have emotional problems; increasing the efficiency with which services are used, by referring individuals appropriately to a variety of care-giving institutions; and increasing the responsiveness of mental health services to the needs and wishes of the community, by encouraging community participation in the planning and operating of centers.

ORGANIZATION

In attempting to attain these objectives and to adapt to the needs and resources of the varying communities they serve, centers have organized themselves in many different ways. A few centers have been created as new and independent entities with newly constructed facilities. Most, however, have come about through the efforts of a preexisting agency, such as a general hospital or a psychiatric outpatient clinic, to expand its services or through the affiliation of two or more agencies. Currently, over 90% of the centers are operated by means of interagency agreements between two or more affiliated agencies, usually housed in a combination of existing, remodeled and enlarged buildings. The agencies have agreed to provide the five essential services in a highly coordinated and nondiscriminatory manner under the leadership of a center director, who is a member of one of the core mental health disciplines (psychiatry, psychology, social work, or psychiatric nursing). Although the number of organizational arrangements is nearly as great as the number of centers, several general patterns stand out. Centers have been created under the auspices of general hospitals, state mental hospitals, outpatient clinics, university teaching programs, and multiple cooperating agencies.

Whatever its organizational pattern, each center makes services available to all people within its catchment area—a geographical area around the center that includes from 75,000 to 200,000 people. This size was selected as large enough to justify the development and financial support of the center's program and at the same time small enough to ensure that the center could be easily accessible to the population served. In sparsely populated rural areas and in densely populated urban areas, exceptions have been made to these population limits. Centers are not limited to serving people within their catchment areas; they may provide services for people living outside their areas as long as priority for services is given to catchment area residents.

COMMUNITY PARTICIPATION

The major responsibility for initiating a community mental health center rests with the local community, which works with the Department of Health, Education, and Welfare regional office and the state mental health authority in developing its plan.

Once a grant has been made and a center established, community members continue to play active roles in the operation of the center. They serve on advisory and governing boards both of the entire center and of particular services or satellite clinics that are part of the center, and they work as volunteers within the center. Eleven percent of all community mental health center staffs are volunteers. The functions of the boards include policy-making and budget-setting responsibilities as well as being the liaison with the community.

FINANCING

The financial support for a center comes from federal grants, state and local funds, third-party payments (insurance, Medicare, and Medicaid), patient fees, and philanthropy. Construction costs for centers average about $1.7 million. Since most centers include construction features and items of equipment that cannot be funded under current legislation, federal participation on the average accounts for only one third of the total construction costs. In some states, construction of community mental health centers has gone ahead without federal assistance. In Indiana, New York, and Oklahoma, for example, the state governments themselves have matched locally raised funds.

On the average, the cost of operating a mental health center is $1.2 million per year. Federal funds, which under previous legislation were available only for the salary costs of professional and technical personnel, covered roughly one third of average operating expenses. Forty percent came from state and local governments, with the remainder obtained from patient and third-party payments and from philanthropies. New legislation (P.L. 94-63) expands the federal role in operating costs in addition to salary costs and may result in some changes in the ratio of federal, state, local, and third-party support. By the close of fiscal year 1974 (June 30, 1974), a total of $231.5 million in federal community mental health center construction funds had been awarded to 413 community mental health centers. During the same period, $731.8 million in federal staffing funds was awarded to 489 centers. As large as these dollar figures may seem, they are dwarfed by the total annual cost for direct mental health care. In 1974 this amount was close to $15 billion, 25% of which went toward support of public mental hospitals.

PRESENT STATUS

The "bold new approach" launched by President Kennedy in 1963 and implemented through the series of statutes described earlier was in effect a "seed money approach." That is, the federal government provided start-up funds to state and local groups to initiate community mental health service programs that would ultimately be supported by other sources. Even after 1970, when the period of federal participation was extended from 51 months to 8 years, the federal grants were still awarded on a declining basis to permit the centers to phase in other incomes as the federal share grew smaller. A recycling of federal funds was envisioned—as centers matured and were able to operate without grants more money would be available to start new centers. With the expectation of continued congressional appropriations for the federal share, the goal of complete coverage of all catchment areas by 1980 was set.

A different interpretation of the seed money approach was adopted with the change of administration. President Nixon, acknowledging that the Community Mental Health Centers Program had successfully demonstrated the value of community-based mental health services, took the position that this success obviated the need for further federal participation. Since the basic concepts were well established and operating programs were available as models, state and local agencies could now proceed on their own to develop programs in unfunded catchment areas. Based on this reasoning, extension of legislative authority for the program was vetoed and the Community Mental Health Centers Act technically expired June 30, 1974. However, a strong body of sentiment in the Congress for continuing the program to meet the goal of national coverage resulted in legislation passed over Presidential veto in July, 1975.

This legislation not only extends the program but makes important changes. In addition to those services required in the past, centers are now also responsible for providing a full range of diagnostic, treatment, liaison, and follow-up services for children and the elderly—groups that were inadequately served by previous resources. In addition, centers are required to provide screening for catchment area residents being considered for referral to state mental hospitals, as well as follow-up care to persons discharged from such hospitals, specifically including a program of community residences and halfway houses. To help initiate these expanded services additional federal grants are authorized, including special support for consultation and education services.

The 1975 legislation initiated a new generation of centers based on the experience of those already in existence. As noted earlier, 547 centers are now fully operational. An additional 56 centers either are providing partial services or are under construction. When all 603 centers that have been funded are operating, they will offer services to catchment areas containing 86 million people, or 41% of the population of the United States. There are centers in each of the fifty states, the District of Columbia, and Puerto Rico. They are located in communities ranging from urban inner-city ghettos to midwestern farmlands and from affluent suburbs to the poorest counties of Appalachia. Nearly one third of the centers are being established in small towns and rural areas, where mental health services have previously been virtually nonexistent.

EVALUATION

We can begin to evaluate the program's impact in several ways. First, by focusing national attention on the need for community-based mental health services, centers have been an influential factor in the increase in the number of general hospitals that have facilities for psychiatric patients. More than 450 general hospitals are now actively affiliated with mental health centers that provide short-term, intensive inpatient care. In a similar manner, centers have influenced many state mental health hospitals to coordinate their services with those available in local communities. Over 160 centers have affiliations with state mental health hospitals, ranging from referral agreements to use of state hospital wards for inpatient services.

Second, the impact of centers is indicated in the wide range of mentally ill patients who are being treated. Patients seen in 1973 ranged in diagnosis from acute brain syndrome to transient situational disorder and from psychoneurosis to schizophrenia. They ranged in age from under 5 to over 75 years. Of these patients, 57% had never before received psychiatric services and 16% had been patients in public mental health hospitals. Thus, centers are serving both as a first line of defense in treating mental illness and as a source of rehabilitation and aftercare.

Third, in addition to treating patients directly, centers have been providing consultation services to other members of the community who give care—teachers, physicians, clergy, police officers, attorneys, and welfare workers. Since many of these care providers serve mentally ill individuals or can affect situations or environments that may be pathogenic, offering them consultation and education promotes prevention, early case-finding, and indirect treatment.

Fourth, centers have changed the perspectives of mental health professionals, government officials, and community residents. Many mental health professionals are now utilizing innovative treatment methods, such as partial hospitalization, family crisis intervention, and 24 hour emergency services. They are looking beyond the individual and the family for pathogenic influences and are examining large-scale institutions and social conditions. Mental health training programs have added courses and experiences in community psychiatry, psychology, or social work to prepare their graduates to meet the challenges of community-based and community-focused systems of care. Within federal, state, and local governments the process of creating and maintaining centers has brought the problems of the mentally ill to the attention of officials and large groups of private citizens in a manner that indicates that these problems can be prevented or ameliorated. The idea of sending mentally ill persons to distant institutions for care is rapidly falling into disfavor. Within the community, residents are finding that by becoming organized they can bring into being the services they need and can influence how these services are administered and delivered.

Finally, centers are affecting the job structures in their communities and are creating new groups of mental health workers. Most centers employ and train community residents, many of whom leave the ranks of the unemployed to join the staff of a center. Because of their knowledge of the community, these staff members help the center provide services in ways that meet the needs, values, and life-styles of community residents and also help make the community aware of the center's services. In-service training equips these community residents to become mental health workers—counselors, aides, educators, consultants, and research assistants. Center officials are assisting civil service personnel boards in redesigning job descriptions so that on-the-job training for educationally disadvantaged residents produces promotions on newly established career ladders. New jobs and new roles as decision makers are helping community residents to replace feelings of frustration and withdrawal with feelings of competence and self-esteem.

PROBLEMS AND CHALLENGES

The centers program can thus point to a solid record of achievement over the past 10 years. Nevertheless, the 1975 legislation raises important new problems to be faced by planners of mental health services at all levels.

1. The possibility of maintaining long-institutionalized patients outside of state hospitals had led, in many places, to the discharge of large numbers of dependent and semidependent individuals before suitable supportive services were available in their communities.
2. Greater public expectation of the benefits of treatment has stimulated activity in the courts, leading to landmark decisions articulating pa-

tients' rights to active treatment, to protection from harm, to least restrictive care modalities, and to wages for work performed—forcing far-reaching reassessment of the structure and capacity of the mental health services delivery system and the resources available to it.
3. A variety of environmental factors has seriously eroded some of our most critical social support systems—most notably the family—with significant implications for the nature and importance of preventive activities and for therapeutic intervention at certain crisis stages in human experience.
4. The prospect of the enactment of a national health insurance program within the next few years carries the obligation to plan now, so that a substantial portion of the services needed to fill responsibly the increased demands of the consuming public will be available.
5. In spite of strong legislative and policy statements, serious inequities remain in the distribution of services geographically and in the delivery of services to particular groups, notably minorities. Cultural and financial barriers will be overcome only by sustained and carefully targeted effort.

None of these issues can be addressed successfully by any single agency. They will require concerted strategies, drawing on the resources of federal, state, and local governments, organized voluntary groups, and concerned individual citizens. The centers program, by bringing these elements together in the organization of local programs, has helped set a precedent for such joint action. In the long run it may well be that the most significant achievement of the program will be the creation of an informed, dedicated constituency, better able to tackle the problems that lie ahead.

REFERENCES

1. Glasscote, R., and others: The community mental health center. An analysis of existing models, Washington, D.C., 1964, Joint Information Service of the American Psychiatric Association and the National Association for Mental Health.
2. Joint Commission on Mental Illness and Health: Action for mental health, New York, 1961, Basic Books, Inc., Publishers.
3. Yolles, S. F.: United States community mental health program. In Freedman, A. M., and Kaplan, H. I., editors: Comprehensive textbook of psychiatry, Baltimore, 1967, The Williams & Wilkins Co.
4. Glidewell, J. E., and Swallow, C.: The prevalence of maladjustment in elementary schools, unpublished report prepared for the Joint Commission on Mental Health of Children, 1968.
5. Levine, Daniel: Cost of mental illness, Washington, D.C., 1974, U.S. Government Printing Office.
6. Ochberg, Frank,: Community mental health legislation of 1975: flight of the Phoenix. Am. J. Psychiatry **133:**56-60, Jan. 1976.

SELECTED READINGS

Koran, L. M.: Mental health services. In Jonas, S., editor: Health care in the United States, New York, 1977, Springer Publishing Co., Inc.

Weston, W. D.: Development of community psychiatry concepts. In Freedman, A. M., Kaplan, H. I., and Sadock, B. J., editors: The comprehensive textbook of psychiatry, ed. 2, Baltimore, 1975, The Williams & Wilkins Co.

10

Measuring the quality of medical care

AVEDIS DONABEDIAN

■ Recently the demand for regulations covering the quality of medical care has become more insistent both from outside and from within the health professions. Many studies have shown the integral relationship between the setting in which physicians work (structure), physician performance (process), and the outcome of medical care (result). Although there are difficulties inherent in any one method used in investigating the standard of health services, Dr. Donabedian indicates that there is an epidemiology of poor (or good) medical care; that is, poor quality care is often seen in certain types of settings and in certain categories of physicians. On the basis of the understanding of this epidemiology, Dr. Donabedian then discusses the components and implications of a professional review system for medical care delivery. His analysis of the potential benefits, such as reduced hospital stays, reduction in unnecessary surgery, and establishment of accepted norms of good medical care, provides a basis for understanding the future expectations and limitations of such a review system.

Physicians in particular and the health professions in general are entrusted with what is possibly the most precious thing of all: life itself. Hence there has always been more than usual concern with the quality of professional performance. In the past, society, in granting the health professional considerable privileges and powers, has expected, in return, that the professions regulate the conduct and competence of their members. In recent years the demand for such regulation has become more insistent, both within the health professions and outside. There are many reasons for this. One is the remarkable development of medical technology and the specialization associated with it. As science places in the hands of the physician increasingly more powerful tools, it enhances both the ability to do good and the potential to inflict harm. The rise of specialization, which has paralleled the development in technology, is one answer to the need for higher levels of competence. However, specialization also creates groups of physicians within the larger profession who have a stake in mechanisms that assure recognition of their particular skills and, equally important, identification of colleagues who do not have these skills.

The growth in technology and specialization has also required increasingly higher levels of organization in the delivery of service. Much of medical care in its most complex and critical phases has moved into the hospital. Increasingly, office practice also is becoming organized into formally constituted groups.[1] Within such organized settings one finds not only the need to regulate and supervise professional performance but also the incentives, the opportunity, and the means to do so. As I have suggested, the incentives arise in large part within the profession itself. They also derive increasingly from external forces. First among these are the changes in society that have brought about a better-informed and more-demanding public. Second are the developments that have led to the purchase of a large share of care through health insurance and government programs.[2,3] Voluntary health insurance agencies (whether private, like the insurance companies, or quasi-public, like Blue Cross and Blue Shield) have tended to avoid being placed in a position of regulating the practice of medicine. At most, they have concerned themselves with discouraging major abuses in use of services and in cost. With a few notable exceptions, such as the federal crippled children programs, the same may be said of the majority of government programs in the past; however, this picture is in the process of undergoing a remarkable change. From the very beginning, Medicare and Medicaid had statutory and regulatory requirements for the supervision not only of utilization and cost but also of the content and appropriateness of care.[4] The 1972 amendments of the Social Security Act brought this line of development to a head by specifying detailed and sweeping requirements for the review of professional practice by local, state, and federal bodies especially constituted for the purpose.[5] The requirements for review apply only to hospital and other institutional care for beneficiaries of specified governmental programs, but through their influence on the voluntary health insurance system and on professional accrediting bodies, it is expected that all care, whether in the hospital or elsewhere, will become increasingly subject to more detailed and exacting scrutiny.

The judicial system, through the machinery of malpractice litigation, has become an increasingly visible regulator of practice, at least when it is most flagrant in its departure from established norms; so much so that the fear of being sued influences medical decisions for good as well as bad, and the rising cost of malpractice insurance has brought many physicians to the brink of catastrophe.[6] The courts, through rulings in particular cases, have also emphasized (but not without exception) the responsibility of the hospital, as a corporate entity, for the care that physicians provide within the hospital.[7] Indeed, one sees in the hospital the convergence of the many developments that collectively signify higher levels of organizational and social control over the practice of medicine. However, the hospitals are not alone in this respect. The organized group practice, the foundation for medical care, and the health maintenance organization are all actual or potential instrumentalities that will render the practice of medicine increasingly less "private," increasingly open to the scrutiny of others. The debate at present is not about whether or not there should be scrutiny of professional performance but about the manner in which and, especially, by whom it should be done. It is for this reason that the organized profession has embarked on a campaign to further strengthen the hold that physicians have over the hospital and to ensure that the implementation of quality supervision is, first of all, the responsibility of the profession itself. It is in this context that one must see proposals to appoint physicians to the boards of hospitals in which they practice and to institute peer review organizations that would allocate to local medical societies supervisory functions on behalf of governmental programs that finance medical care.[8]

DEFINITION OF QUALITY

Any attempt to assure the quality of medical care must logically begin with some degree of agreement on what "quality" signifies. Unfortunately no simple definition is forthcoming. Fundamentally, this is because the notion of quality embraces all the values, desires, prejudices, and aspirations of anyone in a position to pass judgment. This includes at least professionals, clients, and administrators. Professionals are likely to emphasize aspects of technical performance in pursuing preventive, therapeutic, or rehabilitative goals. Clients may define these same goals differently, place them in a different order of importance, have a limited understanding of the technical means used to attain them, and place greater emphasis on interpersonal and social aspects of care. Administrators are in a position to appreciate both the perspectives of professionals and of clients. They are also likely to add ingredients that they perceive as particularly relevant—efficient operations, for example, or acceptability to community leadership. In addition to the three major perspectives—professional, client, and administrator—there is likely to be a great deal of difference between individuals within each category in what they value and the order of their preferences. Quality is also seen differently, depending on whether the concern is with the care received by individuals or with the system that is meant to provide care to groups or communities. In the former instance, the focus is on performance by individual professionals or institutions. In the latter instance, there is additional emphasis on access to care, the quantity of care that is delivered, and the optimal distribution of such care. For example, a system that provides excellent care to a limited segment of a community can be seriously deficient because significant numbers of people have limited access to any care. Similarly, a system that provides less-than-excellent care to all persons may rate higher in quality than one that provides unexceptionable care to some and no care or poor care to others.

This chapter will not deal with the effectiveness of the medical care system as a whole but with the performance of physicians as they provide care. Accordingly, I shall adopt as a point of departure the definition offered by Lee and associates in their classic study for the Committee on the Costs of Medical Care almost 40 years ago: "Good medical care is the kind of medicine practiced and taught by recognized leaders of the medical profession at a given time or a period of social, cultural and professional development in a community or population group."* Clearly, this is a definition that recognizes the primacy of the professional viewpoint. However, it does not necessarily confine attention to technical features and exclude the social, the psychological, or even the organizational aspects of care. In fact, as further elaborated by Lee and Jones in their eight "articles of faith," the definition was meant to include cooperation between public and practitioners, the treatment of the individual as a whole, close and continuing personal relations between physician and patient, and coordination with social work and all types of medical services.[9] The relevance of the definition is further increased by the realization that, at least in certain settings, higher value is placed by clients on technical quality and by physicians on patient satisfaction than one would ordinarily suspect.[10]

A definition that ties judgments of quality to the opinions of recognized leaders in the profession has some further implications. First, obviously, it rests on what is perceived to be the ideal rather than on what is actually practiced even by these same "leaders." Second, it assumes that there is sufficient agreement among the leaders as to what constitutes proper performance in each instance under consideration. Third, it must recognize that as medical science and professional expectations change, the standards of what constitutes acceptable performance will also change. Finally, the definition raises the question of how valid the opinions of professional leaders are. To the extent that there is agreement among leaders, their opinions acquire what has been called consensual validity. One can make a case for the view that the

*Lee, R. D., Jones, L. W., and Jones, B.: The fundamentals of good medical care. Publications of the Committee on the Costs of Medical Care, No. 22, Chicago, 1933, University of Chicago Press, p. 6.

obligation of the physician is to practice not the "best" medicine in some absolute sense, but the "best" medicine as defined, no matter how provisionally, by recognized experts in his field. However, it must also be recognized that the ultimate proof of validity of professional opinion is in the demonstrated contribution of medical care to human health and well-being. Professional opinion can be accepted only to the extent that there is assurance that it is constantly subjected to this final test. Furthermore, it would be reasonable to insist that health and well-being are concepts or states that can be defined not by professionals alone, but by professionals and clients acting collectively within a broader social context.

APPROACHES TO EVALUATION

With quality defined essentially in terms of validated professional opinion, it follows that evaluations of quality must initially rest on examination of the process of management and on judgments concerning that process. As will be seen later, many studies of quality are performed in precisely this way. However, in many situations it is either not possible or not practicable to subject the process of care to direct or indirect scrutiny. Other methods are then used that permit inferences to be drawn concerning professional performance. One such approach is to examine the structure of care, and another is to examine the end results, or outcomes, of care. By "structure" is meant the reasonably stable set of arrangements under which care is provided. For example, one may assume that a large hospital affiliated with a medical school and staffed by specialists is more likely to provide "good" care than a small, unaffiliated hospital staffed by general practitioners; or one might postulate that the university hospital is more likely to perform better in the technical aspects, and the community hospital to perform better in the interpersonal aspects of management. Needless to say, the validity of such statements is subject to verification by observing, more directly, the management of patients. The use of end results, or outcomes, appears to have a greater degree of validity because it examines the extent to which care has brought about states of health and well-being in clients. The problem here concerns mainly the element of attribution, namely, the extent to which it is possible to establish that prior care can be credited with the states of health and well-being that are observed. In many situations there are so many variables that influence health, in addition to medical care, that it is not possible to say that good health means good medical care without adding a large number of reservations. This does not mean that health cannot be used as an indicator of the quality of professional performance; it merely means that it must be used with great care. For example, Williamson has shown that it is possible to specify how much improvement (or lack of deterioration) is expected to occur in specified illness situations under optimal care. The extent to which expectations for improvement, or lack of deterioration, are attained can then be used as the measure of the quality of care.[11] This approach, although conceptually very satisfying, does not remove the many problems of specifying expected outcomes, measuring health states, and attributing observed results to physician performance. It is clear that no one approach is free of conceptual or methodological limitations. In fact, it is quite likely that the best and most useful assessments of quality would be those that use all three approaches. In this way the judgments are likely to be more valid, and one obtains some understanding of what may be wrong so that it can be corrected.

SOME STUDIES OF QUALITY

In recent years there has been much debate about the quality of medical care in the United States, how the United States compares with other countries that are at reasonably similar levels of economic development, and whether or not the United States is improving over its own past record and whether it is gaining or falling behind in comparison with its "competitors." Unfortunately, it is not possible to give convincing answers to any of these questions. There are no nationwide studies of professional performance in this or any other country. Even if there were, one could, by varying the nature of the criteria and the stringency of the standards, arrive at any answer desired. In a real sense, the quest for quality is a never-ending effort, since as knowledge improves, expectations are set that much higher. As to comparisons between nations, these rest largely on measurements of morbidity, mortality (infant mortality, in particular), and longevity.[12-15] There are, in addition, reports of international studies on use of services,[16-19] the incidence of surgery,[20] and the incidence of symptoms and the receipt of care in response to symptoms.[17,21,22] A careful examination of these reports would lead us far afield. Suffice it to say that from none of them can one conclude unequivocably that the quality of care in the United States is inferior or superior to that in comparable countries. This is not meant to explain away differences that are observed between countries. It is merely a recognition of the fact that there are so many problems of concept and method that firm conclusions concerning quality of physician performance or even effectiveness of medical care systems are not yet possible. The findings of international comparisons at this stage are more appropriately inputs into further research than legitimate contributions to the politics of national decision-making.

More is to be learned from an examination of some specific studies in the United States. A selection of such studies will be classified and reviewed in part to indicate the variety of methods used, limitations in method, the nature of the findings, and some lessons concerning the organization of health services. Since many of the landmark studies selected were done many years ago, it should be clear that the levels of quality revealed are not necessarily applicable today. I believe, however, that because standards would today be set that much higher, the essential findings remain reasonably relevant. The studies reviewed will be divided into studies of office care, studies of hospital care, and studies of incremental system effects. Under hospital care will be examined (1) studies of adverse outcomes, (2) the justification of surgery, (3) studies of elements of performance, and (4) case reviews or audits. Although these different categories are not totally distinct, they do help in ordering the material.

Evaluation of office care

Among studies of office practice the major representative is the study of rural general practitioners in North Carolina by Peterson and his co-workers.[23] The object was to determine what characteristics of physicians, including aspects of prior medical education, were associated with successful performance in general practice. In order to answer this question it was necessary to obtain a measure of performance. Since records in general practice tend to be rudimentary, it was necessary to resort to direct observation of practice. A representative sample of general practitioners who accepted the invitation to participate was visited by an internist who observed patient management and who arrived at his own conclusions about the quality of care rendered. The observer was guided in his observations and judgments by a protocol that listed the kinds of activities that needed to be included and the manner in which they were to be rated. Nevertheless, there was much room for the exercise of independent judgment by the observer. The findings were rather shocking: 44% of physicians were considered to be performing at a level considered to be below average, and in most instances, the deficiencies noted were gross and striking. The methods developed in this study have since been used in Canada and in Australia, with findings not too unlike those in North Carolina.[24,25] One wonders, therefore, whether isolated general practice everywhere is not subject to serious deficiencies in quality. However, in all these diverse locales, there remain general practitioners who practice good medicine, even under adverse circumstances.

Among the factors that were associated with good practice in North

Carolina, the most important was a certain minimum of training in internal medicine subsequent to graduation from medical school. Practitioners who had access to laboratory services and those who maintained an appointment system also were more likely to perform better. Younger physicians also were likely to perform better, but it is not possible to say whether this was caused by younger physicians' being better trained, by loss of competence with aging, or by both. Neither income nor medical school attended were factors, and higher standing in medical school appeared to have a positive effect for only a few years subsequent to graduation. All these attributes may be seen as aspects of structure that influence performance and could, provided other studies yield similar findings, be used as indirect evidence of the likelihood of good performance. At least one of these—training subsequent to medical school—has also been found to be a critical factor in the performance of family physicians in group practice.[26]

Several observations can be made concerning the methods used in the study of general practice in North Carolina. First, this is obviously a study of the process of care itself and of the relationships between physician characteristics (structure) and performance (process). The outcomes of care were not measured. We cannot, therefore, answer the question, "What difference does it make?" Second, although there were guidelines for evaluation, the standards for evaluation were largely those that the internist had acquired in his own training. One finds that the degree to which criteria and standards are specified and made explicit varies a great deal from study to study. In this instance an intermediate position was taken. One can also bring up for debate the extent to which standards derived from specialist practice in a teaching hospital can apply to rural general practice. More generally stated, the relevance of a particular set of standards to a particular practice situation is a matter of critical importance. There also is the general problem of reliability in largely subjective judgments of this kind. For example, to what degree might two observers differ in their judgments of the same process of management? Finally, one can ask, "Does not the presence of the observer, no matter how careful he is not to interfere, alter the behavior of the physician who is being observed?" All these questions are raised, not to be critical of this one study, but to identify questions that may be raised about many of the methods used in assessing the quality of medical care.

Evaluation of hospital care

Studies of adverse outcomes. Under the more general rubric of studies of hospital care, the first category that I have set up is the evaluation of adverse or undesirable outcomes. The case selected to represent this category is a landmark study of perinatal mortality conducted under the aegis of the New York Academy of Medicine.[27] The object was to discover what factors contributed to such deaths and the extent to which, by appropriate action, deaths could have been prevented. Information concerning each death in the sample was assembled from hospital records and was evaluated by a committee that represented several specialties. The findings were profoundly disturbing: 44% of deaths in mature infants and 29% of deaths in premature infants were associated with preventable contributing factors. In 80% of all deaths with one or more preventable contributing factors, there were errors of medical judgment. Several features of the medical care system were found to be related to the likelihood that preventability factors were associated with perinatal death. For example, in relation to deaths in mature infants only, the percent of deaths in which preventable factors were found was lowest in the voluntary teaching hospital and highest in the municipal nonteaching hospital; it was higher for deliveries in the ward than for those in the private service and for deliveries under the care of a member of the hospital's house staff than for those under the care of an obstetrician. Such observations obviously are useful, but they cannot be interpreted fully unless one is certain that the cases in each of these categories are comparable in their social as well as clinical characteristics. For example, deliveries attended by house staff in the wards of municipal hospitals are likely to be at high risk. The precise nature of the preventable factor and the responsibility for it become critical in specifying the nature and degree of nonprofessional performance and, even more important, in instituting corrective measures.

The study of perinatal mortality just described is one among a family of studies that take as their point of departure some undesired event. This could be a postoperative death, any death in the hospital, a complication in the course of treatment, and so on.[28–31] The frequency with which such events occur can in itself be an index of quality, provided one can be certain that an allowance has been made for factors other than medical care that influence outcome. More definitive judgments can be made if, as in the study of perinatal mortality, each event is scrutinized and the factors associated with it are evaluated. Such studies are concerned, to use our terminology, with the relationships between outcome (adverse event), process (medical management), and structure (the setting within which care is provided).

In the particular study previously cited, there are several aspects of method that are of general importance. First, the information is derived from patient records. Unlike the study of general practice in North

Carolina, most studies of quality have depended on recorded information rather than on direct observation of care. In this way, one removes the effect of the observing monitor, but there are introduced other questions concerning the completeness and the veracity of the record itself. Often one hears the criticism that such studies are evaluations of the record rather than of the care rendered. Recording is, of course, an ingredient in management that deserves independent evaluation. There also is reason to believe that good records and good care are correlated.[32–34] Nevertheless, judgments of quality are so dependent on the availability of true and complete records that every effort must be made to make the record suitable for this purpose. A subsidiary but important issue is whether the record evaluation is favorably or adversely influenced by knowledge of the hospital and the physician who provided care. When possible, such identification should be removed prior to evaluation. The question of reliability remains. It is necessary to know how closely independent evaluations of the same record are likely to agree on the rating of quality. In the study cited, committee judgments were used in questionable cases to iron out disagreement. It may be preferable to obtain an average measure of independent evaluations by several judges. As the number of judges that evaluate each record increases, the stability of the composite judgment also increases.[35]

Justification of surgery. A second variety in the category of hospital studies deals with the justification of surgery. Such studies have disproportionate representation in quality assessments partly because the situations and the relevant criteria are rather sharply defined. More important, however, has been the pioneer work of the American College of Surgeons in instituting and developing the surgical audit.[36] The justification of surgery can be conducted at several levels of thoroughness and sophistication. At the simplest level one is guided simply by whether or not the tissue removed is abnormal or whether or not it sustains the preoperative diagnosis—assuming, of course, that the judgment of the pathologist is to be trusted. Justification is more complete and defensible when all the circumstances of the case, including the tissue findings, are weighed by an independent expert judge. Examples in the latter category are found in the early studies by Doyle of unnecessary hysterectomies[37] and the later, more highly structured approach developed by Lembcke.[38] These studies are not very different from the case review method of evaluation.

My selection for discussion is a simpler study that uses as its only criterion whether or not the tissue removed is considered by the pathologist to be abnormal.[39] The study was carried out in Baltimore. It com-

Table 16. Percent of appendectomies that are unnecessary or doubtful in university and community hospitals

Pay status of patients	Percent of appendectomies that are unnecessary or doubtful: In university hospitals	Percent of appendectomies that are unnecessary or doubtful: In community hospitals
Welfare (N = 96)	33	40
Private pay (N = 186)	35	42
Insurance other than Blue Cross (N = 165)	35	50
Blue Cross Insurance (N = 555)	34	55

pares appendectomies performed in two university hospitals and three community hospitals among patients who were categorized by the source of payment for hospital care. The findings are shown in Table 16, which gives the percent of primary appendectomies classified as unnecessary or doubtful based on tissue examination.

Several aspects of the findings are worthy of note. First, even in university hospitals, which presumably maintain high standards, about a third of primary appendectomies are not clearly justified, on the basis of lack of tissue abnormalities alone. Presumably, this represents the margin of "error" in current technology. A second feature is that in university hospitals the likelihood of removing normal appendixes is not influenced by the method of payment. Examination of the records of the community hospitals reveals a different picture—the likelihood of removing a normal appendix is higher, and the likelihood of this event is increased for some persons, depending on the form of payment. In community hospitals, appendectomies performed for persons financed by welfare payments are least subject to being unnecessary, and those performed for persons with Blue Cross insurance are most subject. Because of insufficient information in the published account, the findings were not subjected to a statistical test of significance. It is not my intent to build too weighty a case on evidence from one study. This example is chosen because it illustrates what many other studies also show—the remarkable sensitivity of physician performance to organizational factors. It is, of course, not possible to say whether university hospitals make good surgeons or good surgeons make university hospitals; it may well be some of each. The example is chosen also because it illustrates interesting features of method. The most important of these is the use of practice in a criterion institution as a standard for comparison. In this way one introduces a larger element of realism into the situation and allows for the margin of unavoidable "error" in the technology or in its application. However, in all such comparisons, one must be sure that like is compared to like. In this instance, for example, we have no assurance that the cases in which appendectomy is considered in each of the eight tabulated categories are comparable with respect to factors that influence success in preoperative diagnosis. Furthermore, the judgment of the pathologist, the radiologist, or any other professional cannot be accepted without question. When such judgments are subjected to independent verification, surprising variability is almost always found.[40] Finally, this study, as others that seek to justify the performance of any interventive procedure, deals with errors of commission only. Errors of omission, namely the nonperformance of a procedure when it is indicated, are not detected. A different and more difficult study would be required to establish the latter.[41]

Comparisons of patterns of care and of outcomes. A third subclass under the category of hospital studies embraces those that may be described as comparisons of patterns of care and of outcomes. Probably the best example is the system developed by the Commission on Professional and Hospital Activities (CPHA) in Ann Arbor, Michigan. The basic elements in the system are standardized abstracts of hospital records that are prepared in each of about 2,200 participating hospitals under the supervision of its medical record librarian. There is room for about 150 items of information on each abstract. The record abstracts are mailed to CPHA headquarters in Ann Arbor, where the information is placed on tape for computer processing. Each participating hospital then receives a number of standard tabulations that give a large amount of information about patient characteristics and the performance of specified professional activities for each patient and for patients grouped in a number of ways. It is possible to compare the practice of individual physicians within hospitals as well as the performance of the hospital as a whole with other hospitals. In addition, the Commission uses data from all its member hospitals to perform and publish special analyses that illustrate the range in practice among hospitals categorized by size or other attributes, and from which can be drawn at least tentative conclusions about the quality of care.[42] Recent publications have included reports concerning length of stay in teaching and nonteaching hospitals, recording of complications, transfusion rates, electrolyte studies in patients given fluids parenterally, performance of electrocardiograms for patients over 40 years of age who are operated on, and time of death after admission of patients with coronary occlusion. Perhaps the major finding of all these studies is the remarkable, almost unbelievable range in current practice. Table 17 illustrates this point.

Table 17. Ranges in care*

Categories of care	Percent of patients cared for in each category	
	In hospitals	**By physicians with ten or more patients in each category**
Primary appendectomies not justified by finding of acute appendicitis in the surgical specimen	32-82	13-100
Diagnosis of diabetes without a record of blood sugar determination	5-55	4-100
Diagnosis of diabetes without record of chest x-ray film	54-96	—
Chest x-ray film not taken in cases of acute lower respiratory infection	5-55	0-75

*From Eisele, C. W., Slee, V. N., and Hoffman, R. G.: Can the practice of internal medicine be evaluated? Ann. Intern. Med. **44:**144-161, 1956.

These findings raise several questions concerning the method used and the inferences to be drawn from the findings. Since the entire system derives from the hospital record, the quality of that record obviously is crucial. Second, the comparisons between hospitals and between physicians must involve consideration of comparability between the kinds of cases under management. Third, deviation from average practice does not in itself constitute poor quality. However, it can and should draw attention to practice that could be questionable. Average practice is, of course, not necessarily the standard of comparison. The method is perfectly suited for use with practice in a criterion institution or practice by a criterion group of physicians as the standard. For example, practice in community hospitals can be compared with that in university hospitals. Nevertheless, in each instance of aberrant practice, the decision on quality must derive from a careful review of all the relevant circumstances by qualified persons.

Case review. Another class of quality studies deals with detailed evaluations of this nature, designated as case review, medical audit, or surgical audit. The example chosen is a study of hospital care received by members of the Teamsters Union in New York City. The study has some interesting features of method. Because a sample of all hospital cases was used rather than a selection of diagnostic categories, the findings represent all the hospital care received. However, the sample only represents care received by a specified population group. Its findings represent neither the care received by the population as a whole nor all the care provided by a specifiable sample of physicians. These distinctions concerning the generalizability of findings are important considerations in all studies of quality. Another feature is the

Table 18. Percent of hospital admissions judged to have received "less than optimal" care, by accreditation status and type of hospital*

Type of hospital	Accreditation status of hospital	
	Accredited	Not accredited
Voluntary, affiliated with a medical school	14	—
Voluntary, not affiliated with a medical school, but approved for training of interns, residents, or both	45	—
Voluntary, not affiliated with a medical school, and having no approved training programs	47	60
Proprietary	57	52

*Morehead, M. A.: Personal communication based on data from Morehead, M. A., Donaldson, R., and others: A study of the quality of hospital care secured by a sample of Teamster family members in New York City, New York, 1964, Columbia University School of Public Health and Administrative Medicine.

use of two experts to review each hospital record independently. Quite unlike the study of general practice in North Carolina, or as advocated by other proponents of medical audits, the judges were not given specific guidelines or standards. They were merely asked to use as a yardstick the manner in which they themselves would have managed each case under review. In 78% of the cases there was agreement between the two judges in assigning care to one of two classes of quality. This was raised to 92% following reevaluation of disagreements in meetings between the two judges. These rather high levels of reliability may be attributed to unusual care in selecting judges who were not only professionally expert but also experienced in the process of auditing.

The findings of this study are summarized in Tables 18 and 19. The best performance was in hospitals affiliated with medical schools, and the worst performance was in unaffiliated proprietary hospitals. Hospital accreditation did not appear to be a potent safeguard in itself. Accredited voluntary hospitals with no teaching programs did perform somewhat better than similar hospitals that were unaccredited. However, accredited proprietary hospitals performed no better than their unaccredited counterparts. Certified specialist status of the physician was not a factor in teaching hospitals. It was, however, an important factor in proprietary hospitals. The worst performance of all was that of physicians who were not specialists and who had privileges only in proprietary hospitals. Seventy-one percent of their cases were rated as less than optimal!

A more recent study, reported by Payne and Lyons, provided an alternative approach to case review, as well as additional information

Table 19. Percent of hospital admissions judged to have received "less than optimal" care by type of hospital and by physician qualification*

Type of hospital	Physician qualifications		
	Diplomate or fellow†	Appointment at municipal or voluntary hospital‡	Privileges at proprietary hospital only§
Voluntary, affiliated with a medical school	14	6	—
Voluntary, not affiliated with a medical school	46	54	—
Proprietary	30	56	71

*Data from Morehead, M. A., Donaldson, R., and others: A study of the quality of hospital care secured by a sample of Teamster family members in New York City, New York, 1964, Columbia University School of Public Health and Administrative Medicine.
†Diplomate of American Specialty Board or fellow of an American college.
‡Not diplomate or fellow, but with municipal or voluntary hospital appointment.
§Not diplomate or fellow and with no appointment at a municipal or voluntary hospital.

concerning the factors that influence physician performance.[43] This work was notable in several respects. It was based on a sample of all hospital care in a natural population, that of Hawaii, even though only twenty-one diagnostic categories, representing 32% of discharges, were included. It attempted to go beyond care in the hospital to include information about care before admission to and after discharge from the hospital. To assess care it used explicit criteria formulated by panels of experts and specific to each diagnosis. As a final refinement, the criteria were weighted, so that the noncompliance with some had a larger negative weighting relative to that of others.

The data, analyzed by Payne and Lyons and also by Rhee,[44] indicated that the quality of care for hospitalized illness was influenced by specialization, type of office practice, and type of hospital, with interactions among these factors. Specialists tended to perform better than generalists, provided the specialists did not step out of the areas in which they were specialized. Physicians associated with larger group practices performed somewhat better, but this superiority was entirely attributable to the fact that such physicians were almost always specialists. Physicians affiliated with a category of smaller group practices not only performed no better than those in solo practice but were suspected of having performed worse. Performance was better in the large, urban teaching hospitals than in the small urban or rural hospitals. Joint effects were evident. Care was best when provided by specialists in large, urban teaching hospitals and worst when provided by generalists in small urban or rural hospitals. Of all three factors, type of hospital was most important, especially in bringing about differences in the practice of generalists than in that of specialists.

These findings tend to reinforce those noted earlier by Morehead and her associates. Taken together, these findings shed further light on the relationship between physician performance (process) and characteristics of physicians and of the settings within which they work (structure). They also illustrate vividly the general observation that the propensity to poor performance is not a characteristic that is randomly distributed throughout the medical care establishment. On the contrary, poor quality is more frequently seen in certain types of settings and in the practice of certain categories of physicians. There is, in fact, an epidemiology of poor (or good) quality that needs to be studied, just as one studies the epidemiology of any disease or social phenomenon. Understanding the epidemiology of quality is the foundation for social action to bring about improvement in care.

Incremental system effects

A final class of quality studies is designed to show the effects of systems of care as they influence successive stages in the process of care. Brook and his co-workers have documented the extent to which the system fails at each step, so that the cumulative effect is a remarkable loss of effectiveness in meeting patients' needs.[45,46] In one study of 100 patients who came to the emergency room of a city hospital with gastrointestinal symptoms, only sixty-seven completed all x-ray examinations, fifty-five had an "adequate" diagnostic work-up, twenty-seven had abnormal findings, and ten had treatment for abnormal findings. When the ten who received treatment were added to the thirty-one who were normal and, therefore, appropriately not treated, the emergency room service, as a whole, was judged only 41% "effective" in managing this category of patients.[45]

The stratagem of using patients with specified conditions to test the strengths and weaknesses of a given system of medical care has been further developed by Kessner and associates[47] under the rubric "tracer methodology." The fundamental principle underlying this approach is that good medical care involves a variety of activities and objectives (such as prevention, case-finding, diagnosis, treatment, and rehabilitation) and that the handling of patients with each of a set of selected conditions (the conditions being the tracers) can be used to obtain a comprehensive picture of the capacities of the systems to perform the activities specified and to achieve the desired outcomes. A partial appliation of this approach to selected populations in Washington, D.C. uggests that there are large deficiencies in the detection of hearing lefects, visual defects, and anemia in children and in the treatment or orrection of these conditions, irrespective of the source of care.[48]

ROFESSIONAL MONITORING OF QUALITY

There obviously are many factors that are necessary to assure the quality of professional performance. Chief among these is likely to be he initial recruitment, education, training, and professional socialization of practitioners as well as their continued educational renewal. A econd group of factors relates to the tools that the professional needs in rder to practice, whether these be facilities, equipment, or the skills of llied and supportive personnel. Another requirement is appropriate inancing that assures access to care proportionate to need and provides a range of benefits broad enough to permit the physician to select the are most appropriate to each situation. Even the manner in which hysicians are paid may be a factor.[49] A large number of other organizational factors are almost certain to influence the quality of performance. These include opportunities for professional exchange and consultation in hospital or group practice as well as the formal and informal educational activities that are a feature of such organized settings. Anything that renders care more visible and more accountable to coleagues is likely to serve as an incentive for better all-around performance. Among these are formal mechanisms for professional review.

In an organization such as a hospital, responsibility for maintaining he quality of care resides in the board of trustees. This responsibility is usually delegated to the organized medical staff, who are recognized as persons possessing the professional competence to make the necessary echnical judgments. In most hospitals of reasonable size the review unction is performed by a special committee of the medical staff. The bjectives of formal professional review are primarily educational. The purpose is to detect deficiencies in performance, identify the factors that contribute to them, and make the necessary changes through the institution of educational activities, changes in procedures or regulations, and the like. In some instances of incorrigible behavior, it may be necessary to take disciplinary action. It is hoped, however, that in most instances this will not be necessary.

There is considerable agreement that professional review is primarily the responsibility of practicing physicians. There is less agreement on the extent to which external agencies, such as health insurance organizations or governmental programs, are responsible for the care for which they help pay and on the need for such agencies to conduct independently what have been called external audits of care. As suggested in the opening section of this chapter, it is believed that such agencies will increasingly demand proof of effective implementation of internal audits by hospital staffs or other peer review groups and that, in addition, they will conduct independent checks, at least on certain aspects of physician performance, especially when these directly influence the cost of care.

An efficient system for monitoring care should probably have at least two components: one that sifts large numbers of cases and identifies those most likely to contain defects of management and a second that subjects questionable cases to detailed and definitive professional evaluation. This model suggests the institution of a statistical system such as that of the Commission of Professional and Hospital Activities, which I briefly described in a previous section. Added to this is the professional committee that conducts reviews of cases that are identified through the initial statistical runs as well as other cases selected through independent sampling or referred for review by internal or external sources. The precise procedures for review may vary a great deal. Some authorities insist that the entire case record be used; others favor the use of case abstracts prepared by a nonphysician, at least for the first run. As I have already mentioned, some would allow the reviewing physician complete discretion in how the chart is reviewed and what standards are applied.[50] Others favor the development, by the medical staff, of fairly detailed minimum standards that serve as a guide in evaluation.[51,52] When such standards are in force, abstracts of records may be quite appropriate as a first step in record review. There is little information about the comparative merits of these various proposals. For routine application in most situations, I would favor the explicit formulation of reasonably detailed procedures and standards. This should make it easier for most physicians, who are relatively inexperienced in chart reviews, to arrive at reasonably reliable judgments. Moreover, the formulation of standards by the medical staff and the periodic revisions that are necessary are likely to serve as an educational experience and increase the commitment of the staff to making the system work.[51,52]

The concept of a system of medical care review, with interrelated and mutually reinforcing parts, is clearly exemplified in the structure and activities of the organizations now being formed under the provisions of the Social Security amendments of 1972.[53] As shown in Fig. 14, the key element in this complex design is the local professional standards review organization (PSRO), which is meant to represent all physicians who practice in a designated area.

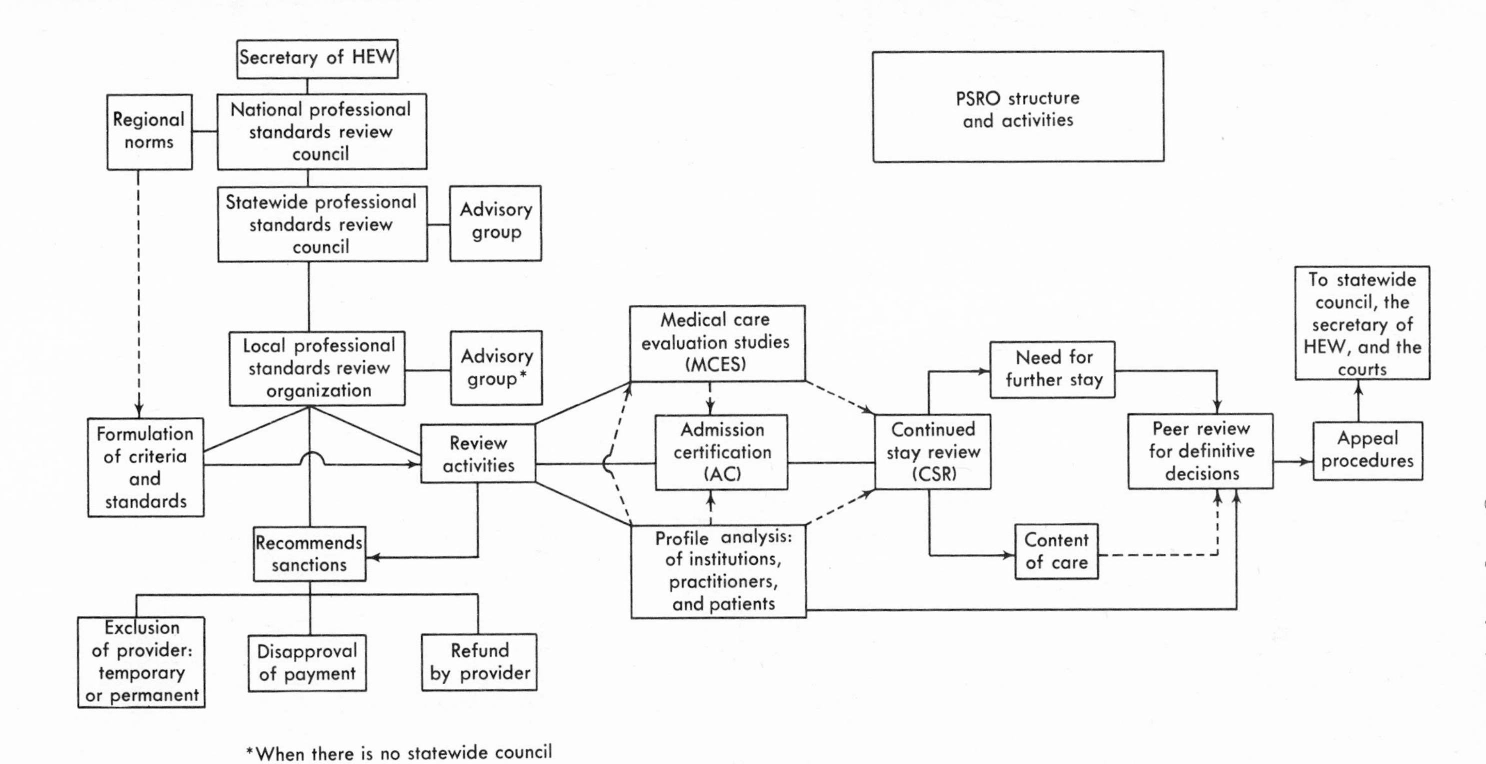

Fig. 14. PSRO structure and activities. (Based on Goran, M., and others: Med. Care, vol. 13, no. 4 (suppl.), Apr. 1975.)

As a basis for its review activities, each PSRO must formulate criteria, norms, and standards that cannot differ significantly, unless justified, from the more widely applicable regional norms promulgated by the national council. Using whatever criteria, norms, and standards are finally adopted, the PSRO is charged with (1) certifying the appropriateness of admission to the hospital, (2) certifying the appropriateness of stay beyond a specified day for each admission on the basis of diagnosis and other patient characteristics, and (3) reviewing the content of care to determine its quality, as judged by its conformity to the preformulated criteria and standards. It is to be emphasized that deviation from standards does not, in itself, constitute evidence of inappropriate or poor care. When there is a deviation, the entire record of care is reviewed by a committee of the physician's colleagues. At the time of review, the physician has an opportunity to explain and justify the actions. Should the physician be considered to have been wrong, the local PSRO may recommend disapproval of payment for care, a refund of payments already made, or, in exceptional circumstances, temporary or permanent exclusion from participation in the care of patients under Medicare, Medicaid, and other governmental programs. It should be clear that the PSRO has no authority either to prevent admissions to the hospital or to mandate discharges. The sanctions it imposes are purely monetary and apply only to the governmental programs that are specified by the law. Furthermore, the physician is protected against ill-considered or arbitrary actions by a variety of safeguards, including due notice, hearings by the local PSRO, the statewide council and the Secretary of HEW, and by recourse, ultimately, to the courts.

The several steps involved in the certification of admissions and length of stay and in assessment of the content of care are shown in greater detail in Fig. 15. In addition to these review activities, the local PSRO (as shown in Fig. 14) must collect and analyze statistical data designed to give a general picture of the care provided by individual physicians, hospitals, or other institutions and of the care received by individual patients from all sources. These "profiles," as they are called, are expected to lead to a better understanding of the patterns of care that are prevalent in a given locality and to reveal weaknesses that may be remedied by modifications in the standards and procedures of review. A similar function is served by the requirement that each PSRO engage in a minimum number of "medical care evaluation studies" that explore in greater detail the care provided for specified illnesses or categories of patients.

While one or more of these activities may be delegated by the PSRO, under specified conditions, to hospitals that are judged capable of per-

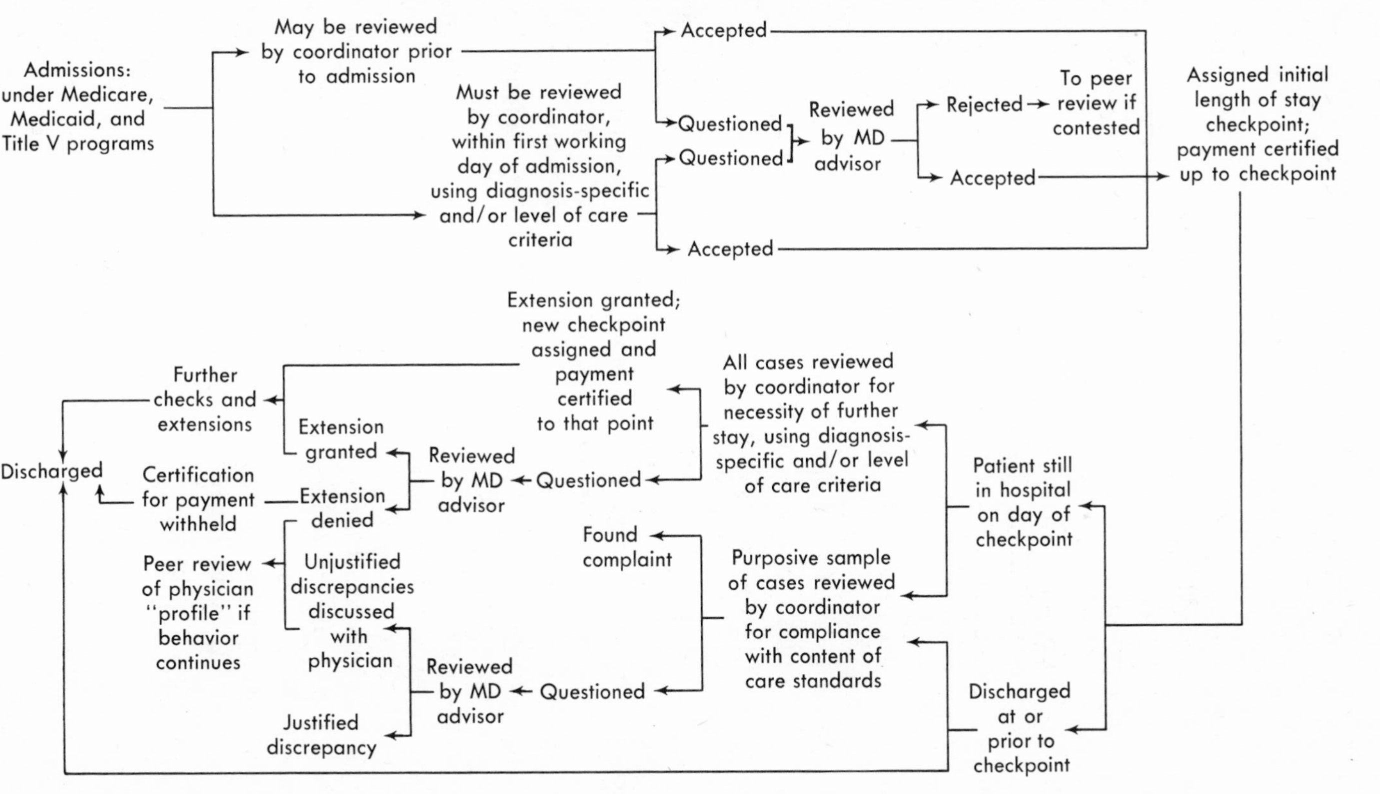

Fig. 15. Certification of admission and stay under PSRO. (Based on Goran, M., and others: Med. Care, vol. 13, no. 4 [Suppl.], 1975.)

forming them, the PSRO remains responsible for the proper performance of all review activities in its area and is answerable in this respect, ultimately, to the Secretary of HEW, who has the power to terminate the agreement with the local PSRO and, thus, to relieve it of its powers and responsibilities.

Not much is known about the costs, the benefits, and the effects of such programs of professional review. The costs include the considerable amount of time that physicians have to spend on formal monitoring activities. The benefits should include savings because of shortened hospital stays and less easily quantifiable benefits in the form of earlier recovery or better health. There are reported instances in which the institution of internal and external monitoring mechanisms has, in fact brought about shortening of hospital stays, reduction in the number of unnecessary surgeries, and even reduction in perinatal mortality. There also are reported instances in which the effect of monitoring systems has been transitory or negligible. At present, little is known about the circumstances under which professional monitoring is effective or ineffective, although speculation abounds. I have discussed what is known about these and other aspects of formal monitoring systems in another publication to which the reader is referred for more detail.[54]

Finally, it is necessary to ask whether formal review mechanisms can pose a threat to professional freedom and the capacity to innovate. I know of no instances in which professional monitoring has been applied in so repressive a manner as to bring about such adverse reactions. On the contrary, my experience has been that professional monitoring is in danger of becoming a pro forma exercise with little commitment to effective implementation. Even then, it is necessary in every monitoring system to make provision for physicians to depart from conventional standards, provided that they serve notice by a note in the chart, for example, that they intend to do so for reasons that they can justify. Furthermore, there always must be provision to judge quality not only by whether or not procedures adhere to conventional knowledge, but also by whether or not they contribute to client health and well-being. In this way, standards of performance are affirmed, refined, or revised by subjecting them to this most valid test of all.

REFERENCES

1. Balfe, B. E.: A survey of group practice in the United States, 1965. Public Health Rep. **84:**597-603, 1969.
2. Mueller, M. S.: Private health insurance in 1974: a review of coverage, enrollment, and financial experience, Social Security Bull. **39:**3-20, Mar. 1976.
3. Skolnik, A. M., and Dales, S. R.: Social welfare expenditures, 1950-1975, Social Security Bull. **39:**3-20, Jan. 1976.
4. U. S. Department of Health, Education, and Welfare, Social Security Administration:

Utilization review plan. In Health insurance for the aged: conditions of participation for hospitals, Washington, D.C., 1966, U.S. Government Printing Office.
5. U.S. Congress, Senate and House of Representatives, 92nd Congress: Social Security Amendments of 1972—P.L. 92-603, Title XI, Washington, D.C., pp. 101-117.
6. U.S. Department of Health, Education and Welfare, Office of the Secretary: Medical malpractice: report of the Secretary's Commission on Medical Malpractice, DHEW Publication No. (OS) 73-88 and Appendix to the Report, DHEW Publication No. (OS) 73-89, Washington, D.C.: 1973, U.S. Government Printing Office.
7. Curran, W. J.: The legal status of American hospitals: point and counterpoint. Am. J. Public Health **61**:177-178, 1971.
8. AMA's stand: review by MDs only, Am. Med. News **13**:1, Oct. 19, 1970.
9. Lee, R. I., Jones, L. W., and Jones, B.: The fundamentals of good medical care, Publications of the Committee on the Costs of Medical Care. no. 22, Chicago, 1933, University of Chicago Press.
10. Smith, D. B., and Metzner, C. A.: Differential perceptions of health care quality in prepaid group practice, Med. Care **8**:264-275, 1970.
11. Williamson, J. W.: Outcomes of health care: key to health improvement. In Hopkins, C. E., editor: Outcomes Conference I-II, Methodology of identifying, measuring and evaluating outcomes of health service programs, systems and subsystems, Conference Series, National Center for Health Services Research and Development, Washington, D.C., 1970, U.S. Government Printing Office.
12. Hunt, E. P.: Lags in reducing infant mortality, Welfare Rev. **2**:1-14, Apr. 1965.
13. Chase, H. C.: International comparisons of perinatal and infant mortality: the United States and six Western European countries, Public Health Service Publication No. 1000, series 3, no. 6, Washington, D.C., Mar. 1967, U.S. Government Printing Office.
14. Lewis, C. E.: A cross-cultural study of patterns of hospital mortality, Med. Care **6**:42-47, 1968.
15. Forbes, W. H.: Longevity and medical costs, N. Engl. J. Med. **277**:71-78, 1967.
16. Anderson, O. W.: Health-service systems in the United States and other countries—critical comparisons, N. Engl. J. Med. **269**:839-843, 896-900, 1963.
17. White, K. L., and Murnaghan, J. H.: International comparisons of medical care utilization, Public Health Service Publication. No. 1000, series 2, no. 3, Washington, D.C., June 1969, U.S. Government Printing Office.
18. Bice, T. W., and White, K. L.: Factors related to the use of health services: an international comparative study, Med. Care **7**:124-133, 1969.
19. Pearson, R. J. C., Smedby, B., Berfenstam, R., Logan, R. F. L., Burgess, A. M., and Peterson, O. L.: Hospital caseloads in Liverpool, New England, and Uppsala, Lancet **2**:559-566, 1968.
20. Bunker, J. P.: Surgical manpower. A comparison of operations and surgeons in the United States and in England and Wales, N. Engl. J. Med. **282**:135-144, 1970.
21. Andersen, R., Anderson, O. W., and Smedby, B.: Perceptions and responses to symptoms of illness in Sweden and the United States, Med. Care **6**:18-30, 1968.
22. Andersen, R., Smedby, B., and Anderson, O. W.: Medical care in Sweden and the United States: a comparative analysis of systems and behavior, Research Series No. 27, Chicago, 1970, Center for Health Administration Studies.
23. Peterson, O. L., Andrews, L. P., Spain, R. S., and Greenberg, B. G.: An analytical study of North Carolina general practice: 1953-1954, J. Med. Educ., vol. 31, part 2, 1956.
24. Clute, K. F.: The general practitioner: a study of medical education and practice in Ontario and Nova Scotia, Toronto, 1963, University of Toronto Press.
25. Jungfer, C. C., and Last, J. M.: Clinical performance in Australian general practice, Med. Care **2**:71-83, 1964.
26. Makover, H. B.: The quality of medical care, New York, 1950, Health Insurance Plan of Greater New York.
27. Kohl, S. G.: Perinatal mortality in New York City: responsible factors, Cambridge, Mass., 1955, Harvard University Press.

28. Stanley-Brown, E. G., Eagle, J. F., and Zinter, H. A.: An analysis of operative deaths in infants and children, Surg. Gynecol. Obstet. **114:**137-142, 1962.
29. Moses, L. E., and Mosteller, F.: Institutional differences in postoperative death rates Commentary on some of the findings of the National Halothane Study, J.A.M.A **203:**492-494, 1968.
30. Roemer, M. I.: Is surgery safer in larger hospitals? Hosp. Manage. **87:**35-37, 50, 77 101, 1959.
31. Lipworth, L., Lee, J. A. H., and Morris, J. N.: Case fatality in teaching and nonteaching hospitals, 1956-1959, Med. Care **1:**71-76, 1963.
32. Rosenfeld, L. S.: Quality of medical care in hospitals, Am. J. Public Health **47:**856-865 1957.
33. Lyons, T. F., and Payne, B. C.: The relationship of physicians' medical recording performance to their medical care performance, Med. Care **12:**714-720, Aug. 1974.
34. Zuckerman, A. E., Starfield, B., Hochreiter, C., and Kovasznay, B.: Validating the content of pediatric outpatient medical records by means of tape-recording doctor-patient encounters, Pediatrics **56:**407-411, Sept. 1975.
35. Sheps, M. C.: Approaches to the quality of hospital care, Public Health Rep. **70:**877-886, 1955.
36. Lembcke, P. A.: Evolution of the medical audit, J.A.M.A. **199:**543-550, 1967.
37. Doyle, J. C.: Unnecessary hysterectomies: study of 6248 operations in thirty-five hospitals during 1948, J.A.M.A. **151:**360-365, 1953.
38. Lembcke, P. A.: Medical auditing by scientific methods, J.A.M.A. **162:**646-655, 1956
39. Sparling, J. F.: Measuring medical care quality: a comparative study, Hospitals **36:**62-68, Mar. 16, 1962; **36:**56-57, 60-61, Apr. 1, 1962.
40. Kilpatrick, G. S.: Observer error in medicine, J. Med. Educ. **38:**38-43, 1963.
41. Howie, J. G. R.: The morbidity of non-operative treatment of possible appendicitis, Scot. Med. J. **13:**68-71, Mar. 1968.
42. PAS Reporter, Ann Arbor, Mich., Commission on Professional and Hospital Activities.
43. Payne, B. C., and others: The quality of medical care: evaluation and improvement, Chicago, 1976, Hospital Research and Educational Trust.
44. Rhee, Sang-O: Relative influence of specialty status, organization of office care and organization of hospital care on the quality of medical care: a multivariate analysis, Doctoral dissertation, 1975, The University of Michigan.
45. Brook, R. H., and Stevenson, R. L.: Effectiveness of patient care in an emergency room, N. Engl. J. Med. **283:**904-907, Oct. 22, 1970.
46. Brook, R. H., Appel, F. A., Avery, C., Orman, M., and Stevenson, R. L.: Effectiveness of inpatient follow-up care, N. Engl. J. Med. **285:**1509-1514, Dec. 30, 1971.
47. Kessner, D. M., Kalk, C. E., and Singer, J.: Assessing health quality—the case for tracers, N. Engl. J. Med. **288:**189-193, Jan. 25, 1973.
48. Kessner, D. M., and Kalk, C. E.: A strategy for evaluating health services, Washington, D.C.: 1973, Institute of Medicine, National Academy of Sciences.
49. Roemer, M. I.: On paying the doctor and the implications of different methods, J. Health Hum. Behav. **3:**4-14, 1962.
50. Morehead, M. A.: The medical audit as an operational tool, Am. J. Public Health **57:**1643-1656, 1967.
51. Payne, B. C.: A criteria approach to measurement of effectiveness of hospital utilization. In Utilization review: a handbook for the medical staff, Chicago, 1965, American Medical Association, Department of Hospitals and Medical Facilities.
52. Payne, B. C., editor: Hospital utilization review manual, Ann Arbor, Mich., 1968, University of Michigan Medical School, Department of Postgraduate Medicine.
53. Goran, M. G., Roberts, J. S., Kellogg, J., Fielding, J., and Jessee, W.: The PSRO review system, Med. Care **13**(4) (Suppl.): April 1975.
54. Donabedian, A.: A guide to medical care administration, volume H, Medical care appraisal, New York, 1969, American Public Health Association.

11

Policy issues in national health insurance

WILBUR J. COHEN

■ Mr. Cohen outlines the ingredients of a national health insurance plan. As outlined in his original chapter in 1969, national health insurance proposals fall within two extremes: on one extreme by programs desiring change only in the financing mechanism of the health industry and on the other by proposals requiring a complete organizational as well as financial overhaul of the health care system. The costs, expenditures, benefits, and realities of the financial and organizational changes of some of the presently proposed national health insurance plans are discussed.

Although public discussion of health insurance on a state-by-state basis began in the United States in the period from 1910 to 1920, it was not until the 1940s that the first significant national health insurance bill (the Wagner-Murray-Dingell Bill, 1943) was introduced into the Congress.

As a result of stimulation arising out of the political threat of federal legislative action in this area from 1935 to 1945 and the economic impact of wage and salary controls during World War II and the Korean War (1950 to 1951), private and commercial health insurance plans began to spread during the period from 1945 to 1965 (Blue Cross, Blue Shield, and commercial plans).

The first Presidential message on health was issued in 1945 by President Truman. Government action in various health and medical areas began to develop at the national level in the postwar period: Hill-Burton hospital construction, 1946; public welfare medical assistance, 1950 to 1965; disability insurance, 1956; and the coverage of physicians under Social Security, 1965. These diverse developments culminated in the enactment by Congress of Medicare and Medicaid in 1965, the professional standards review organization legislation in 1971, and the National Health Planning and Resources Development Act in 1975.

The Medicare legislation of 1965 changed the entire nature of the public policy discussion with respect to the financing, organization, delivery, and reimbursement of medical services. An ideological Rubicon was crossed in 1965 that resulted in a quantum leap, precipitating nationwide acceptance not only of the general idea of some kind of national health insurance, but also of proposals for the reorganization of the health delivery system and changes in the methods of insurance reimbursement to physicians and hospitals.

While the detailed outlines of what is likely to develop are at present shrouded in mystery, it is probable that public policy in the immediate years ahead will discard two specific approaches: first, the exclusive reliance on the private voluntary insurance mechanism to handle all the responsibilities of assuring an adequate handling of costs, controls, and the availability and effective delivery of care; second, complete reliance on a public medical service approach, such as Great Britain, the Soviet Union, and several other countries employ, in which the costs are financed wholly or largely out of general revenues and reimbursement of physicians is not on a fee-for-service basis.

The provisions of the various legislative proposals introduced in Congress in recent years not only tend to support this "discard" contention but also indicate that some kind of a "mixed system" most likely will evolve, at least initially, in the United States, utilizing both the public and the private sectors. Most probably the evolution will proceed on some kind of disjointed incremental basis with very pragmatic considerations because of the diversity in the components of the American medical care system.

The allocation of public and private responsibilities in any new national health insurance legislation could take the form incorporated in the Medicare program: public financing through payroll contributions and general revenues with use of private agencies as "payment" agencies as distinct from "insuring" mechanisms. In other words, the federal government would perform the "insuring" function; the private agencies could perform the payment function under conditions specified by federal law.

The evolution of the future American health and medical care system seems less clear in view of the various different methods of handling key policy and management problems. One way that has been suggested is the initial coverage of catastrophic medical care costs along the lines of major medical insurance coverage. Another is the comprehensive coverage of all child and maternity costs. These two elements could be joined into various combinations of coverage and costs, including reducing Medicare eligibility from 65 to 60 years of age. The major point is that there are various ways to arrive at comprehensive coverage.

The financing of medical costs will continue to be an issue on which there will also be considerable differences of opinion. For the employed person, there appears to be widespread acceptance of the view that the employer should pay a major portion of the cost of medical coverage as a wage supplement. This has been a significant change over the past 30 years. Originally, employers were of the opinion that they should finance only a small portion of the total cost of health protection for their employees and families. As a result of collective bargaining, the general attitude has changed. It is now widely accepted that employers should contribute two thirds to three fourths of the cost of comprehensive medical care coverage, since employers can deduct such costs as business expenses. The AFL-CIO endorses the principle that employees should contribute a portion of the cost of national health insurance to assure their earned right to benefits without a test of need. Practically all the major proposals introduced in Congress indicate that substantial general revenues will be needed to assure coverage for low-income persons. It is thus possible, and even probable, that the plan eventually adopted will utilize multiple sources of financing.

Every major national health insurance proposal assumes that the financing of the plan would come from four sources: employer and employee contributions, federal general revenues, and state (and possibly local) revenues.

Two major policy issues arise in this connection:

1. How much of the total costs should be assessed on each of these four sectors, for what purpose, and on what rationale?
2. Would the employer and employee contributions be collected by nongovernmental agencies or by state and/or federal public agencies? What implications would flow from various alternatives?

COSTS AND EXPENDITURES

There is general recognition that any national health insurance plan will involve some additional costs. But there are substantial differences of opinion on both the short-run and long-run cost-expenditure effects of various proposals.

Experience with Blue Cross, Blue Shield, Medicare, Medicaid, and other health insurance plans, especially during a period of rising prices, has made legislators and others wary of estimating future medical care costs. Many employers and taxpayers fear that costs will rise much more than estimated. Many physicians, however, believe that a national health insurance plan will tend to hold down expenditures through control of physicians' fees and hospital reimbursements. Some health professionals believe a much better distribution of services could be achieved within the monetary totals presently being expended if there were changes in the health delivery system.

One of the key issues to be decided by Congress is whether the reimbursement-control features of any legislation will be handled by (1) providing funds *directly* to providers as in Medicare, with or without intermediaries acting as fiscal agents of the federal government; (2) allotting funds to the states, which will have the responsibility of keeping reimbursements and control of costs within bounds; or (3) assigning private insurance carriers to handle these responsibilities.

Substantially different results are likely to develop depending on which approach or variation is authorized. It is not clear at this time which approach will be favored by consumers; federal, state, and local agencies; professional associations; or congressional policy makers.

The *additional* cost of various major national health insurance proposals was estimated in 1974 by the Social Security Administration (SSA). Utilizing 1975 as a base year, the SSA estimated that the present existing health care system resulted in a total personal-health expenditure of $103 billion. The additional cost ranged from $4 billion for the proposal introduced by Senator Fannin to $13 billion for the Kennedy proposal. The percentage increase was 3.9% for the former and 12.6% for the latter. The bill then supported by the AMA was estimated to involve an increase of $9.8 billion. The Ullman-AHA–sponsored bill was estimated to increase costs by $11 billion.

Table 20. Transfer and increase of costs under the 1974 national health insurance proposal sponsored by Representative Ullman (in billions)*

Source of funds	1975 Expenditures without bill	1975 Expenditures with bill	Increase (+) or decrease (−) in 1975 expenditures
TOTAL	**$116.4**	**$127.4**	**+$11.0**
1. Private	63.8	64.2	+ 0.4
a. Out of pocket	30.1	16.1	− 14.0
b. Employer contributions	19.9	35.4	+ 15.5
c. Employee contributions	6.7	9.1	+ 2.4
d. Other plans	7.1	3.6	− 3.5
2. Public plans	39.2	49.8	+ 10.6
3. Nonpersonal	13.4	13.4	

*National Health Insurance, Hearings before the House Committee on Ways and Means, 1974, vol. 2, p. 673. Data submitted by the Department of Health, Education and Welfare, Estimated health expenditures under selected national health insurance bills, 1974, pp. 631-707.

To illustrate how various components would be affected, Table 20 shows the estimates of both increased and transfer costs of the Ullman-AHA bill.

Differences of opinion over the cost of any national health insurance plan center largely on the impact of the particular provisions of the plan on the elasticity of demand for medical services and the methods for reimbursing providers. Any plan that provides medical services to persons not now receiving them is reasonably certain to increase costs.

Critics of the option calling for the public sector to assume costs usually claim that any plan that relies solely or substantially on governmental responsibility will decrease public interest in conservative financial administration. Thus, there are substantial reasons to believe that any national health insurance plan will increase costs; the question is, how much?

On the other hand, there are those who believe that a national health insurance plan with appropriate provisions could serve to constrain cost increases. They argue for limitations on fees, restraints on hospital utilization, budgeting of institutional costs, salary payments instead of fees, group practice plans instead of solo practice, and other changes in the delivery of services.

Irrespective of what one thinks *should* be done to change the health delivery system, it would be prudent to expect some increase in expenditures under any national health insurance plan. By phasing in the scope and coverage of services, it might be possible and desirable to keep the increase to about $5 billion a year for each of 3 years (at 1975 prices) for a total of about $15 billion for a very comprehensive plan.

DIFFERENT APPROACHES

The formulation and administration of a national health insurance plan raise a host of complex issues. Some are so personal or so diffuse that it is not possible to isolate all the forces and factors involved. Health is a service and not a commodity. It is not only a sensitive service, but also the most important service rendered by an individual to or for another individual. It really cannot be compared in importance with any other service. Its evaluation in the mind of the health professional, patient, economist, taxpayer, or legislator may be based on a weighing of different factors. This is in large part why physicians and other persons have such divergent views on unnumerable aspects of the health insurance issue and find it difficult to comprehend the logic or conclusion of those who differ strongly on key matters of policy.

A review of the many different national health insurance plans that have been proposed over the past 40 years indicates that, despite numerous variations, they can be classified under the following eight broad general models*:

1. Utilizing federal tax credits and subsidies to encourage universal acceptance of coverage on a voluntary basis
2. Utilizing the Social Security system to collect contributions from employers and employees and to pay benefits, with federal general revenues to cover the remainder of the population to provide universal coverage
3. Mandating employers to cover employees and their families under private plans, with federal general revenues to cover the remainder of the population to provide universal coverage
4. Extending Medicare to cover employees and the self-employed under the Social Security system for major medical insurance coverage (catastrophic) and to provide a federally financed system of medical care coverage for low-income persons, with the residual coverage handled through the voluntary system
5. Utilizing federal subsidy incentives and requirements, so that individuals and employers can choose from a limited number of federally approved private (and public) health insurance plans
6. Utilizing federal tax and subsidy arrangements to require each state to provide health insurance coverage to its citizens—with a variety of options to states and individuals
7. Broadening the coverage of Medicare on a population-age basis by reducing the age and/or extending coverage to children and other groups, such as mothers.
8. Allowing individuals and employers to voluntarily be covered under a broadened Medicare plan

In any of these plans there is the possibility of incorporating any or all of the following features separately or in some combination:

1. Utilizing private plans (Blue Cross, Blue Shield, commercials) as fiscal intermediaries of the federal or state government to provide for the payment of benefits on a managerial-fee basis
2. Utilizing state agencies as insurance carriers or fiscal intermediaries
3. Utilizing health maintenance organizations according to the choice of the employer, employee, or collective bargaining
4. Providing for reimbursement of physicians through a variety of methods, such as fee-for-service, capitation, salary, per session (time), or some combination
5. Establishing one or more public health insurance plans as benchmarks or standards for comparison

*For a summary of various types of national health insurance proposals introduced from 1939-1961 see The health care of the aged: background facts relating to the financing problem, Appendix D, pp. 138-159, U.S. Department of Health, Education, and Welfare, Social Security Administration, Division of Program Research, 1962, pp. 159. For a summary of more recent proposals see National Health Insurance Proposals, compiled by Saul Waldman, Provisions of Bills Introduced in the 93rd Congress as of Feb. 1974, U.S. Department of Health, Education, and Welfare, Social Security Administration, Office of Research and Statistics, DHEW Pub. No. (SSA) 11920, 1974.

THE ROLES OF THE PUBLIC AND PRIVATE SECTORS

Proposals for national health insurance give rise to extended and critical remarks on the volatile issue of the respective advantages and disadvantages of public and private responsibilities. This has been a persistent and controversial topic in many issues in social policy in American history. In discussions of national health insurance proposals, this aspect has raised special and often emotional and ideological arguments.

While political and ideological elements are frequently discussed in general terms relating to power, authority, and responsibility, many other elements come into play in discussing national health insurance, such as the merits of centralization versus decentralization or pluralism, and their implications for financial costs, managerial effectiveness and economy, and adaptability to local circumstances and attitudes.

The basic view of the AMA with respect to national health insurance may be simply stated as being antigovernmental, or being in favor of as little governmental participation in the program as feasible. Most physicians, as independent professional-business, self-employed individuals, have indicated their belief in the philosophical position that "that government is best which governs least." There is also a strong belief that government is generally more wasteful, inefficient, and expensive than private enterprise, and that the regulatory function exercised by government results in rigidity and inappropriate rules in relation to varying and special circumstances. These same views are generally shared by insurance companies, by pharmaceutical manufacturing companies, and to a large extent by proprietary hospitals and nursing homes.

On the other hand, the proponents of public sector responsibility in a national health insurance plan believe that only through the public sector can equity to all participating individuals be assured. By equity is meant assurance of similar treatment of individuals in similar circumstances with respect to financing costs, access to the delivery system, adjudication of grievances, and similar matters.

To simplify the issue it may be said that there is a significant difference in approach between those who emphasize efficiency and those who emphasize equity in the implementation of a national health insurance plan. Neither group excludes the consideration of the other's values, but there is an important difference in the weight given to each of the two elements.

Recourse to history, foreign experience, domestic programs, "human nature," and implications for the future make objective evaluation of these two elements imprecise. Moreover, since personal values come into play so prominently, it is difficult to avoid emotional discussion of the respective merits of various elements in any national health insurance proposal.

Efficiency and equity mean different things to different people. Neither concept is pushed by its adherents to an ultimate conclusion. Stated differently it may be said that there appear to be limitations or expectations that the adherents of each concept make with respect to given elements in a proposal.

Thus, those who may strongly support a proposal that they argue will cost less because it will be handled by nongovernmental agencies do not carry the argument to the logical conclusion of advocating a single agency for the collection of premiums in order to save millions of dollars in administrative costs. Nor do those who believe that a governmental plan will ensure equitable treatment of patients and contributors necessarily accept the providers' conception of equity as applied to them. For instance, do uniform or differential payments to providers meet the test of equity?

There are separately identifiable tasks that could be handled by nongovernmental agencies under any plan. For instance:

1. Check writing and mailing
2. Initial handling of complaints
3. Computerization of data
4. Auditing services
5. Actuarial services
6. Management analysis
7. Program evaluation
8. Outside legal services
9. Building maintenance services
10. Preparation of annual report
11. Fraud investigations
12. Maintenance of fee profiles of physicians
13. Hiring of temporary employees

THE PHASED-IN SCHEDULE

My experiences in implementing health, education, and welfare programs, especially during the 1960s, has led me to the strong conviction that trying to put into effect large-scale programs all at once can lead to administrative difficulties and disappointment. Unforeseen problems develop; errors of judgment occur; personnel and facilities do not quite work out as intended; delays occur; costs rise; local, state, and individual problems develop that require solutions. Hence, it is best to plan for a step-by-step implementation that takes into account the realities of human administration.

Table 21 presents an outline of one approach to implementing a comprehensive national health insurance program under existing conditions.

Table 21. Outline of a possible step-by-step development of major provisions of national health insurance legislation with due regard to administrative feasibility

	Provision	Number of months from enactment
	Congressional deliberations from time of reporting bill out by the House Committee.	-10
1.	Enactment of the National Health Insurance law.	0
2.	Selection and appointment of members of the National Health Insurance Board, Senate hearings, confirmation.	1-3
3.	New board members assume office; appropriation requests, congressional hearings and action on appropriations.	4
4.	Broaden membership in Health Insurance Benefits Advisory Council; consultation with them on major policy matters.	5-8
5.	Broaden Medicare coverage; use of state or regional fee schedules for payments to physicians; prospective reimbursement for institutional providers; and strengthening of state agencies for a more effective role.	6
6.	Begin health education program.	7
7.	Extension of home health services and outpatient services to entire population.	9
8.	Coverage of major maintenance prescription drugs for Medicare; reduce Medicare age to 60.	12
9.	First Annual Report to Congress; congressional review.	17-22
10.	Coverage of physicians' services for entire population; no coinsurance or deductibles for maternity and children.	18
11.	Coverage of hospital services for entire population.	24
12.	Implementation of experimental arrangements for long-term care, including skilled nursing care, intermediate care, and family home care.	27
13.	Second Annual Report to Congress; congressional review.	29-34
14.	Conversion of Medicaid to a federally administered low-income program.	30
15.	Coverage of dental care for children under age 6.	32
16.	Extension of major maintenance prescription drugs to entire population.	36
17.	Revision of long-term care programs with adoption of new approaches.	40
18.	Third Annual Report to Congress; congressional review.	41-46
19.	Coverage of dental care for children under age 18.	42
20.	Coverage of dental care for adults.	48

ESSENTIAL ELEMENTS IN AN EFFECTIVE NATIONAL HEALTH PROGRAM

In my opinion, there are four broad lines that medical care in the United States may take. On the one hand there is a continuation of the present system as it is; on the other, there is the transformation of the present system into a full-time salaried service with practitioners becoming employees of a governmental enterprise—usually called "socialized medicine." There is a third approach of "mandated" private plans with government regulation such as the proposal advocated by the AMA and other groups. I do not favor any of these three approaches. I favor a pragmatic approach that builds upon the last 40 years of experience in the United States with Social Security and Medicare.

I believe that the establishment of a national health insurance plan is inevitable during the next 5 years. Such a plan would cover everyone in the nation from birth to death—the rich, the poor; the young and the old; the middle-income earner and the middle-aged; blacks and whites; everyone living or working in the United States—in urban or rural areas, in large corporations or small businesses, in domestic service or migratory labor.

The essential elements in a responsible and responsive national health insurance plan are the following:

1. *Breaking the barrier between paying for health care and eligibility for service.* One of the key purposes of a national health plan is, as far as possible, to arrange to prepay health costs while the individual is working so that basic financial considerations are not a major problem during illness.
2. *Requiring the employee and self-employed to pay part of the costs.* This would assure the individual of a statutory right to benefits without a means test. By large numbers of people paying small amounts over a long time, all individuals can be assured of coverage for comprehensive medical care protection. Such a plan would, as Sir Winston Churchill said, "Bring the magic of the averages to the rescue of the millions."
3. *Requiring the employer to pay a substantial part of the costs so the immediate financial burden is not so great on the individual.* The employers' contributions are deductible from federal and state taxes as a business expense while employees' contributions are not deductible. Hence, the employer can and should pay substantially more than the employee. Moreover, the employer should be involved in the planning of community health services and be concerned about adequate access to health services for employees and their families.
4. *Requiring the government to contribute a significant part of the cost.* This would enable individuals without incomes or with low income to receive equal access to health services on the same basis as those with more adequate incomes. Thus, the stigma of poverty and welfare would be removed from the medical care system. Medicaid could be substantially reduced.
5. *Requiring employee and employer contributions to be handled as part of Social Security contributions.* This would greatly reduce the cost of collecting contributions, which now takes place through hundreds of separate and costly administrative arrangements. A single system of collecting contributions would be more economical than the present system

and would reduce the costs of universal coverage by about a billion dollars a year.

6. *Providing for universal coverage and eligibility to services solely and simply by virtue of residence in the United States.* Universal coverage would simplify the eligibility process, reduce accounting, and keep administrative costs to a minimum. One eligibility card and one reimbursement form for physicians would be feasible and desirable.
7. *Assuring that access to service for all persons throughout the nation would be determined by federal rules.* Uniform nationwide contributions to the health security system should be accompanied by uniform nationwide standards of access to services. This would assure an individual of a fair hearing on matters in dispute before a federal agency and an appeal for judicial review on matters of law by federal courts. Thus, due process and equal treatment would be assured every individual irrespective of color, age, sex, education, or background.
8. *Providing for a broad range of medical services with specific arrangements for extending services over a reasonable period of time.* While comprehensive and complete medical service is a desirable objective, it is not feasible to attain that goal immediately as part of eligibility under a national health program. Hence, any national health program should include specific provisions for a step-by-step expansion of such services as out-of-hospital prescription drugs, nursing home care, dental services, and similar services, which require planning and organization for their universal availability. Such planning must be coordinated with plans for training of health personnel, building appropriate facilities, recruiting and redeploying personnel, and developing health maintenance organizations.
9. *Providing for new, innovative, economical, and efficient methods of organizing and delivering medical care.* Financial incentives should be provided for expanding ambulatory and outpatient care, improving emergency services, establishing health maintenance organizations, increasing salaries and capitation payments, encouraging multiphasic screening and periodic examination, and coordinating community-sponsored plans for health education, family planning, nutrition, and environmental concerns. Nurses and other health personnel should take a more effective leadership role in community health education programs.
10. *Encouraging and accelerating plans for more effective increases in health personnel.* Financial incentives should be provided for expanding the training of physicians, nurses, dentists, and other health personnel including physicians' assistants, aides, technicians, and allied health personnel. Particular attention should be paid to training more persons from minority groups and more women for opportunities to participate in the health care system. Medical, nursing, and other health schools training health personnel must establish incentives and arrangements to assist in the more rational distribution of personnel and services.
11. *Providing opportunities for the consumer as taxpayer and patient to play a significant role in policy formulation and administration of the health system.* Health care is too important to allow it to be the sole province of any one professional or bureaucratic group, no matter how well trained

or well intentioned. Many matters of vital importance are of concern to consumers: the effectiveness with which their money is spent, the efficiency of administration, the manner in which they are treated, the assurance of dignity and privacy, the determination of priorities, and other factors in addition to the diagnosis and treatment of disease or disability. A more effective partnership between the professional, the consumer, and the bureaucrat must be developed.

12. *Assuring health personnel reasonable compensation, opportunity for professional practice, advancement, and the exercise of humanitarian and social responsibility.* The various components in a national health program should be designed so as to foster the highest quality of medical care, with individual and group responsibility for initiative, professional advancement, and a sense of creative and social responsibility. Individuals providing services should receive fair and reasonable compensation in relation to their abilities, responsibilities, and productivity, and should be able to choose a method of remuneration. Compensation should be adjusted periodically in relation to changes in costs and productivity. Various incentives should be provided to encourage the establishment of groups including health maintenance organizations.
13. *Encouraging effective professional participation in the formulation of guidelines, standards, rules, regulations, forms, procedures, and organization.* There should be widespread participation by all health personnel in the formulation of policy at every level of administration. A cooperative sense of participation should be fostered that would overcome hierarchical considerations and invidious distinctions based on income, education, or prestige. The nursing profession should take a leadership role in relating services to individual, family, and community needs.
14. *Requiring a state and area health agency to take more affirmative leadership in providing for effective delivery of medical services.* A nationwide plan should utilize state and area health agencies to stimulate the availability and coordination of services, to set standards for personnel and services, and to handle complaints, grievances, and local problems.
15. *Fostering a pluralistic system of administration.* There are widely divergent ideas in the different parts of the United States and among various groups as to how medical care should be administered. As science and technology continue to develop new methods of diagnosis and treatment, new drugs, and new systems of delivery, we should be willing to adapt our arrangements to new needs and new styles.

SUMMARY

A national health security plan is not a panacea for all the problems of medical care. The continued increase in demand for medical services while the increase in supply remains inelastic will certainly create increasing price and cost pressures for the foreseeable future. Changes in organization, delivery, and access to services will not occur overnight. Changes in school curricula, admissions, and orientation are underway but will take time.

Health education and preventive health care must be expanded in order to make it possible for the available medical personnel and facilities to handle acute and chronic sickness and disability.

Meanwhile, we must make a more effective effort to distribute medical services in a more rational and socially conscious manner than at present. A national health security plan is a mechanism to focus our planning and our priorities toward a more intelligent distribution of health care to the entire population.

CONCLUDING OBSERVATIONS

1. Based on past experience, Congress is most likely to include some important and unexpected elements in any final piece of legislation that takes into account the forces at work in the legislative process.
2. Providers and consumers should be fully consulted in both the legislative and the administrative process to assure successful and acceptable administration of the entire program.
3. A comprehensive public information and health education program is vitally necessary to obtain public support and understanding of the key issues and to avoid excessive demands on the medical care system. Such a program should begin substantially before any new significant benefits begin.
4. Important new benefits should begin preferably between April and October in order to avoid paying for services during high morbidity periods (November to March).
5. Benefits under national health insurance should be phased into operation by a predetermined schedule that takes into account the progress made under the health resources law and any federal personnel legislation.
6. The federal administrative authority should be held by a board consisting of three to five persons rather than a single administrator. The federal board should be functioning a number of months before any major new benefits or policies are put into effect.
7. A separate health appropriations bill should be processed by the Congress to ensure that all health legislation is considered in relation to all aspects of health and medical care.

12

Financing and cost controls in medical care

I. S. FALK

■ Medical care is a commodity about which the provider of service largely determines need and supply, price and cost; and thus it does not function by the dynamics of the free marketplace. Mechanisms of health care financing that provide only additional funds, therefore, intensify the demand on available resources. Dr. Falk stresses the relationship between the financing and the organization of health services. Cost controls and financing of health care that will be both adequate and equitable can be achieved only if they are also the means for effecting improvements in the delivery of personal health services. A good financing program should provide for national eligibility, public financing, private provision of services, fiscal support for the development of needed personnel, health care facilities, medical care organizations, and public participation.

THE SETTING OF THE CURRENT NATIONAL PROBLEM

Medical care in the United States is "in crisis," as are various other major sectors in our society and economy. Medical care has the distinction of having come into crisis before others, of having been in this unhappy state longer, and of being in difficulty for reasons inherent in its own system and not merely from sharing in general economic recession. "Crisis," however pejorative, is almost uniquely applicable to medical care because it reflects that circumstances worsen and that they will not spontaneously improve as a result of the play of forces in the general marketplace. The longer national action is delayed, the more heroic the remedies will have to be.*

The most evident reason for crisis in medical care is rising costs—

*Unless otherwise explicitly indicated, the term "medical care" is used throughout this chapter to refer to the whole spectrum of personal health services and goods—the services of physicians, dentists, other personal providers, hospitals, and nursing homes and drugs, medicines, and appliances. The term "personal health services" excludes community-wide public health and related services, capital investments for construction of medical facilities, and the costs of professional and technical education, training, and research.

increasing at a rate 50% to 100% higher than the rate of increase for the costs of other necessities. Medical care has been progressively pricing itself beyond the reach of tens of millions of people who need it. For many its high and steadily rising costs have become one of the most common causes of economic insecurity, burden, or even catastrophe.

Another reason for crisis is that the "system" of medical care has become incapable of self-regulation and of serving the public need. This crisis is occurring despite steeply escalating prices, costs, and expenditures, and despite congressional efforts in the 1960s to deal with the evident problems through limited categorical programs. Thus, there is nearly a consensus in the United States that resolution of the problems of medical care requires both improvement in the financing of the service and improvement of the system itself.

We are confronted by a national dilemma because among those who agree on the need to improve the financing of medical care, there are many who do not recognize that more money for medical care will not, of itself, resolve the problems. Decades of experience demonstrate that the main effect of providing more money to pay for medical care is escalation in price and cost without contributing substantially to actual general availability and delivery of services. If this is not in keeping with the usual canons of market behavior and *laissez faire,* it only reflects that medical care does not function by the dynamics of the marketplace but by the dynamics of the *medical-care* market—a quite different phenomenon. Medical care is a field in which the providers of service—the physicians—largely determine both need and supply, both price and cost; a field in which the physicians' responsibility and power extend not only to their own services but also to most other goods and services responsible for major medical care costs. Here is a market in which monopoly controls the dynamics in which the consumers often know little about their true needs—perhaps even less about the value of what they buy and pay for—in which consumer "demand" has little effect on the availability of "supply," and in which increase of expenditures has had little if any effectiveness in overcoming barriers or hurdles to the availability and receipt of medical care.

Not many years ago, medical care involved the expenditure of about 3.5% to 4.0% of national income and was responsible for an average of about 3% to 4% of family expenditures. As recently as a decade ago, medical care expenditures were about $33 billion a year, about $180 per capita, and accounted for 5% of a gross national product of $700 billion. In the fiscal year 1974 to 1975, when total national health expenditures were over $118 billion, personal health services were over $104 billion, $480 per capita, and accounted for 7.3% of a gross national product of

$1,425 billion. The annual rate of escalation for personal health services was 13.9%, more than one and a half times the rate for the general economy.*

The impact of medical care costs is unlike that of any other essential commodity because families do not incur them in regular, repeated, and thus foreseeable amounts, but in uneven and potentially unforeseeable frequency, and because their enormous range of size for individuals and families makes them unbudgetable by the individual family. These are the basic reasons why it has long been evident that the costs of medical care demand *group payment*—whether via insurance, taxation, or both—allowing for the distribution of costs among groups of people and over periods of time and providing a group of people with a foreseeable, budgetable average cost to supplant the variable and unbudgetable costs of the individual.

This need for group payment was the incentive for the development of insurance against these costs and, in the absence of governmental compulsory health insurance, for the growth of private voluntary insurance. In the course of the 40 years since the modern movement for medical care insurance began, private insurance (through both for-profit commercial companies and nonprofit Blue Cross and Blue Shield plans) has been successful in effecting massive sale of group and individual insurance—to the point that nearly everyone who has need for protection against medical care costs has some insurance. At the same time, however, private insurance has been grievously unsuccessful in effecting adequate insurance—presently all the private health insurance combined covers only about one third of the private costs incurred for personal health services—and for more than a decade has effected little or no improvement in the adequacy of insurance protection for Americans. Nor has this picture of extensive but inadequate reach of private insurance substantially improved since 1965 when the federal government, by the development of Medicare, relieved the insurance industry of the need to cover the high risk population of older persons.

The failure of private insurance to effect *adequate* coverage has been compounded, year after year, by some unintended but disastrous effects of its coverage design. By providing coverage principally for the costs of inpatient hospital care and for surgery—the categories easiest to insure and indemnify—while providing minimal, limited, or no coverage for many ambulatory services or for preventive care, private insurance has

*For general source data, see Mueller, Marjorie Smith, and Gibson, Robert M.: National health expenditures, fiscal year 1975, Social Security Bulletin, Feb. 1976, pp. 3-21. For provisional estimates for the fiscal year 1975 to 1976, see Forward plan for health by 1978-1982, DHEW Pub. No. (OS) 76-50046, Aug. 1976, p. 30.

fostered hospital services and surgery to scandalous levels. Also, by largely, if not wholly, eschewing intrusion into quality standards of clinical performance, private insurance has provided fiscal supports for the status quo of the delivery system and for monopolistic control by the medical profession, and for the almost unyielding preservation of an inherited design with which physicians, hospitals, and most other providers are comfortable.

When national health insurance was first being advocated in the United States—as a constituent element in the Social Security Act of 1935 and through other legislative proposals in subsequent years—some argued that such a system should not be instigated until the organization of the services was first improved—lest the system embed undesirable practices and thus delay needed reforms. Others argued that since organizational change comes very slowly, improvement of financing should not wait—it should provide fiscal supports to stimulate and accelerate organizational change—and that national health insurance should not be postponed. The former view prevailed; national financing was not instituted, leaving a clear field for the rapid expansion of private insurance to serve an urgent nationwide need. Organizational improvements then proceeded at a snail's pace, while private insurance providing more and more powerful bulwarks for solo practice and fractionating specialty services, supported by fee-for-service payments and strong stimuli for excessive and excessively expensive inpatient care, effected precisely what had been feared when arguing against national insurance.

That debate is now ended, because neither the financing nor the reorganization objective can wait any longer. Even more importantly, there is nearly a consensus now that national financing and system improvement are inseparable needs, each for its own objectives and each a necessity for the other.

If we were merely to provide additional financing for the purchase of more private insurance, while postponing systems improvements, we would surely intensify the demands on the available resources for service and probably further the excessive use of hospitals and increase medical care prices and expenditures. If we were to continue to postpone instituting a financing system and only focus on improvements in the system, it is a foregone conclusion that these improvements would be limited, categorical, and minimally financed, totally incapable of containing medical care costs that must then be expected to keep rising above the recent $104 billion annual level toward levels that within a few years would compel truly heroic remedies. The point must be emphasized that any program that would well serve the national need must be targeted simultaneously to both adequate financing and adequate rationalization and modernization of the system of medical care.

Finally, it should be clear that the objectives fixed by these lessons and guidelines are attainable only through strong and directed measures of social policy and public law. The magnitude of the expenditures involved compels the financing of an adequate system of medical care for the whole U.S. population to have its base in the national economy. The needed redirection of the national expenditures requires the authority of public law in order to allocate the impact of the costs according to the individual's ability to contribute to the national funding, independent of the individual's ability to buy needed care. The needed redirection in the organization of the services demands sufficient financial resources to assure adequate operational support funds for the system as a whole and to provide incentive support for the needed changes. These prescriptions lead to the conclusion that adequate financing of medical care can be effected only through national funding from national resources.

DESIGN OF A HEALTH SECURITY PROGRAM

In light of these conclusions, it may be useful to specify the major elements of an adequate, national program that would serve the dual objectives of financing and systems improvement for availability of care. The primary social goal is the availability of all needed services for health maintenance and medical care to everyone in the United States, as far as this is practical initially and with comprehensiveness increasing as much as expansion of resources and services makes feasible. Obviously, since the intent is to start with the resources available and move toward greater adequacy as the resources become more adequate, the progression would be on an evolutionary course,[1] according to the following guidelines:

1. As an article of social policy, the whole population should be eligible for all the benefits of the program, according to the need for health care, without financial tests or barriers—i.e., with no required insurance contributions history, no means tests, and no payments to be made by the patient at the time service is received
2. As a corollary of national eligibility for services, the financing of the program should be national, with as equitable allocation of the costs as may be feasible, and with built-in provisions not only for quality assurance but also for national cost controls on budget bases which are geared to trends in the national economy as a whole
3. While the financing and fiscal management should be national, indeed "monolithic" as in our national social insurance, the availability and provision of the medical services should be private and "pluralistic"

through self-elected diversities among providers of service as to their location, organization and selection of professional activities, subject however to requirements to assure the worth of the services supported by public funds
4. Alternative patterns of organization for the provision of services should be not only permitted but even encouraged, especially toward the development of organized provisions for the availability of comprehensive care on a prepayment basis and especially through group practice of the providers of care
5. The financial resources should include special earmarked provisions of adequate dimension to support improvements in the availability of medical care, especially with respect to shortages and maldistributions of health manpower and of facilities for primary and ambulatory services and in organization for the delivery of care
6. Administration of the public program should involve not only the public authority but also representatives of consumers and providers of the services at all levels from policy making to ombudsman, with mandatory provisions to assure periodic public accounting of program operations, performances and evaluations

Obviously, these specifications do not encompass all the requirements for a legislative proposal or for an administrative design. Those would require a long array of details which are not necessarily germane to this discussion.*

It is no oversight that there is no explicit provision included here regarding the role of private insurance carriers. A system whose financing and administration can be adequate through budgeted national funding abolishes the fiscal "risks" that are the usual basis for private insurance or reinsurance. Whether there is or is not a place in this pattern for the insurance industry—to serve not as carriers of risk but as claims takers or fiscal intermediaries—is not a question of logic or necessity but of political feasibility. Massive national experience shows that the insurance industry adds billions in cost and distorts sensible patterns of service and expenditure, while contributing little in administration and less in quality and cost control that could not be done at least as well, and probably better and at lesser cost, by public administration.

For emphasis, it should be noted that these specifications intend:

1. *Universal automatic eligibility for needed health care from all available qualified provider resources*
2. *Public financing*
3. *Private provision of services with*

*See, for example, the Health Security Act, 95th Congress, 1st Session: H.R. 21, 22, and 23, by Representative Corman and others: Congressional Record, p. H. 79, Jan. 4, 1977; and S. 3, by Senator Kennedy: Congressional Record, pp. 468-501, Jan. 11, 1977.

4. *Organizational improvements*
5. *Fiscal supports for development of needed personnel, facilities, and organization*
6. *Public participation and accounting*

Among the various congressional proposals for national health insurance, only the health security program conforms to these specifications, though a few of the alternative proposals allege some of these objectives but stop short of presenting manageable or promising designs.

The first principle, that of universal eligibility, reflects a broad acceptance that everyone in the United States should have access to good medical care as a matter of right. Failure to accept this principle is a fatal weakness in the alternative proposals, complicating—if not defeating—the other major objectives. For example, starting with coverage for employed persons and with employer-purchase of private insurance, as do most of those alternatives, would perpetuate the very designs and practices largely responsible for current difficulties. Such a starting point would lead to prescribing separate (and generally unequal) service provisions for population groups to be covered—for those who change employment status, for the self-employed and the nonemployed, for the poor and near poor, for the geographically mobile, and for other groups; it would precipitate unmanageable problems for absolute or comparative equity in premium payments, deductibles, copayments, income tests of eligibility for coverage and services in relation to public fiscal supports and to the impacts of costs; it would require extreme regulatory controls for the availability of services, payments to providers, and benefit and fiscal accounting; and it almost surely would result in lack of needed leverage to effect quality assurances, general systems improvements, or meaningful professional and public participation. Since such proposals cannot escape fractionations of persons, services, and costs, they would result in incomprehensible complexity for those who would have to participate in the proposed administrative and service provisions and for the public. Every such proposal would encourage the continuance of the disastrous separate systems of medical care for the self-maintaining, for the elderly, and for the poor and near poor.

Variants of the employer-purchase-of-private-insurance plans propose similar functions for a federal agency—to purchase or arrange contracts for such groups as the nonemployed aged, the self-employed, and the poor. And a variant of the wholly national pattern proposes participation by state commissions to authorize and control federally subsidized (mainly hospital-based) health care corporations. These proposals promise administrative and service—and even federal-state—complexities as prices for attempts to achieve some limited quality controls or cost containments, while avoiding conflicts with the vested interests of the private insurance industry, the hospitals and other providers of services, and the state agencies. It is hard to believe such proposals would be acceptable.

Some proposals are based on the improvement or reorganization of Medicare (our national health insurance for the aged and disabled). But these proposals are only tinkerings since they do not deal with the basic weaknesses of that system—the lack of adequate service coverage, cost controls, or even legal authorization to deal with system needs for the 10% of the U.S. population that this insurance must serve. Development along these lines would not effect improvements for the other 90% of the population.

Some proposals intend improvements for maternity services and for the medical care needs of children, especially in the area of preventive health services. By covering relatively small proportions of medical care expenditures, such programs could have no substantial capacity for system improvement and, at best, could lead only to undesirable further increase of categorical programs that would be subject to the basic deficiencies of the system. Some proposals intending to effect urgently needed improvements in Medicaid (our federal-state medical care quagmire for the poor and the medically indigent) would, at best, encourage already disastrous separate provisions for the disadvantaged and, at worst, merely tighten the rationing of available services according to ability to pay.

Proposals for "tax credit" devices would authorize credits against federal income-tax obligations—to be measured by premiums paid in purchasing private insurance—and Treasury vouchers to help in such purchasing by families with no or insufficient tax obligations. These proposals have been strongly advocated, and a recent variant proposed tax credits not for private insurance premiums but for direct medical expenses. Such designs are usually without provisions for financing and would merely reduce income to the Treasury or increase demands on the Treasury. In addition, the voluntary and noncompulsory character of these programs—well advertised as a virtue—becomes difficult to reconcile with how federal general revenues are derived. These proposals have been advanced with little or no controls for the costs (eligible premiums or expenditures), quality standards, or system improvements, and as such they become invitations to the expenditure and cost dilemmas that were discussed earlier. It is doubtful that they could be found acceptable for meeting the national need.

Proposals for "catastrophic insurance" are presently being advocated—to provide protection against very high cost cases of medical need. Unfortunately, advocates of this approach do not seem to realize that requiring large deductibles or prior expenditures as a precondition to eligibility for catastrophic benefits inevitably biases the program toward those who can afford or already have broad basic insurance, that is toward those of considerable means.* Advocates of these proposals also seem to be unaware of—or indifferent to—the undesirable effects such proposals may be expected to have on overall medical care organization and cost—*inviting* expensive surgical, hospital, and other services, at least up to the qualifying deductible levels—further strengthening extremes of specialism, and not only contributing nothing to system improvement but even strengthening resistance to needed provisions. Such effects could be disastrous for the medical care scene, both from the proposed program *per se* and from its role in delaying more comprehensive action.

PROBLEMS OF FINANCING

Each proposal for national health insurance demands inspection of its probable costs, its financing, and its impact on the costs and financing of other sectors of the economy. There are serious questions that deserve serious answers—not merely the play of politically inspired numbers games or exercises in rhetoric or semantics. Above all else, these fiscal discussions require explicit clarity as to whether the costs and financing of a particular program refer to the *added* or *induced* costs of the proposal or to the continuing national costs and their financing, and—equally important—as to whether they refer only to initial program costs or to prospective costs, including both initiation and continuation of the program.

No major proposal presently advocated proposes a roll-back of medical care prices, costs, and expenditures to levels of previous years, and each proposal starts with the level of expenditure expected at the time of program implementation. At the current levels of expenditure, this would mean for fiscal year 1975-1976 about $139 billion for all health care services and about $124 billion for the personal health services, thus the added or subtracted costs of a newly operating program would affect these totals only by a small proportion of those amounts, if at all.

* For example, the "catastrophic" insurance benefits (like those in Medicare) in the program sponsored by Senators Long, Ribicoff, and others would be available to those who have already incurred medical expenses of at least $2,000 or have been hospitalized for at least 60 days, or satisfy both of these requirements.

Thus, for example, the Office of the Actuary, Social Security Administration, recently estimated total medical care expenditures (federal, state, and private) for the year 1975, assuming first that no national health insurance plan would be in effect and then, alternatively, for each of seven then-current national health care schemes under consideration.[2] With no new plan, the total cost was $103 billion; with the hypothecated programs the totals ranged from $107 billion to $116 billion, with subordinate items showing how much of the total would be within the scope of the plan and by how much expenditures financed from one source or another would be affected. The general concept for the comparisons was sound, but unfortunately the methodology was not altogether faultless. Since the study assumed uniform pricing for all programs and paid no discernible or adequate attention to built-in provisions for new system improvements or cost controls, the results were biased against programs that emphasized controls of both unit prices and utilization volumes. Also, being addressed to comparisons for only a single year, the study failed to account for program impacts on prospective costs, and thus treated with equal neglect proposals with provisions for containing cost escalations and those with provisions that would invite escalations. It is not difficult to demonstrate reversals in the comparative *prospective* program costs by taking into account such differences in the specifications.[3]

Sponsors of particular programs provide studies of their program costs, but in most cases these present only particular elements of the costs.* Perhaps the most common form of this practice is to show how much the program would require from federal general revenues, while disregarding other, vastly larger costs: how much it would leave as premiums to be paid by employers, employees, states, and others who come within the framework of the intended program; how much it would leave for out-of-pocket expenditures to be made by the insured patients by reason of noncoverage of services or for payment of deductibles or copayments for covered services; how much it would escalate costs for those who would be required to purchase private insurance; or how much it would be for costs incurred for the care of the poor or the near poor. In the case of catastrophic insurance proposals, the relatively low cost figure for the program—a few billion dollars a year initially—merely reflects that few would be served by the program. Those served would mainly be the fortunate or well-to-do, who could

*See, for example, data cited by Davis, Karen: National health insurance: benefits, costs, and consequences, The Brookings Institution, Washington, D.C., 1975, chapter 6, pp. 129-150.

afford insurance with deductibles that at current prices would cost about $8,000 to $15,000 in an individual case as a precondition of eligibility for medical and hospital benefits. Moreover, as indicated earlier, such a low cost figure would be taking no account of the much larger cost that would result if (as may be expected) the specifications of the programs invited widespread escalations in costs to reach the deductible amounts so that more cases would qualify for the insurance benefit.

Thus, a partial or limited proposal, or a part of a broader proposal, may *per se* have a seemingly small price tag; but if it adds to the current and prospective levels of national expenditures without effecting improvements in the system and without reasonably promising cost controls, it may cost too much. On the other hand, a comprehensive proposal that intends to provide comprehensive health care may have a relatively large price tag; but if it would provide the means to improve resources and delivery while financing current costs and also containing prospective cost escalations, its overall expenditure may nevertheless be sensible and acceptable. The seriousness of these considerations is evident from the following fiscal facts: the total national health care expenditures—$118.5 billion in fiscal year 1974-1975 (double what they were only 6 years before)—were still escalating at an annual rate of 13.9%, and the total is approaching $200 billion or more in the biennium 1978-1980. With a continuing double-digit rate of escalation, these expenditures threaten to increase from about 8.3% (one twelfth) of the gross national product toward 10% or even more.* And there is no end in sight to the steep escalation because there is no natural ceiling on what can be spent for health and medical care and because the forces for such escalation are inherent within the present medical care system. As expensive as intervention and cost containment are now, they will be more expensive in the future.

The health security program is especially useful to illustrate the problems of health care financing because it encompasses most health services without requiring deductibles or copayments. Initially this program will cover about 66% to 70% of all current expenditures for personal health services, having some limitations in dental and medicine utilization, long-term nursing home care, and nonmedical mental disease institutional maintenance. As medical availability increases, expansion of services in many of these areas is planned toward coverage of 80% to 90% of what is included in current expenditures.

Accordingly, the costs to be incurred under the health security pro-

*See footnote on p. 190.

gram would be initially about 66% to 70% of *the then current level of expenditures for personal health services;* and, in the course of time, they would move toward 80% or more of such a figure, escalated annually *not* by the recent and current rate for health care expenditures but by the same annual percentage as for the economy in general. The crucial proposal for adequate cost containment is that *medical care expenditures will be limited by the general economy's level,* not by the unrestrained demands of the physicians, the hospitals, and other services. It would reflect that the financing of the program's costs would be effected by a manifold of tax revenues designed to produce, for a trust fund, the annual amounts needed to budget for the expected levels of expenditure—those levels being determined by an adopted public policy rather than by the demands of the monopolistic medical care industry.

There are two other essential considerations in this formulation. The first is that the fiscal considerations assume no *net* increase in costs from instituting the program, except by reason of population growth or escalation in the economy generally. The feasible expansions of services for underserved fractions of the population and for underused categories of service can and would be offset by the savings and economies that the program design makes possible. Any doubts on this score can be resolved by considering the extreme savings that are evident from comprehensive prepaid group practices. While providing a substantially open-end spectrum of services, they reduce two of the most expensive and steeply escalating categories of service—inpatient hospital utilization (by about half) and common categories of surgery (by even more)—through more adequate provision of preventive care, ambulatory services, orderly referral arrangements from primary practitioners to specialists, consulting second opinions prior to nonemergency major surgery, and other provisions. These facts were formally recognized when Congress recently enacted the Health Maintenance Organization Act of 1973 (P.L. 93-222) and authorized funds to support development of such programs and other organizational variants of the group practice design. Some statisticians and actuaries have focused attention on increases in services and costs for the aged under Medicare and for the poor under Medicaid (both being programs with minimal cost controls and with almost uncontrolled guarantee of paying free market billings) and have applied these so-called induced increases to estimates for a total population. While adding, they have failed to subtract and have shown no faith in the potentials for cost controls that may be extended to the prevailing solo and fee-for-service pricing practices of physicians and the full-cost reimbursements of hospitals and other institutions despite the urgency of the need.

The second, a corollary of the first, is that the program's provisions for system improvement could come into play immediately after legislative enactment. Supported by appropriations from general revenues in the first 2 to 3 years between enactment and the effective dates for benefit availabilities, such measures would begin to effect augmentations in needed personnel and facilities, make a concerted effort to overcome and correct geographical and specialization maldistributions, and greatly accelerate the development of organized group practice. Such program activities would be continued, supported by formula-fixed allocations from the total health funds securely in permanently appropriated trust fund accounts. Thus, these innovative or special activities would be assured of supportive funds.

The health security program does not contemplate or require an increase in total expenditures for personal health services, for it involves a rerouting of expenditures through a proposed system of public financing. This rerouting is designed to come from private insurance, from noninsured private individual payments, and from local, state, and federal expenditures presently being incurred for various public programs like Medicaid and Medicare. The details of financing are controversial as program design seeks a justifiable and potentially acceptable manifold of taxes for a program to be supported by public financing. In light of the objective of universal population eligibility for the benefits of the program, the tax structures being explored are targeted to the national economy. In light of historic and current impacts of the costs of medical care and of their financing patterns, consideration is given to impacts on individuals, families and employers and on the general revenues of governments at all levels.*

The history of Social Security financing, the closest available precedent, argues for at least a limited role of payroll taxes as a relatively stable source of revenue and as a protection for "benefits as a right" and as a barrier against the injection of means tests. The national interest in health care and in the relief of governmental budgets from committed expenditures (for current ongoing and prospective programs that would be absorbed by the proposed program) dictates sharing from the general revenues of government—especially of the federal government—while intending to give fiscal relief to state and local governments for medical care programs like Medicaid that they administer and that they finance

*For analysis of source data, prospective costs, system for financing, calculation of tax rates, and other related topics, see Falk, I. S.: The costs of a national health security program and their financing, Hearings on National Health Insurance Proposals, Committee on Ways and Means, House of Representatives, Ninety-Second Congress, First Session, Oct. 28, 1971, Part 3, pp. 524-578 and 583-586.

in part or in whole. Overall, there is a desire to achieve equity as well as progressivity in the impacts of the taxes.

The tax structure first developed for the health security program (1971) proposed the following sources of the funds to flow into a permanently appropriated trust fund: 50% from federal general revenues (by formula appropriation) and 50% from health security taxes (75% from employers and 25% from individuals). After estimates were developed for the expected annual total dollar needs, these appropriations were applied to give tax rates* and to compare the potential impacts of the taxes with costs currently being met by the prospective taxpayers.

In light of a downturn in the economy, consideration has been given to three major changes in the financing of a health security program:

1. Reduction of the support from federal general revenues—from 50% to 33⅓%
2. Retention of the current Medicare taxes on employers and employees (justified since all of the Medicare benefits and costs would be absorbed into the health security program)
3. Raising the ceiling on earnings taxes, reflecting escalations in wages, salaries and payrolls, and the need for offset against reduction in the contributions from general revenues.

Many other details of tax structure are omitted here, especially since with delay in enactment of the program and the continuing escalation of medical care costs (at steeper rates than escalation of the tax bases), relationships have been changing so as to require reinspection of the proposed tax structure in general and of the tax rates in particular.

An important point to remember, however, is that tax supports for the health security program or for any similar program that is geared to *then current* level of costs and expenditures *is not proposing new gross expenditures* and—if equitably constructed—*is not proposing new fiscal demands on the economy or new burdens on taxpayers.* What is involved is mainly a *rechanneling* of expenditures already being made, while striving to make those expenditures more effective, more productive, and less burdensome. Equally important is a financing design that has built-in cost containment provisions for the medical care of the United States. The tax structure is intended to support comprehensive and quality health care for everybody and, at the same time, reduce what the nation would otherwise spend for medical care in the future.

*Rates, as slightly amended in 1975:

On employers' total payrolls	3.5%
On wage and salary receipts, up to $21,150 a year	1.0%
On self-employment income, up to $21,150 a year	2.5%
On nonearned income, up to $21,150 a year	2.5%

"STAGING" INITIAL DEVELOPMENT OF THE PROGRAM

The question is frequently raised whether a national health insurance as broad and inclusive as the health security program (or as any other major proposal) can be instituted on a single "effective date," or whether—in light of the size and complexity of the medical care industry—it would need to be implemented in stages. Some have raised the question on fiscal grounds and then advocated staging, being moved by concern about the potential rapidity of the consequent fiscal changes, especially about the rapidity with which a new demand would be placed on the federal general revenues. For example, if federal sharing were to be 50% of the total cost of the health security program, in fiscal year 1975-1976 that demand would have been about $38 billion. Were this sharing to be reduced to 33⅓%, it would become quite manageable, since in the same fiscal year health expenditures from federal general revenues were already $25 billion, and $11 billion to $12 billion were earmarked for federal general revenue expenditures which would be absorbed by the new program.* If Medicare taxes were retained in a year when the program cost $76 billion, earmarked health security and Medicare taxes would provide $53 billion, federal offsets would equal about $11 billion, and the net cost to federal general revenues would be about $12 billion.

Others who have proposed staging on the ground of "easing into" the program have been moved by other considerations, such as the magnitude and complexity of the program, technical difficulties, and needs for administrative staffing and educational preparations. Their proposals usually take the form of bringing various benefits into operational stages in successive steps. For example, in staging by population categories, the system would be applied to the aged and the disabled under Medicare or to mothers for maternity care and to children before being extended to others. The objection, obviously, is the inequity and inadequacy of such proposals for the national population as a whole, and the inability of such limited categorical approaches to provide the opportunity or the means for improving the organization and effectiveness of the medical care system as a whole.

Still others have proposed staging by categories of services: start with hospital coverage before undertaking to provide physicians' services, or *vice versa;* improve or extend Medicare, such as by lowering the age for eligibility by a few years before extending benefits to people of all ages; defer dental benefits, out-of-hospital prescription medicines,

*Medicare supports, from general revenues, a large share of federal Medicaid financing, expenditures for maternal and child health, crippled children's programs, and others.

or nursing home care until other benefits have become available. Such staging is objectionable on three grounds: (1) under Medicare, the public agency already has statutory authorizations and contractual and fiscal relations with a large proportion of all hospitals and related institutions and of all physicians and many other personal health providers—though Medicare covers only slightly more than 10% of the population—and the basis for national fiscal relations with those providers of care is already operational; (2) any staging of the major services invites further and potentially disastrous escalations of utilization and costs—for example, starting with hospital care but not physicians' services as prepaid benefits invites augmented "dumping" on the hospitals, as happened in Canada when they pursued this course[4]; or, starting with physicians' services but not hospital care invites continuation of the most steeply escalating medical care service, since hospital costs are already approaching 50% of total costs for personal health services and in recent years have been escalating at 12% to 18% per annum; (3) every such fractionation of coverage (by categories of service) reduces the capacity of the financing system to exert leverage toward effecting improvement of the system.

In short, staging or phasing-in of benefits—unless most carefully designed—could operate to defeat the duality of objectives: to effect rational and adequate financing of the needed services *and* to effect improvements and cost containment for the system. To the contrary, a carefully designed staging process could provide a basis for initial program *cost controls* without damage to the program objectives, if effected through some limitations on particular service benefits so as (1) not to seriously damage the value of the benefits and (2) to be readily removable when no longer justified on grounds of costs.

CONCLUSION

This discussion of financing and control of medical care costs started with "crisis" and proceeded toward means of achieving resolution. There is urgency in the need for constructive action because the rates of escalation of these costs and the absence of any ceiling to which they can rise threaten the very survival of our system of medical care.

The fiscal problems are at the center of controversy, but they do not stand alone. Cost control and financing that are both adequate and equitable can be achieved only if they are also means for effecting major improvements in availability and delivery of personal health services. These are separate but intertwined objectives because only the power of the fiscal resources can overcome the resistance of vested interests against substantial changes in the system itself. Exhortations for voluntary undertakings, the institution of new but limited categorical service programs, reliance on regulatory controls by governmental and professional agencies, and consumer outcries about inadequacies of needed services and against steeply rising costs have been ineffective. Indeed, they have been largely exercises in futility for the more than four decades since the course of developments toward the present state of medical care was first foreseen.[5,6] Continuation of this impasse is not likely to be acceptable much longer. It would therefore be better for the United States to deal with this "crisis" now through a carefully considered program of dimension and design suited to the need rather than through hastily improvised or emergency measures later.

Of the program proposals now being considered by Congress, only the health security program was designed in response to identified needs and without major dilutions through compromises to avoid the resistance of those who have comfort in the *status quo.* It proposes a partnership of governmental financing and private provision of services. It intends system improvements for adequacy and quality of care for the population as a whole simultaneously with cost controls and with financing through national resources. Its fiscal demands would be feasible because they depend mainly on rerouting expenditures already being made rather than on incurring new expenditures.

There are representatives, especially from the medical profession, the hospitals, and other provider groups, who counsel moderation, voluntary effort, and continuing reliance on the marketplace. But these counsels of caution are from those basically content with the *status quo* and with their dominance in the existing system, reflecting policies that have been accepted for decades and that have not proved to be counsels of wisdom.

In the presently troubled political scene, with the economy in serious difficulty, it is not clear what measures may be expected through congressional action or how soon. If, as it appears despite disagreements, there is nearly a consensus in public opinion that the medical care system needs broad governmental intervention now, it is to be hoped that the actions to be undertaken will be determined not by compromises for political convenience but by decisions on needed public policy for the health of the people of the United States.

REFERENCES

1. Falk, I. S.: Financing for the reorganization of medical care services and their delivery, Milbank Mem. Fund Q. **50**(4, Part 2): 191-221, 1972.
2. Estimated health expenditures under national health insurance bills, a report to the Congress, July 1974.

3. Woodcock, Leonard: National health insurance, Hearings of the Subcommittee on Health, Committee on Ways and Means, Washington, D.C., Nov. 5, 1975.
4. Andreopoulos, Spyros, editor: National health insurance: can we learn from Canada? The Sun Valley Forum on National Health, Inc., New York, 1975, John Wiley & Sons.
5. Medical Care for the American People: The Final Report of the Committee on the Costs of Medical Care, Chicago, 1932, University of Chicago Press. (Reprinted 1972, U.S. Department of Health, Education, and Welfare, Community Health Service.)
6. Falk, I. S., Rorem, C. Rufus, and Ring, Martha D.: The costs of medical care, Chicago, 1933, University of Chicago Press.

13

Legislative realities of national health insurance

EDWARD M. KENNEDY

■ Senator Kennedy outlines the present health care problems in the United States: a cost inflation of over 13% a year, lack of coverage for 40 million Americans, and lack of health professionals in 5,000 American communities. The Senator constructs a program of legislative recommendations that involve universal coverage, emphasis on preventive care, provisions for continuing health education and national licensure, and funds for attracting health professionals to medically indigent areas. These legislative recommendations would also ensure that the United States would evolve a unique but cohesive health care system, a system that guarantees that the federal government does not own our hospitals, employ our physicians, assign patients to physicians, make medical judgments, or operate another monolithic federal agency.

In the United States today, medical care is in crisis because the present methods of getting and paying for health care are dangerously near total collapse.

Americans are spending too much for care. The quality of care is not what it should be. The care is not available to many who need it most. Present health insurance pays less than one third of the health bill for those covered, and millions are not covered.

The best indicator of overspending is that today the average American spends 1 month's pay for health care, a considerably higher total than is spent by the average citizen of any other industrial country.

One major reason for the overspending results from the nation's failure to control runaway costs. In fiscal year 1974, for example, total health costs in the United States were $104 billion, an increase of 10% over fiscal year 1973. This was during a period of price controls. Following the lifting of controls on April 30, 1974, inflation of health costs accelerated at an annual rate of 18%, much faster than even the general inflation.

During the previous 5 years, total health costs for the country increased an average of 12.8% a year. The total cost increase during the past 8 years was over $56.1 billion—from $47.9 billion in fiscal year 1967 to $104 billion in fiscal year 1974. Thus, the nation's total health bill jumped well over 100% in 8 years.

The lack of quality and availability of health care is indicated by America's failure to keep up with other industrial countries in such important health care indices as infant mortality, maternal mortality, and life expectancy. By all these measurements, the United States ranks farther behind other industrial countries than it did 15 or 20 years ago.

America's public-private partnership in health has never been an easy relationship in the past, and it is not today. The relationship is full of tension, because it is never easy in our society to draw rigid lines or build high walls between the public and private sectors. However, it is increasingly evident that after more than 30 years of trying, private health insurance has failed to come even close to meeting the nation's need for adequate coverage, since it pays less than one third of the health costs. The rest either comes out of the individual's pocket or is paid by the government.

After 30 years of trying, private health insurance has failed to provide universal coverage. About 40 million Americans have no health insurance. Millions of additional working people and their families do not have the security of knowing their hospital and medical costs will be paid during layoffs and periods of unemployment.

In order to begin to resolve these problems, legislation is necessary to assure Americans of health security, even as legislation of the 1930s assured them Social Security. The basic role of a legislative program would be to establish a broad system for health care in the United States, not just to set up a method of paying the bills for doctors, hospitals, and other health services.

It would be equally concerned with making sure health services are available to all Americans, improving the quality of care, and holding the costs of the care within reasonable limits.

The program would be a working partnership between the public and private elements of our society that are concerned with health care. Care would be provided by physicians, hospitals, and other private providers in much the same way it is done today, but it would be financed through the government.

Under the program, the funds made available would finance and budget the essential costs of good health care for all Americans. These funds would also build a new capacity to bring adequate, efficient, and reliable health care to all.

This legislation, in other words, would provide every American with enough insurance to purchase health care as needed; it would also assure that good health services would actually be made available to each of us where and when we need them, and in a form that we can understand and use.

THE HEALTH CARE CRISIS

There are many aspects to this crisis in health care in America. But the aspect known best by every American is the crisis in costs.

The crisis in costs

Hospital costs have risen. Doctor bills have risen. And insurance premiums have risen to keep pace. Every American family feels the pressure of this inflation. The average wage earner works 1 month a year just to pay health care and health insurance bills.

And there is no limit in sight. There is nothing at present built into our health care system that will assure an end to this inflation. Unless the United States takes action to slow this progress, health care will cost Americans more and more each year.

The answer to this problem is not to cut back on benefits, to raise insurance premiums even more, or to simply offer more insurance to more Americans. The answer is to reform our health care system and bring these costs under control.

The key to cost control is to couple effective budgeting mechanisms throughout the health care system with expanded and improved services. The lesson of Medicare and Medicaid is that attempts to offer piecemeal solutions to segments of the population without attending to the overall system results in increased inflation, which robs Americans of much of the intended benefit. Effective budgeting depends on the federal government becoming the health insurance agent for the nation.

This system would allow us to pursue two principal objectives. First, it would assure the same comprehensive coverage to all Americans. Second, since resources are limited, and health does compete with other social goods, it would enable limits to be set on the resources spent on health. It would make the most of these limited resources by controlling costs, by developing a more efficient health care system, and by more wisely allocating health dollars among health services.

Costs can only be controlled and rational allocations made if public budgets are established that focus public scrutiny and debate on the key question of the allocation of scarce resources. This approach forces both Congress and the taxpayer to weigh increased benefits against increased taxes and to make responsible decisions.

Ultimately, I believe American consumers know there are no "free rides." Consumers know they will have to pay for health care, whether in the form of insurance premiums or taxes or dollars from their pockets at the time they need the care. The real question involves keeping these costs down to levels that both the worker and the government can afford. There is no way to use the private health insurance industry to control costs. There is no way the nation can use this industry as a lever to encourage change and reform in the health care system. It is for these reasons that the federal government should be the health insurance agent and cost control mechanism in a national program of health security. The billions of dollars that are currently paid to insurance companies would be paid to the federal government under the program. Likewise, since this program covers all essential health services without deductibles, coinsurance, or limitations, billions of dollars that Americans currently pay to physicians, hospitals, laboratories, dentists, drugstores, and other providers would also be paid to the government.

The government would collect these funds and serve as Americans' agent in paying these bills. Americans will pay no more health insurance premiums, few or no physicians' bills, few or no hospital bills, fewer dental bills, fewer drug bills, and less of many other health care costs.

Instead, Americans will pay taxes geared to their income. The average family, in the early years of the program, will pay the government roughly the same amount for health care that it is currently paying insurance companies, physicians, and others. The difference will be that the average family will have a far better insurance policy and will get broader services for its money.

The crisis of disorganization

But the health care crisis in America is not a matter of inflation and rising costs alone. The crisis is also evident to the 5,000 American communities that have no physician, and to patients who wait in city hospital emergency rooms 6 or 8 hours for help because they have no physician or because they cannot reach their physician after hours. Legislation can establish funds, planning procedures, and incentives to build accessible facilities to attract health professionals to every community —and to allow imaginative professionals to offer health care in new ways, designed to meet the special needs of these rural and urban communities.

Health security legislation can encourage health professionals to reorient their efforts toward preventative care and to offer more tightly organized forms of health care to Americans who choose it. It does this by building in long-term economic incentives to professionals who start health maintenance organizations, foundations, and other new forms of care—as well as by offering the resources needed to underwrite the start-up and initial operating losses of some organizations.

The crisis in quality of care

The crisis is evident, too, to Americans who suffer needlessly because they cannot get to the skilled services of facilities they need, or because they receive less than the best quality care. The fact is that the quality of health care varies greatly in America. Some studies suggest that there is too much unnecessary or ill-advised surgery performed and that there are too many missed diagnoses. This is not necessarily the result of greed, incompetence, or carelessness. It is simply that the United States is trying to offer sophisticated twentieth century medical care through nineteenth century organizations.

Health professionals are, for the most part, still licensed on a once-and-for-all basis, while medical knowledge has literally exploded during recent decades. Continuing education of physicians, whose training was completed decades ago, has not been required—and more importantly, minimal efforts have been made to establish continuing programs to meet these physicians' particular needs and problems.

A health security program should establish national licensure and continuing education requirements—as well as the resources for conducting these programs. A national commission on the quality of care in the Department of Health, Education, and Welfare could be established to gather statistics, establish guidelines, and set standards of quality based on the advice of health professionals, and it could strengthen local peer review organizations to review services in their areas in the light of these standards. The program could also establish referral requirements to assure that a variety of treatments would be considered before subjecting a patient to lengthy or costly procedures. All of these features are aimed at providing incentives and resources to health professionals to reorganize health care in a way consistent with the enormous complexity of modern medicine—and assuring every American the best health care possible.

The crisis of inadequate health insurance

But perhaps the crisis in health care is most obvious to Americans whose health insurance has run out, who cannot get insurance because of their medical history, or who simply cannot afford to buy good insurance. Many Americans of all incomes have been bankrupted by health care costs that continue after their insurance runs out. They then join the ranks of Americans whose medical history makes it impossible to buy good insurance at all, and millions of other Americans of low income, who are not eligible for group plans and cannot afford decent insurance.

For these Americans with no decent insurance, every illness can turn into a financial disaster. Since every penny comes out of already limited incomes, they weigh every decision as to whether or not to seek a physician—and sometimes they wait too long and suffer needless pain.

There is no way to tell how many children have grown up in America with needlessly twisted limbs, dulled minds, or other handicaps simply because fear of the cost kept their parents away from the physician for too long. There is no way to tell how many Americans suffer needless pain and even early death simply because good health costs too much. It is clear, however, that these things can and do happen all too often for a country as advanced as America.

The problem is the hopelessly fragmented health insurance system that encourages insurance companies, in the name of profit, to exclude Americans who need care the most—or to limit their policies to the most profitable benefits that the companies can market. This crazy-quilt system also frustrates the providers of care. Physicians and hospitals are faced with providing expensive services to millions of Americans whose insurance may or may not pay—knowing that if the insurance does not come through, there is little hope of the patient being able to pay the bill.

Providers deserve fair fees for their services. The answer to the health insurance dilemma is not to require the provider to offer free care, but rather to create an insurance system that assures that every American is covered for basic health care. If we insist that health professionals offer help to everyone who needs it, and Americans do insist on that, then we should make sure that every American is covered by an insurance policy that will pay the provider a fair fee for services.

Insurance coverage should not influence the provider's method of treatment. Too often providers are encouraged to hospitalize a patient so that insurance will cover the cost. Insurance should be comprehensive enough to cover whatever course of treatment the physician considers medically appropriate.

The health security program would assure this by covering all Americans with comprehensive health insurance coverage from the federal government. If this legislation is passed:

No American family will be bankrupted by the cost of care
No American will be kept from needed care for fear of the cost
Physicians and hospitals will not be forced to write off bills or hire bill collectors. They will bill one source on one form and know that they will be paid.
Providers will be freed to offer care in the most medically accepted way, without regard to insurance coverage.

This program would free the patient to seek health care, and it would free the provider to be a physician rather than an accountant.

Crisis in medical research

Equally critical choices must be made for the future in the area of medical research. For 20 years the federal government has invested heavily in biomedical research. This aspect of the public-private partnership in health has produced the finest medical research in the world. This growth of medical knowledge is unparalleled, and Americans take well-deserved pride in these achievements.

However, under the pressures of the tighter federal budget, more and more public dollars are being directed now to research cancer and heart disease, while basic and applied research face diminishing support.

Public funding of medical research continues to be based partly on the legitimate public hope that cures for specific diseases can be found, so that the eternal longing of the public—to be spared from the crippling and killing effects of illness and disease—can be fulfilled.

In many cases, research has yielded sophisticated new technologies against disease. But often, the technologies are only half successful. They are literally too expensive to provide to everyone in need. Too little emphasis has been placed, for example, on research in the prevention and causes of heart disease. Instead too much emphasis has been placed on developing expensive surgical procedures to ease the patient who already has the disease. Too often in medicine and in other areas, both dollars and priorities have been directed toward picking up the pieces, instead of toward preventing the fall.

Of course, research results cannot be commanded or even planned with any real precision. It is not the government's role nor the intent of Congress to command biomedical research in this way. Instead, the role of government is to set priorities for spending the limited public funds available.

Within the area of funds for health research, the dilemma of the budget is to set priorities in a way that encourages payoffs against disease, without depriving basic research of the freedom to pursue its goals, wherever they may lead. This is an area that requires cooperation, in order to strengthen the creative, continuing partnership of government and medical research.

America's health professionals are the backbone of health care in the nation; none of the health care problems in America will ever be solved without their strong and creative efforts.

The health care crisis in the United States is as apparent to providers as to patients. Providers are concerned with disorganization of services, with quality of care, with inadequate and fragmented insurance coverages, and with the shortage and maldistribution of health professionals and facilities. These problems frustrate providers' attempts to serve the people who need care the most. They involve the providers in a tangle of cumbersome referrals and cross-referrals and occasionally leave them without proper facilities and associates. The insurance red tape frequently turns the physician into a bookkeeper.

The health security program does not intend to take responsibility for reform away from the providers. Rather, it would offer providers the incentives and resources they need to bring about the reform both they and their patients so badly need. Indeed, the program would create a lever, which I hope providers would help to use responsibly, to bring about change.

Let me offer a series of guarantees to protect the fundamental principles important to American physicians.

The first guarantee is that the federal government in the United States must not own the hospitals or employ the physicians. I do not want to build a British health care system in the United States. I do not want socialized medicine in America.

I believe in maintaining the free enterprise system in this country and in American medicine. In fact, I would like to see even more variety and more competition in the health care system between different forms of health care. I look forward to a day when physicians can practice in solo practice, in HMOs, in medical foundations, in large groups, or in any other way that is efficient and beneficial to the patients and physicians, too. It is possible to create a uniquely American health care system that will preserve free enterprise for the physicians, and still offer patients the financial support and adequate care they need.

The second guarantee is that Americans must not be assigned as patients to one physician or another, or to one organization or another for their health care. Americans should have maximum choice in this regard. Only in this way can a system be produced that is fair to physicians and patients alike.

My third guarantee is that the federal government must not make medical judgments or interfere in the clinical decisions between physicians and patients. Physicians must be encouraged to take the actions necessary to assure Americans that they are receiving the finest possible care that American medicine can offer.

The fourth guarantee is that an overarching federal agency telling every area and community in this nation exactly how to offer health care must not be created. What must be done is to set national guidelines and standards, within which local agencies can develop the best possible health care programs for the physicians and patients in their areas.

I subscribe completely to these guarantees, and I am confident that they will be at the heart of any national health care legislation that Congress may enact.

The United States has the potential for higher levels of health than any other nation because of our far vaster health care resources and the brilliant record of American medical research. I believe the health security program is a uniquely American approach to organizing health care that will capitalize on these strengths and preserve the basic values of physician and patient alike.

The health care crises of high costs, maldistribution of resources, inconsistent quality of care, inadequate insurance coverage, and conflicting future directions of medical research are undeniable, but can be met. To meet them is the goal of legislation in health care today.

14

The Canadian health care system—its impact on the health of the society

MARC LaLONDE

■ Since the introduction of the National Health Care Scheme in Canada in 1968, maternal mortality has dropped from 27 to 11 per 100,000 live births; infant mortality, which was only 5% lower than the United States in 1968, is now 14% lower. In addition, the physician to population ratio has gone from 1 to 769 to 1 to 618, with substantial increases in the number of primary care physicians in rural areas. Personal health care costs in Canada between 1971 and 1973 declined from 6.5% to 6.1% of the gross national product, compared to a stable 6.4% in the United States. To most Canadians and to the Canadian federal government, the initial objective of universal accessibility of medical care has been reached, and new directions are beginning to be undertaken—directions aimed at prevention rather than sickness care.

To an outside observer trying to grasp the total Canadian reality, Canada appears as a complex mosaic, made up of a variety of elements —geographical, cultural, social and political. We in Canada have learned to live with this phenomenon, with pride even, since it represents one of our greatest national assets. This richness and diversity of social components making up the Canadian nation do, however, bring with them certain peculiar constraints.

On the political level, for example, the provinces have considerable power. In fact, in some fields, such as education, these powers are virtually absolute. The political history of the Canadian nation, therefore, is in large part a history of seeking and maintaining the best possible balance between the political power of the provinces and that of the central government.

Despite the decentralization of political power in Canada, multiculturalism, linguistic duality, the vastness and diversity of the geography—centrifugal forces that are more significant than in many other countries—Canada is a country with a very strong feeling of belonging and of national identity. This very diversity is something distinctively Canadian and a source of pride.

In my opinion, the main force that has gradually shaped and unified the country, while preserving the diversity, is the particular style of federalism that is ours. This style is characterized by a flexible but energetic leadership on the part of the central government. I believe the action of the federal government in the health field constitutes one of the major elements that has contributed to the shaping of the united society that we are constantly seeking to create and improve.

I should like to review how the Canadian health policy has developed, especially in the last 20 years, and attempt to project what the future policies will be. In this way I hope to give an idea of the leadership role exercised by the federal government and the influence this role can have both on the health of Canadians and, more broadly, on the structure of Canada. It is important to evaluate our health policy and its development within this broader sociopolitical context, for health policy does not operate in a vacuum; it is greatly influenced by the broader context.

HISTORICAL PERSPECTIVE

In any examination of the evolution of Canadian health policies to the present day, it must be remembered that at the time of Confederation in 1867, the role of the state in health care delivery was virtually nonexistent.

In the 70 years that followed, state involvement remained at a minimal level, and what little form it did take was as a sort of benevolent paternalism. From 1928 on—the year that a House of Commons committee started to examine the possibility of state run health insurance—the federal government became interested in this question, and various attempts were made to set up health insurance schemes.

It was, however, only after World War II, when there was a rise in the cost of personal health care and when an increasingly powerful and complex technology emerged, that concrete decisions could be made to assure all Canadians of access to personal health care.

In the Canadian constitutional context, the prime responsibility for health matters rests with the provinces. On the other hand, as I mentioned earlier, the federal government has always felt a major responsibility for national unity and has always seen uniformity of social security programs and equality of opportunities for all Canadians as one of the cornerstones of this national unity. It was for this reason that the federal government did not hesitate to take the lead in the implementation of uniform hospital and medical care insurance programs across the whole country as soon as it became clear that a number of provinces were ready to follow the example of Saskatchewan and adopt such programs. Saskatchewan was the first government to adopt insurance programs—a hospital insurance program in 1946 and medical care insurance in 1962. However, it was naturally expected that the federal government would assist in this field. One important objective was to assure the development of a health care system homogeneous and coherent from one province to the other and equally beneficial to all Canadians. This orientation was based on the principle that access to health services, in particular medical and hospital care, is a basic *right* of *all* Canadians.

Cost sharing was the instrument used by the federal government to assume this leadership and to realize acceptable uniformity of programs. At the federal level the government offered to pay, to those provinces setting up public programs meeting certain requirements, approximately half of the cost of the services rendered in the provinces. Such federal legislation was put into effect in 1958 for hospital services and in 1968 for medical services. The federal requirements in these legislations were basically that the programs should cover everybody, that they should offer a complete range of services, that they be publicly administered, and that the benefits be transferable from one province to the other in the case of interprovincial migration.

As a result of these initiatives by the Canadian government, the entire population of Canada is at present insured within public insurance plans for both hospital costs and physicians' fees. The federal contributions for these plans come from general revenue. Sources of provincial contributions differ from province to province—coming from general revenue, sales taxes, insurance premiums, or some combination of these. The coverage offered is total, in that there is no financial limit to insured services as long as they are medically required. Also, at present, there is no payment required from the patient at the time of treatment.

In addition to these basic medical and hospital care programs that are cost shared through joint federal-provincial programs, each province has added other services on an individual priority basis, such as home care, community health centers, dental care for children, ambulance service, prescriptions for older people, and so on. The nature of these complementary services varies from one province to another.

THE HEALTH OF THE NATION

What has been accomplished as a result of these programs? It is difficult sometimes to measure the impact of a major public program because methods of measuring the success or failure are not precise. The various mortality rates are commonly used but these do not depend solely on the adequacy of health care.

There have been some dramatic improvements in certain indicators. Maternal mortality dropped from 27 per 100,000 live births in 1968 to 11 in 1973, which is one of the lowest in the world. During the same period, our infant mortality dropped from 20.8 per 1,000 live births to 15.5, bypassing the United Kingdom, Australia, New Zealand, and France in ranking. In 1973 infant mortality in Canada was 14% lower than in the United States, while in 1968 it was only 5% lower. These marked changes, of which we are very proud, are not unrelated to the considerable improvement in both physical and financial access to necessary care, which resulted when the medical insurance program was added to the preexisting hospital insurance program.

In addition to this, the hospital insurance plan solved the acute financial problems that were being experienced by many hospitals in the late 1950s, and this more stable and more rational financing contributed to a marked improvement in the quality of hospital care.

Moreover, despite predictions that medical health insurance would provoke a mass exodus of Canadian physicians to other countries and would dry up immigration of foreign physicians, not to mention decreasing the attraction of medicine as a career, the number of physicians has in fact increased since 1968, the year the scheme was inaugurated. This growth rate has been much higher than the general growth rate of the population. In 1968 the physician to population ratio was 1 to 769. By January 1974 this ratio had become 1 physician to 618 inhabitants. This surpassed the optimum ratio of 1 to 650 that the 1964 Royal Commission on Health Services had set as a goal for 1991. In fact, there is presently concern among some people (including physicians themselves) that there could be a surplus of physicians in the coming years. Provincial governments have become concerned about the rate of growth in the number of physicians, and measures have now been taken to severely control the immigration of physicians. Even though there are still problems concerning the distribution of physicians throughout the country and between specialties, medical care insurance has made a great contribution to this situation in that now the practice of medicine has become economically viable in any location where the population is sufficient to justify the presence of a physician.

For example, the physician to population ratio of Newfoundland (the poorest province) increased from approximately 1 to 1,500 the year before Medicare to almost 1 to 900 in 1974, 5 years after Medicare. In addition to an improvement in the overall supply of physicians, the province has more practitioners settling in smaller communities. In the last 2 years alone, the physician community of St. John's (the province's capital, a university city with a medical school) increased by only 5%, whereas in rural Newfoundland, during the same period, the rate of increase was more than 30%; so that at present, the number of doctors in rural Newfoundland is roughly equal to that of St. John's. The other "have-not" provinces and the Northern Territories have also shown major increases, in general substantially greater than the richer provinces.

COST

Of course this progress has not been made without cost. In fact, the phenomenon of increased health costs has been a general one in all industrialized countries over the past 20 years, even in those without public health insurance. Canada has not escaped this; in the period from 1960 to 1971 the cost of institutional care and medical care rose from 3.7% to 5.3% of the gross national product. The financial involvement of the government in the dispensation of these two types of care has no doubt contributed to the government's major concern with these unexpected increases.

Over the past 6 years the federal government has responded to this new challenge. In particular, two study reports were completed to serve as guidelines for discussion and implementation by the provinces. The first report was by the Committee on Costs of Health Care Services,[6] which identified major factors of excessive costs in the system and made recommendations on methods of financial restraint and control. The second, a report on community health centers,[2] gave important emphasis to the establishment of comprehensive ambulatory care facilities as a means to control costs and to develop low cost alternatives to hospital services, which would simultaneously improve the availability and accessibility of personal health services at the community level. Many of the recommendations of these reports are now being implemented at the provincial level.

In the early 1970s, the problem of increasing costs became less acute. For example, in 1971 personal health care services in Canada represented 6.5% of the gross national product. Provisional figures for 1974 show that personal health care costs in Canada comprised 6.7% of the gross national product. During this time, however, personal health care costs in the United States rose to almost 8.0% of the gross national product.

More recently, largely as a result of present inflationary pressures, the price of personal health care has again begun to rise. During the fiscal year 1974-1975 expenses for the hospital insurance plan were 24.3% more than in the previous year, and an additional rise of close to 22.5% for the fiscal year 1975-1976 is predicted. All evidence indicates that the government must take steps to slow down this skyrocketing of costs. In fact the health insurance programs are sufficiently well developed that a limit to their growth rate is justified. Indeed this is the objective of legislation recently passed by Parliament that establishes a ceiling on the rate of increase of federal financial contributions to the medical care program in the coming years.

With this in mind, the federal government has entered into negotiations with the provinces, which will eventually produce a redefinition of the agreements between the provinces and the central government regarding the financing of health insurance programs. The objective is the greatest possible cost effectiveness of health services given to the population, primarily through the substitution of less costly alternatives to medical and hospital care, wherever this is possible without detriment to the quality of care. Such alternative services include home care, services provided at the community health centers, nursing homes, convalescent hospitals, and the like. To attain this objective of effectiveness, it is our intention to provide the system with more flexibility in order to allow—and even encourage—the provinces to develop these substitutes for higher cost care as their needs and priorities dictate. In the long run this is one of the essential means of controlling costs.

Even though the federal government does not intend to decrease its financial support to the health insurance programs, the objective of greater flexibility will most likely lead to greater autonomy and latitude in this area being given the provinces.

The initial objective of the federal government, at the time of its adoption of the measures to establish health insurance schemes, was to make medical and hospital care financially accessible to all Canadians. This objective has been reached, and the schemes concerned are so much a part of the total social organization that a backward step such as stopping or reducing these programs is totally unthinkable. At the present time no group in Canada would suggest or even contemplate such a backward step. No political party or health professional group and certainly no members of the public are advocating such a retrogressive policy.

The federal government is proud of these universal health insurance schemes and is proud that they are publicly administered. If the government had the whole thing to do over again, knowing what is now known, it would again choose universal public plans, since they seem to be the most efficient way to ensure health services. The collection ratio for Canadian private health insurers in 1969 was $1.25 for every dollar of benefits paid. By 1973 this ratio had increased to $1.55 for every dollar in benefits paid. As for the United States, one report indicated that in the health insurance industry in 1972 the collection ratio was $1.22 for every dollar in benefits paid.[1]

In contrast to the data from the private sector, 97.7¢ of each dollar spent by Canadians in the form of taxes or health insurance premiums in 1973 went to pay hospitalization or medical care costs. In this case the collection ratio is only $1.03 for every dollar in benefits paid.

I do not wish to accuse private insurers of inefficiency. However, they are constrained by all sorts of expenditures such as premium collection, commissions, and maintenance of a cash reserve that the government simply does not have. In Canada private health insurers are still important for certain risks such as loss of income, dental fees, drugs, and private hospital rooms. But for an essential public service such as health care, where universal accessibility is important, public health insurance is the best answer.

FUTURE ROLE OF THE FEDERAL GOVERNMENT

Since the initial objective of these schemes—universal accessibility—has been reached and there is no danger of it not continuing, the federal government deems it compatible with its role of leadership in this field to now transfer a larger part of the responsibility for the development of these programs to the provinces. Indeed, the government does not consider its role of leadership as being connected to a specific way of administering programs or to any specific program; rather it identifies it as a philosophy of action and a form of presence that must be maintained in the name of national unity and equality of opportunity for all Canadians.

My remarks must in no way be interpreted as bringing down the curtain on federal government participation in the health care field. On the contrary, the future will, I believe, bring about a broadening of the federal government's actions and role in the health care field. It is this future that I wish to describe now.

Once the considerable effort had been made to set up the health insurance schemes and see them through a breaking-in period, and once it was obvious that these schemes were on solid footings, it was necessary to have a period of reflection and evaluation to examine the total situation in the health care area. This led to the publication of a working document entitled "A New Perspective on the Health of Canadians," which was tabled in 1974 before the House of Commons.[5]

The analysis contained in this document is based on a health field concept that is made up of four broad elements, namely the health care delivery system, life-styles, environment, and human biology. Over the last 15 years Canada has made considerable strides in the first of these elements—the health care delivery system.

Indeed, the analysis of the epidemiological data made in this report shows clearly that it is not weaknesses in the health care delivery system that affects morbidity and mortality in Canada but rather the life-styles and the physical and social environment. Here I am referring, for example, to poor eating habits, excessive use of alcohol, cigarette smoking, lack of exercise, careless driving, the urban environment, the work environment, and so forth.

The fact that these have now become the dominant factors in explaining the nature and level of mortality and morbidity in Canada constitutes the basic premise of this working document. It is on this premise that the government of Canada has based its desire to now develop a health promotion policy, a policy aimed at improving life-style and environment. Work in this new direction has begun with the same determination and the same general objectives of improving the overall health of Canadians that initiated the effort 20 years ago to seek to supply Canadians with easy access to personal health care. The leadership role of the central government therefore evolves as circumstances change and especially as certain stages are reached, but the ultimate objectives and the underlying philosophy remain constant and unchanging.

The social implications of this orientation or new perspective are, however, extremely important, and it is essential that they be fully recognized before comprehensive policy in this new direction is inaugurated.

THE MOVE TOWARD PRIMARY PREVENTION HEALTH POLICIES

At the risk of oversimplifying the situation, it can be said that up until now, as stated in the *New Perspective,* the bulk of our efforts in the health field, especially since the introduction of the hospital care and medical care systems, has been to offer services to people who are already sick and thus within the health care delivery system. The working document suggests that while this effort should be continued, the time has come to consider some innovative approaches—approaches that are not directed principally toward people who are already ill but toward the population in general, which for the major part can be considered as healthy.[5]

In addressing the issue of the population at large, and especially people who are *not sick,* it is necessary to face the basic or fundamental reality that these persons are not usually, at least as users, inside the health care delivery system (the sickness system). Consequently, they are not persons on whom the health care delivery system—the system the government controls—has an easy direct influence. In any event, the influence that the system in its present organization can have on people who are not sick, and thus are within other systems, is negligible compared to its influence and even control on people who are sick.

This means that if the basic orientation proposed by the working document is to be followed, namely to develop primary prevention aimed at environmental and life-style factors contributing to illness and death, two approaches must be considered. First is the direct approach addressed to the individual, trying to modify certain behavior or life-style patterns. Second is an indirect approach through the other systems in which people are integrated, or which have influence on people. These other systems, including work place, urban environment, education, transport, and so on, over which the health system has no direct control, would be persuaded to include health aspects in decisions relating to their regulatory, administrative, or legislative context.

It is evident, then, what a broad and complex problem is being confronted. When we in the health field speak of modifying life-styles, we are speaking ultimately of influencing values and, indeed, the total culture. When we speak of influencing systems other than the health care system—that is, the other government institutions or private institutions that control the environment—we are speaking of affecting the entire social organization.

In fact, the type of change that it now seems necessary to make resembles a cultural revolution much more than an administrative reform. For example, when, in *A New Perspective,* I invite my fellow Canadians to take personal responsibility for the maintenance and development of their own health, what I am proposing to them is a profound change of attitude. In fact, most of us have abdicated that responsibility for our health, passing it over to the extemely complex and specialized health care delivery system. In doing this we have, moreover, followed the example of the approach our industrial society has adopted to integrate technology in almost all areas of human activity. A whole series of specialized systems has been created, all of them of considerable size and with considerable power over the individual. I refer to such elements as the extremely compartmentalized activities making up the systems of work, recreation, education, transport, and, of course, health care.

So that their administrators may have greater satisfaction and peace of mind, these systems are more or less closed ones, inaccessible and isolated, to a great extent, from one another. The systems divide up the fields of activity or territories among themselves by establishing control on distinct portions of a person's life.

This is how the health care system has, in industrialized societies, established its control over individuals when they are sick. The most characteristic example of this is the phenomenon of hospitalization. Hospitalization requires that individuals accept opting out of all the other systems (work, recreation, transport, and so on) in which they normally operate and which control them to give themselves over to the health care system. This system will exercise a control over them that will be at least as rigid as was the control of the other systems, dictating when to wake up, when to go to sleep, and what to eat. It even supplies garments that will identify them as sick people and decides what examinations and treatments they will have.

It is, all in all, a system that bestows enormous power on those who control it and that often gives the impression that it operates much more along the lines of therapeutic logic or administrative logic than in consideration of the human needs that it must meet. What, in fact, is proposed is to protect the technical excellence of this system while placing it back within the human perspective.

This must not, however, be interpreted as a criticism specifically directed at the health care system. What applies to the health care system also applies to other systems. Ivan Illich's not entirely unfounded criticism of the education system[3] is no less severe than his criticism of the health care delivery system.[4] What goes on in the transport field is also an illustration of this domination of technology over human beings.

THE INDIVIDUAL AND HEALTH

Those who travel enough realize that nowadays they no longer really travel. What they do is get transported from one place to another. To get from point A to point B, especially using modern airports, they are first directed, probably by a moving walkway, to a "container" and are unloaded into the cabin of a giant aircraft (which is really nothing more than a flying movie theater). This will deposit them into another "container," which will take them to another air terminal, practically identical to the first. From there they take a bus and are deposited at the door (or probably in the underground garage) of an airtight, air-conditioned hotel like a hundred others they have been deposited at in a hundred other cities. All this is far from the old notion of travel with its adventure, exploration, discovery, contact with nature, possibilities of the unexpected happenings, and dependence on personal initiative.

This type of organization has deprived individuals of a sizable portion of control over their activities, even such simple activities as walking, eating, finding their way around, looking at things, and discovering.

Individuals have a decreasing sense of being able to dominate their immediate environments and even a decreasing desire to do so. Our surroundings are no longer of a human dimension but are part of vast systems. There seems to have been a break in the balance of power between the individual and the environment. It is this balance that must be reestablished because it is necessary for maintenance of the feeling of individual responsibility.

In the area of health this abdication of control over the environment and of individual autonomy has given rise to the following phenomenon. Since people have developed an inordinate confidence in, and enormous psychological dependence on, the health care system, they do not always see why they should be concerned with the influence they can have on their own health. They can go ahead and eat to excess, drink without restriction, drive carelessly—what does it matter? All that is the responsibility of a highly sophisticated and all-powerful system that will have to pick up the pieces, if need be.

As a consequence, when people are told that they must assume responsibility for their own health, free themselves of the myth that the technical system of health care is all-powerful, regain their awareness that they hold the key to physical and mental well-being in their day-to-day lives, this is not simply an attack on the organization of the health care delivery system, not a simple administrative reform of that system, but instead is a real sociocultural revolution.

In our world with its pigeonholes for everything, its specialization, it will not be any easier to involve other systems outside the health care system with concern for true health. To prove this statement it is only necessary to have to examine our own behavior within the health system.

How do the administrators of the health care system react to suggestions, coming from other social systems, that they make room in the institutions for other human needs, such as recreation, education, and family life? And yet all these activities are part of a whole that is inseparably and profoundly integrated at the level of the individual. Efforts have been made, however, to separate them for purposes of administrative simplification at the level of social systems and institutions.

Seen from the specialized point of view of health care, and not within the overall view of the total human being, these activities that are not health care activities often appear conflicting. I have often been told, for example, of the incessant conflicts between faculties of medicine and teaching hospitals where, it would seem, there is enormous difficulty in reconciling the objectives of teaching and the objectives of health care.

Therefore, I am not unaware of the difficulties there will be in persuading private enterprise and public agencies to always include the health variable in their decisions, especially when protection of health is not in the interests of economics.

The task is vast and complex, and is not being approached with eyes closed and without awareness of the magnitude and complexity of the task. This endeavor is a broad one, because its aim is not to reach only, or primarily, sick people (who represent at any given time a minority of the population), but to reach all the population in order to encourage it to preserve and improve its health on its own.

This task is complex and arduous, because the elements that must be dealt with are concerned on the one hand with living habits, or culture, and on the other hand with social organization, or the social forces that are a result of the interests of the various groups or social institutions.

Finally, the task is complicated even more by the fact that it is no longer possible in this area to act exclusively through a system controlled administratively by health system personnel. It is also necessary to go through other systems, or even to use them as intermediaries.

It may seem that the transformations that have been made in the last 20 years in the health care delivery system have been very significant. I am convinced, however, that the changes Canada hopes to accomplish in the next 20 years are still more significant and certainly more basic. I am convinced, too, that the results will be proportionately more important.

Considering the vast scope of the job at hand, it appears necessary to develop a strategy for action and to determine a critical path. The federal government has already made considerable progress, working along with the provinces, in the development of this strategy for health promotion, or primary prevention.

The aim of this effort is to identify the fields in which priority actions should be taken and on which to concentrate, at least at the start, in order to gain experience while also attaining the necessary success for a general extension of this preventive approach. The choice of priority areas will be made in the light of two main criteria: the significance of the problem in relation to the health of Canadians and the probability of success in dealing with the problem. Using these criteria, certain areas and problems have already been identified as ones against which to take rapid action. I am thinking in particular of the areas of automobile accidents and occupational health. These two problems, obviously, are within systems other than the health care system.

The first of these two problems constitutes an excellent example of a priority in the area of prevention. According to reports, expenses related to traffic accidents in Canada reach about $2 billion each year, including the cost of health care and hospital treatment of the victims. These accidents require a total of more than 2 million hospital days. A conservative estimate of the cost of hospitalization for the victims of traffic accidents is $200 million a year, and other medical care is another $100 million. This represents to the country some 6% of the expenses in these areas. The bill to be met is increased still further by legal expenses, public liability, property damages, absences from work, and compensation for permanent disability. At the present time, automobile accidents in Canada represent the first-ranking cause of mortality, when measured in lost years of potential life. This is explainable by the large number of deaths and by the fact that a large proportion of fatalities are in the 25 year and under age group. Moreover, measures that significantly decrease the fatalities and injuries from car accidents are already known, such as requiring the wearing of seat belts, lowering speed limits, supervising highways, and educating the public. This is why actions have already begun in this area. At the present time, with the support of the Department of Health, the federal Department of Transport is proceeding with an intensive advertising campaign on automobile accidents and the advantages of wearing a seat belt. On a federal level attempts are being made to convince the provinces to introduce provincial legislation making the wearing of seat belts compulsory. Some success is already evident in Ontario and Quebec, which now have such laws.

CONCLUSION

The sustained effort of the federal government, backed by the cooperation of the provinces, has provided Canada with a health care delivery system of prime quality, accessible to all Canadians.

At this point in time, there is a distinct belief that this is the end of a significant stage. The *New Perspective,* within which the government intends to work in the future, is based very strongly on what has been accomplished to date—accomplishments that must be preserved at all costs—but it is opening up new horizons that should prevent complacency.

Despite the scope and complexity of the task that remains, the federal government is confident that the factors that allowed it to come this far will allow it to continue to offer Canadians a level of health and a quality of life that are among the world's highest and that will continue to improve.

REFERENCES

1. Bodenheimer, Thomas, Cummings, Steven, and Harding, Elizabeth: Capitalizing on illness: the health insurance industry, Int. J. Health Serv. **4**(4):583-598, 1974.
2. The Community Health Center in Canada, report of the community health center project to the health ministers, Ottawa, 1972, Information Canada.
3. Illich, Ivan: Deschooling society, New York, 1970, Harper & Row, Publishers.
4. Illich, Ivan: Medical nemesis, Toronto, 1975, McClelland and Stewart, Ltd.
5. LaLonde, Marc: A new perspective on the health of Canadians, Ottawa, 1975, Information Canada.
6. Task Force reports on the cost of health services in Canada, Ottawa, 1970, Queen's Printer.

INDEX

A

Accidents, automobile, 226-227
Accountability, hospitals and, 125
Accreditation programs, 111
Action for Mental Health, 143
Advisory Committee to Senate Subcommittee on Health of the Elderly, 78
Age
  elderly and; *see* Elderly
  infant mortality and, 54; *see also* Infant mortality
Alcoholism, 144
AMA; *see* American Medical Association
Ambulatory care, 123
American Indians
  death rates and, 58
  health care and, 62
  infant and maternal mortality and, 55
  mental illness and, 57
American Medical Association, 178, 181
Americans, health status of, 39-40
  allocations to improve, 45
Appointment system, 158
Assignment of benefit, 70
Audits of care, 168
Augmented medical care, 89
Automobile accidents, 226-227

B

Blacks
  death rates and, 58
  disease rates and, 56-57
  health status of, 39-40
  hospitals and, 110
  infant mortality and, 54
  life expectancy and, 56
  mental illness and, 57
Blue Cross and Blue Shield
  economy and, 22
  health maintenance organizations and, 136
  hospitalization rates and, 38
  influence on hospitals and, 111, 127
  Medicare and, 67, 71-72
  national health insurance and, 177, 180
Boards of trustees, 113, 167
Businessmen in government, 26-27

C

Canadian health care systems, 215-228
  alternative services and, 220
  cost of, 219-221
  future government role and, 221-222
  health of nation and, 217-219
  history of, 216-217
  individual and health and, 224-227
  primary prevention and, 222-224
Case review, 163-166
Certificate-of-need legislation, 128, 129
CHAMPUS; *see* Civilian Health and Medical Program of the Uniformed Services
Children; *see also* Infant mortality
  community mental health centers and, 144, 147
  health care and, 59
  pediatrician visits and, 94-95
Chinese-Americans
  death rates and, 58
  infant mortality and, 54
Civilian Health and Medical Program of the Uniformed Services, 75
Class structure, 10-17
  communication and, 17
  distribution of, 11-12
    in labor force, 25
Clients; *see also* Consumer involvement
  of community mental health centers, 146, 148
  hospitals and, 107-108, 109-110, 126-127
  impersonalization of, 121
  progressive patient care and, 123-125
  quality of care and, 153
Co-Care, 136
Commission on Professional and Hospital Activities, 162, 168
Commission on the Quality of Health Care, 49, 51
Committee on Costs of Health Care Services, 219
Committee for National Health Insurance, 47
Communicare, 136
Community clients; *see* Clients
Community health centers; *see also* Community mental health centers
  in Canada, 219, 220

Community health centers—cont'd
coordinated family care and, 95
risk groups and, 97
Community involvement; *see* Consumer involvement
Community mental health centers, 141-150
agencies affiliated with, 145
catchment areas and, 145
clients of, 148
community participation and, 146
consultation services of, 148
evaluation of, 148-149
financing of, 146
goals of, 144-145
history of, 142-144
interagency agreements and, 145
mental health perspectives and, 148-149
organization of, 145
present status of, 147-148
problems and challenges of, 149-150
services of, 142
workers in, 149
Community Mental Health Centers Act, 141, 144, 147
Comprehensive Health Planning Act, 111
Consensual validity, 154-155
Consumer involvement, 42-43, 46-47, 51-52
community mental health centers and, 146
hospital policy-making and, 125-126
lack of, 42-43
Medicare and Medicaid and, 77-78
national health insurance and, 50-51, 185-186, 193, 194
Consumer Price Index, 73
Continuing education, 210
Controllers, health sector and, 13-14
Convalescent hospitals in Canada, 220
Coordinated family care, 94-95
Corporate assets, distribution of, 21
Corporate economic power, 19
Corporate system and state, 26-29
Cost of Living Council, 116
Cost benefit measurement, 128-129
Cost controls, 45-46, 49-50, 188-205
budgeting and services and, 208
current national problem in, 188-192
health security program and, 192-196
problems in, 196-201
staging initial development of, 202-203
under Medicare and Medicaid, 75
public policy and, 77
Costs, 37-39; *see also* Cost controls
of Canadian health care system, 219-221
community mental health centers and, 146
crisis of, 208-209
economy and, 199, 200, 201
for elderly, 69, 73-75
health maintenance programs and, 131-132, 136-139
of hospitals, 113-120
Federal Planning Act and, 128
number of beds available and, 120
per day, 113, 114
per stay, 113, 114
relative to other health care, 115, 116
specific aspects of, 116-120
measurement of benefit and, 128-129
Medicare and Medicaid and, 68-69, 72-75
Costs—cont'd
of physicians' services, 74-75
total, for medical care, 189-190, 197-198, 206-207
impact of, 190
CPHA; *see* Commission on Professional and Hospital Activities
CPI; *see* Consumer Price Index

D

Deaths; *see* Mortality
Decision making process, consumers and; *see* Consumer involvement
Delivery of health care; *see* Health care and delivery
Disabilities, 56
Disability insurance, 175
Disease rates, poverty and, 56-57
Disease risk, primary care and, 97
Drugs
addiction to, 144
costs of, 73-75
elderly and, 69
Dual choice options, 138, 139

E

Economy
financial capital sector and, 19-22
health sector and, 19
legitimization and defense of, 29-30
market or competitive sector of, 18
medical care expenditures and, 189, 199, 200, 201; *see also* Costs
national health insurance and, 31; *see also* National health insurance
planned or monopolistic sector of, 17-18
power and, 16-17
corporate, 19
private enterprise and, 30-34, 213
state sector of, 18-19
Education
class structure and, 17
hospitals and, 110
life expectancy and, 55-56
morbidity and mortality rates and, 59, 62-63
primary care and, 97
Elderly
community mental health centers and, 147
costs for, 73-75
hospitalization of, 69
Medicare and Medicaid and, 66-79; *see also* Medicare and Medicaid
physicians' visits and, 69
Emergency rooms, 92, 109
Employee benefit provisions, 71
Environment, Canadian health care and, 222, 223
Ethnic groups
deaths and, 58
hospitals and, 110, 127
Evaluation
of quality of care, 155-156, 162-163, 170; *see also* Quality of care
of hospitals, 158-160
Expenditures; *see* Costs
Experimental Health Delivery Systems, 112
Experimental Medical Care Review Organization, 112

Extended care, 71
External audits of care, 168

F

Family
medical care costs and, 190
primary care and, 94-95
responsibility for care of, 96, 105
Family Health Program of Southern California, 136
Family-oriented care, 94-95
Family practitioners, visits to, 94-95
Fannin proposal, 178
Federal Planning Act, 128
Financial institutions, control of, 17-22
Financing and cost controls, 188-205; *see also* Cost controls; Costs
current national problems in, 188-192
health security program and, 192-196
problems in, 196-201
staging initial development of, 202-203
Findings and Purpose of the National Health Planning and Resources Development Act, 112
First contact care, 90; *see also* Primary care
Foster home with nursing supervision, 124-125
Free enterprise system, 30-34, 213

G

General practitioners
evaluation of, 157-158
visits to, 94-95
Generalists, visits to, 94-95
Goals, health care; *see* Health care goals
Government
Canadian; *see* Canadian health care systems
corporate system and, 26-29
fiscal policies and, 29
guidelines and standards of, 214
hospitals and, 107-108, 111-112, 128-129
medical research and, 212
Medicare and Medicaid and; *see* Medicare and Medicaid
national health insurance and, 175-177, 180, 181-182, 184, 200-201; *see also* National health insurance
priority for health expenditures of, 45
quality of care and, 152, 167
regulations of, for health care
effective, 46-47, 51-52
ineffective, 43-44
Group, responsibility for care of, 96, 105
Group payment, 190
Group practice
costs and, 199
prepaid, 77, 135
quality of care and, 153

H

Halfway houses, 147
Health
concept of, 3
society and, 3-8
Health care
accessibility to, 5, 44, 101-102
national health insurance and, 48, 185
physicians' and hospitals' responsibilities for, 44-45, 48-49
utilization and, 76-77, 156
Health care—cont'd
augmented, 89
basic, 92; *see also* Primary care
services related to, 92
in Canada; *see* Canadian health care systems
consumers and; *see* Clients; Consumer involvement
costs of; *see* Cost controls; Costs
and delivery, 9-35, 40-41
allocations to improve, 45, 49
class structure and, 10-17
corporate system and state and, 26-29
crisis in; *see* Health care crisis
deficiencies in, 40-41, 76-77, 85
financial and health delivery institutions and, 17-22
health distribution institutions and, 24-26
health reproductory institutions and, 23-24
legitimization and defense of system and, 29-30
national health insurance and, 184, 185, 186, 200; *see also* National health insurance
organization of; *see* Organization of health delivery system
owners, controllers, and producers of services and, 13-14
persons employed in, 13
private enterprise system and, 30-34, 213
redirection in organization of, 192
economic system and; *see* Economy
evaluation of, 155-156, 170
first contact, 90; *see also* Primary care
goals of; *see* Health care goals
hospitals and; *see* Hospitals
in infancy, poverty and, 59; *see also* Infant mortality
integrationist for, 91
levels of, 86-89
longitudinal responsibility for, 90
primary; *see* Primary care
quality of; *see* Quality of care
regulations of
effective, 46-47, 51-52, 128
ineffective, 43-44
research and, 9-10, 212-214
scope of, 89-93
subsystem, 89
supportive services for, 91
systems of; *see also* Organization of health delivery system
estimated waste in, 38
institutional, 121-129
new, 122
problems in, 40-41
quality of care and, 166-167
Health care crisis, 188-192, 208-214
in costs, 208-209
of disorganization, 209-210
of inadequate health insurance, 210-212
in medical research, 212-214
in quality of care, 210
Health care goals, 36-52
current problems and, 37-44
national health security and, 47-52; *see also* National health insurance
objectives in, 44-47
Health centers; *see* Community health centers; Community mental health centers

Health institutions; *see also* Hospitals
  class structure and, 13-14
  for distribution, control of, 24-26
  financial institutions and, 17-22
  reproductory, control of, 23-24
Health insurance; *see* Insurance
Health Insurance Benefits Advisory Council, 73
Health Maintenance Organization Act, 133, 136-139, 199
Health maintenance organizations, 131-140
  certification requirements for, 138-139
  demographic trends in, 133-135
  dual choice options and, 138, 139
  federal policies for, 136-139
  federal strategy for, 132-133
  future of, 139-140
  national health insurance and, 48, 185, 186
  organizational patterns of, 135-136
  quality of care and, 153
Health personnel, 13; *see also* Physicians
  mental, 149
  national health insurance and, 185, 186, 193, 194
Health sector
  class structure and, 13-14
  economy and, 19
  income distribution in, 14, 15
  providers versus consumers and, 25-26
Health Security Act, 47-52
Health Security Action Council, 47
Health Security Board, 51
Health Security Program, 47-52, 192-196; *see also* National health insurance
Health status, 39-40
  allocations to improve, 45, 49
Heart, Stroke, and Cancer Act, 111
Hill-Burton hospital construction, 175
Home care
  Canada and, 220
  hospitals and, 123-125
Home health agencies, 77
Hospital insurance; *see* Insurance
Hospitalization, phenomenon of, 224
Hospitals, 107-130
  in Canada, 218
  centralization and decentralization of, 121
  change and, 126-129
  client interests and, 107-108, 109-110, 126-127
  controlling interests and, 113
  costs and, 113-120; *see also* Costs
  elderly and, 69
  evaluation and, 158-160
  governing bodies of, 113, 167
  health maintenance organizations and, 136
  health security program and, 199
  institutional medical care system and, 121-129
  Medicare and, 69, 112; *see also* Medicare and Medicaid
  merging of services of, 120
  private insurance and, 190-191
  progressive patient care and, 123-125
  provider interests and, 107, 108-109
  psychiatric facilities and, 148
  quality of care and, 152-153, 164, 165, 166
Hospitals—cont'd
  size of, 120-121
    quality of care and, 165
  societal requirements and, 107-108, 111-112
  third-party payer interests and, 107-108, 110-111
  utilization review and, 125-126
Hypertension, 56-57

I

Incomes; *see also* Wealth
  class structure and, 10
  differentials in, 14-17
  distribution of, 12-13
    in health sector, 14, 15
  median, 12
  poverty and; *see* Poverty
Incremental system effects, 166-167
Indians; *see* American Indians
Individual
  primary care and, 94-95
  responsibility for care of, 96
Individual practice association, 135
Infancy, health care in, 59
Infant mortality
  Canada and, 215, 218
  comparative, 39
  poverty and, 53-54, 56
  priorities and, 45
  quality of care and, 156, 159-160
Inflation, 72-74; *see also* Cost controls
Injury, risk of, 97
Innovation, review mechanisms and, 172
Institutional medical care system, 121-129; *see also* Hospitals
Institutions, value systems of, 24
Insurance
  Blue Cross and Blue Shield; *see* Blue Cross and Blue Shield
  Canada and, 216-217
  community mental health centers and, 146
  disability, 175
  hospital
    Canada and, 216-217
    Medicare and, 66; *see also* Medicare and Medicaid
  lack of coverage and, 41-42
  morbidity and mortality rates and, 59
  national health; *see* National health insurance
  poverty and, 60-61
  private, 72
    adequacy of, 72, 190, 207, 210-212
    Canada and, 221
    development of, 190
    Medicare and Medicaid and, 71-72
  quality of care and, 152, 167
Insurance companies
  commercial, 19-22
  provider, 22, 31-32
Intensive care, 123
Intergroup Prepaid Health Services, Inc., 136
Intermediate care, 123
Internal audits of care, 168
Internists, visits to, 94-95
InterStudy surveys, 133-134, 137
IPA; *see* Individual practice association

J

Japanese-Americans
death rates and, 58
infant mortality and, 54
Joint Commission on Mental Illness and Health, 143

K

Kaiser Foundation Health Plan, 131, 133, 135
Kennedy proposal, 22, 47, 178

L

Labor, organized, 18, 36-37, 113, 126-127
Labor costs, hospitals and, 113
Labor force, 17-19, 20
class distribution of, 25
Laboratory services, 158
Licensure of physicians, 210
Life-styles, Canada and, 222, 223
Long-term care, 123-125
Longevity, quality of care and, 156; *see also* Elderly

M

Malnutrition, 57-59
Malpractice litigation, 152
Management, judgments of, 155
Maternal mortality
in Canada, 215, 218
poverty and, 54, 55
Maternity care costs, 116-120
Median incomes, 12
Medicaid; *see* Medicare and Medicaid
Medi-Cal, 134
Medical audit, 163
Medical care; *see* Health care
Medical information system, regional, 125
Medical research, 9-10, 212-214
Medical schools, 3-6
quality of care and, 158
Medicare and Medicaid, 66-79
administration of, 67
benefits and gaps and, 69-71
cheating under, 75-76
community mental health centers and, 146
cost controls and, 75; *see also* Cost controls
costs and, 68-69, 72-75
deficiencies in delivery of services and, 76-77
formulation of public policy and, 77-79
health maintenance organizations and, 134, 136-139
hospitals and, 112
inflation and, 72-74; *see also* Cost controls
national health insurance and, 175-176, 200, 201, 202, 203
private health insurance and, 71-72
private physician care and, 109
quality of care and, 152
risk-sharing contracts and, 137-138
Medicine, roles of, 3-6
Mental health centers, community; *see* Community mental health centers
Mental health perspectives, 148-149
Mental health workers, 149
Mental hospitals, 147
Mental illness, poverty and, 57
Mental Retardation Facilities Act, 144
Middle class, 11-12
Minority groups; *see also* specific group
deaths and, 58
hospitals and, 110, 127
Morbidity, quality of care and, 156
Mortality
Canada and, 215, 218
infant; *see* Infant mortality
maternal
in Canada, 215, 218
poverty and, 54, 55
perinatal, 159-160
quality of care and, 156, 159
rates and causes of, 58

N

Narcotic addiction, 144
National Drug and Therapeutic Index, 94
National health insurance, 47-52, 192-196
administration of, 50, 176, 178, 180, 182, 186, 193, 194
availability of health care and, 48-49
catastrophic medical care costs and, 176
commercial insurance companies and, 22, 31-32
comprehensive coverage and, 176
cost controls and, 197-198; *see also* Cost controls
costs of, 29, 177-179, 192, 196-201
economy and, 31
efficiency and equity and, 181-182
eligibility for, 192, 193, 194
employer and employee responsibilities and, 177, 184, 194
facilities and, 193, 194
freedom of choice and, 213
health agencies and, 186
health maintenance organizations and, 140
legislative realities of, 206-214
health care crisis and, 208-214; *see also* Health care crisis
organization of services and, 193, 194
policy issues in, 175-187
costs and expenditures in, 177-179
different approaches to, 179-180
essential elements and, 183-186
phased-in schedule and, 182-183
professional participation and, 186
public and private sectors and, 176, 181-182
prerequisites for, 77-79
proposals for, 178
weaknesses in, 194-196
quality assurance and, 192
range of health services and, 185, 192-193
reimbursement-control features and, 178-179
specifications for, 192-194
summary of types of, 180
tax structure for, 201
National Health Planning and Resources Development Act, 175
National health policy, need for, 45
National health security, 47-52; *see also* National health insurance
National Institute of Mental Health, 141, 143, 144
NDTI; *see* National Drug and Therapeutic Index
"A New Perspective on the Health of Canadians," 221
Nursing care, long-term, 71

Nursing homes
  Canada and, 220
  Medicare and Medicaid and, 71
Nutrition, 57-59

O

Objectives of health care; *see* Health care goals
Occupational distribution, 11-12
Occupational health, 226-227
Office care, 157-158, 165
Office visits; *see* Physician visits
Organization of health delivery system
  crisis and, 209-210
  national health insurance and, 193, 194
  redirection of, 192
Outcomes; *see* Evaluation
Outpatient departments
  hospitals and, 123-125
  Medicare and Medicaid and, 109
  visits to, 93

P

Paraprofessional, 14
Patient care; *see also* Clients; Health care
  impersonalization of, 121
  progressive, 123-125
Pediatricians, 94-95
Performance standards, regulations and, 51; *see also* Professional standards review organizations; Quality of care
Perinatal mortality, 159-160; *see also* Infant mortality
Personnel, 13; *see also* Physicians
  mental health, 149
  national health insurance and, 185, 186, 193, 194
PGP; *see* Prepaid group practice
Physician visits
  elderly and, 69
  estimated primary, 91, 92, 93
  Medicare and, 70
  poverty and, 59
  primary care and, 94-95
Physicians
  autonomy of, 172, 213-214
  in Canada, 215, 218
  characteristics, performance, and settings for work of, 166
  charges of, 74-75
    reasonable and customary, 67
  continuing education of, 210
  distribution of, 59
  health maintenance organizations and, 132, 135-136
  licensure of, 210
  preparation of, 3-6, 158
  primary care
    shortage of, 40
    training of, 5-6
  provider interests in hospitals and, 107, 108-109, 126
  quality of care and; *see* Quality of care
  roles of, 3, 4, 5
  in rural areas, 61
  visits to; *see* Physician visits
Physicians' service review organization; *see* Professional standards review organizations
Pluralism, political, 28
Policy-making, hospitals and, 125-126; *see also* Consumer involvement
Political pluralism, 28
Political power, 16-17
Population statistics; *see* Statistics
Poverty, 53-65; *see also* Incomes
  health status and, 40
  infant mortality and, 54-55
  life expectancy and, 55-56
  morbidity and mortality rates and, 59
Prepaid group practice, 77, 135
Prescriptions, 73-75
Preventive medicine
  Canada and, 222-224
  primary care and, 93-94
  priority-setting in, 226-227
  need for, 45
Primary care, 83-106
  access to, 101-102
  attributes essential in, 86-89
  definition of, 83
    approaches to, 98-99
    consensual, 99-104
    need for, 83-85
    questions in, 85-98
  disease orientation and, 93-94
  extent of responsibility and, 96-97
  functional areas of, 102, 105
  functions, qualities, and equity of, 100-101
  health orientation and, 93-94
  history of, 84-85
  hospital care and, 124
  injury risk and, 97
  innovative change in, 103-104
  interventions other than personal health care and, 97-98
  physicians and
    shortage of, 40
    training of, 5-6
  priority-setting and, 99-103
  scope of, 89-93
  unit of attention appropriate to, 94-95
Primary Health Care Study Program, 99
Priority-setting, 45, 99-103, 226-227
Private enterprise system, 30-34, 213
Private health insurance; *see* Insurance, private
Producers of services, 13-14
Production, class structure and, 16-17, 20
Professional Activity Service, 121
Professional freedom, 172, 213-214
Professional monitoring of quality, 167-172; *see also* Professional standards review organizations
Professional service review organizations; *see* Professional standards review organizations
Professional standards review organizations, 76, 112, 168-170
  assessment of content of care and, 170-172
  capacity for innovation and, 172
  certification of admissions and length of stay and, 170-172
  costs, benefits, and effects of, 172
  hospital changes and, 126
  hospital size and, 121
Professions, 26
  quality of care and, 153

Profiles, 170
Progressive patient care, 123-125
Property, class structure and, 16-17
Provider interests, 107, 108-109, 126
PSROs; *see* Professional standards review organizations
Public funding; *see also* Government; Medicare and Medicaid
  of medical research, 212
  of national health insurance, 192, 193; *see also* National health insurance
Public policy, formulation of, 77-79
Public utilities, 122
Public welfare medical assistance, 175
Puerto Ricans, 55

Q

Quality of care, 151-174
  administrators and, 153
  consensual validity and, 154-155
  crisis and, 210
  definition of, 153-155
  evaluation of, 155-156
  factors in, 167
  legislation and, 128
  Medicare and, 75-76
  physicians and, 75-76
  primary care and, 100-101
  professional monitoring of, 167-172
  public policy and, 77, 214
  size of hospital and, 120-121
  studies of, 156-167
    hospital care and, 158-166
    incremental system effects and, 166-167
    office care and, 157-158
Quality assurance, 192

R

Race; *see also* American Indians; Blacks
  discrimination and, 62, 110
  life expectancy and, 55-56
  morbidity and mortality rates and, 58, 59
    infant, 54, 55, 56
Records, evaluation of, 160, 168
Regional Medical Program, 112
Regionalization, 111, 112, 119, 122, 125
Research, 9-10, 212-214
Resources Development Fund, 49
Retirement, employee benefit provisions and, 71; *see also* Elderly
Rights to health care, 44
Risk of disease and injury, 97
Risk-sharing contracts, 137-138
Roemer's law, 120
Rural areas, 59, 61
Rural Health Associates, 61

S

San Joaquin Foundation for Medical Care, 135
Screening for state hospitals, 147
Self-care, 123
Senate Subcommittee on Health of the Elderly, 78
SMI program; *see* Supplementary medical insurance program
SMSAs; *see* Standard metropolitan statistical areas
Social class structure, 10-17, 25
Social legislation, alienation and, 29
Social mobility, 14-17
Social Security
  coverage of physicians under, 175
  national health insurance and, 184-185, 200
  poverty and, 60
Social Security Act
  health maintenance organizations and, 133, 136, 137
  national health insurance and, 191
  professional reviews and, 152, 168
Social services, legitimization and defense of economic system and, 29
Social utilities, 122-129
Society
  and health, 3-8
  health care and delivery and, 9-35; *see also* Health care and delivery
  hospitals and requirements of, 107-108, 111-112
  quality of care and, 152
Spanish-Americans, 110
Special care units, 109
Specialization, 151-152, 165-166
Standard metropolitan statistical areas, 134
Standards
  of performance, regulations and, 51; *see also* Professional standards review organizations
  for quality of care; *see* Quality of care
State, corporate system and, 26-29
State agencies, class structure and, 17
State mental health authority, 146
State mental hospitals, 147
Statistics
  Commission of Professional and Hospital Activities and, 168
  hospital costs and, 113-120
  medical information system and, 125
  professional standards review organizations and, 168-172
Subsystem medical care, 89
Supplementary medical insurance program, 67
Supportive services, 91
Surgery
  costs of, 73
  health security program and, 199
  incidence of, 156, 160-162
  private insurance and, 190-191
Surgical audit, 163
Symptoms, international studies of, 156
Systems of care; *see* Health care, systems of

T

Taxation
  corporate system and, 29
  national health insurance and, 201
Technology, 151-152
Third-party payers, 107-108, 110-111, 127
Tissue findings, surgery and, 160-161
Tracer methodology, 166
Training
  medical school, 3-6, 158
  subsequent to medical school, 158

U

Ullman-AHA proposal, 178
Unions, 18, 36-37, 113, 126-127
Urban areas, 62
Utilities
  public, 122
  social, 122-129
Utilization review, 125-126

V

Value systems, 24
Voluntary planning agencies, 111
Volunteers, 146

W

Wagner-Murray-Dingell Bill, 175
Wealth; *see also* Incomes
  class structure and, 10
  distribution of, 12-13
  monopolistic sector and, 19
  owners and controllers of, 11
Welfare state, 29-30
Working class, 11
  health sector and, 14
World Health Organization Expert Committee on Mental Health, 142